Table of Contents

Fewer Blacks Means the Need for More Poverty Grants

- *Turning Death Into Dollars: How the City and Cops Make Money From Black Homicide*

The "Racial Gap": Concepts and Characteristics

- *Basis of the Racial Gap: Recurring Racist Activity as Normative Behavior*
- *The Racial Gap: "Two Societies, Separate and Unequal ..."*

Community Development

- *Example: The Urban Development Action Grant*
- *The "Empowerment Movement"*

Education

- *American Student Exodus*
- *Higher Education in Nebraska: In Trouble Once Again*
- *"The Cultural Proficiency Journal and OPS": Critique*
- *The Cultural Proficiency Journal Itself: Ecological Fallacies*

Property Taxes and Land Manipulation

- *The Farmland Crisis*

Health Care Industry
A Skewed Department of Corrections: One More Problem
Crime, The Judiciary and the Penal System
Social Services

- *Goodwill Industries, Susie Buffett and Big Bucks For White Males*

Conclusion
References

PREFACE

Throughout the statewide and even national elections of 2016, the claims were made that Nebraskans were "independent." This is not only a contemptible lie, but also flies in the face of the evidence of chronic dependence, ineptitude and outright administrative buffoonery that will be pointed out by the Triple One Neighborhood Association and Parents Union (TONAPU), the largest African-American neighborhood group in the state of Nebraska.

Independence is defined as, "freedom from outside control of support." As you will see on the pages that follow, Nebraska is hemorrhaging money, is steeped in administrative error on a continuous basis, and is losing its ranking in the world as the beef producing capital. The "invasion of the booty snatchers" is what is keeping the state afloat, pilfering from and pimping Federal grant programs, taking advantage of the minority and the poor and outright theft. All of these allegations are supported in this book.

"Cultural competence" is defined as, "Cultural competence can be defined as the level of knowledge-based skills required to provide effective … care to… individuals from a particular ethnic or racial group." Since Nebraska is sorely lacking in real diversity and therefore in culturally competent analysis, reports and policies, this report should be viewed as perhaps the first one to view the state as it really is: culturally, economically, socially, politically, educationally and ethically.

Any sane person performing their "due diligence" before doing business of any kind with or in the state of Nebraska would be shocked at the levels of mismanagement, nepotism and outright buffoonery that permeates the government, the various state departments and its largest city, Omaha. But most of the consultants, advisors and others who are brought in to assess the state or a particular institution are themselves lacking in cultural competency. Nebraska has a national reputation for being rife for the plucking when it comes to spending huge sums of money and not getting much back in return. Outsiders can tell this because they have met the representatives that the state sends to Washington.

"Due diligence" is defined as, "reasonable steps taken by a person in order to satisfy a legal requirement, especially in buying or selling something" or, in terms of the orientation and gist of this book, it refers to "a comprehensive appraisal of a business undertaken by a prospective buyer, especially to establish its assets and liabilities and evaluate its commercial potential."

When it comes to social services, issues of race, and various "services," Nebraska's on-going racial mistakes, discriminatory actions and outright racism and sexism that pervades and saturates the state's decision making apparatus. It is as Michael Bradley wrote in his incredible insightful book, *The Iceman Inheritance*,

> Generations of slavery and lack of social and educational opportunities for black and Amerind fulfillment had inevitably resulted in poor development of these people and their offspring in comparison with the whites. The **cultural gulf** between these blacks and Amerinds and whites was presented as evidence of natural biological and moral inferiority. Their inferiority and consequent slavery, was a matter of natural law. (p. 38 – emphasis added).

What Bradley refers to as a "cultural gulf" is, at least in my view, synonymous with the more current term of "racial gap," which is what this book is all about. In this case the "gulf" has the contemporary label of "disparity," and the state of Nebraska, like numerous other parts of the nation, have found a way to maintain these disparities, convince the public that those in power are fighting to eliminate the disparities while, at the same time, generating millions of dollars in free money (grants) to "continue the fight."

Nebraskans for the most part, are a culturally arrogant people. As a result, they are lacking in other intellectual areas. That is why even though these conservative curmudgeons believe in the death penalty, most of them were so ignorant (read: stupid) that they had to have the wording of LB 268 "translated" or "interpreted" for them. According to one blurb, "The purpose of Legislative Bill 268, passed by the First Session of the 104th Nebraska Legislature in 2015, is to eliminate the death penalty and change the maximum penalty for the crime of murder in the first degree to life imprisonment. Shall Legislative Bill 268 be repealed?"

But that was too advanced for the typical Nebraska hick; they were having issues figuring out the difference between the terms "retain" and repeal." Check it out:

> A vote to "Retain" will eliminate the death penalty and charge the maximum penalty for the crime of murder in the first degree to life imprisonment by retaining Legislative Bill 268, passed in 2015 by the First Session of the 104th Nebraska Legislature. A vote to "Repeal" will keep the death penalty as a possible penalty for the crime of murder in the first degree by repealing Legislative Bill 268, passed in 2015 by the First Session of the 104th Nebraska Legislature.

People who are this lacking in intellect should not be people who are hired to run the state, to head an agency or to supervise a staff. And yet these same people wonder why Nebraska is falling by the wayside as increasing numbers of individuals obtain jobs, stay long enough to generate a healthy nest egg, and then either quit or intentionally do something so stupid they know they will be terminated. And then they receive a huge severance check and then live happily ever after. This is a survival tactic in a state that is slowly but surely getting poorer and poorer. So they generate money on the backs of the minority, the low-income and the neglected.

Remember, as you read the words that follow, that the "invasion of the booty snatchers" has existed for centuries. At the root of it is the profit motive and the fact that the American system will do ANYTHING for profit. On the morning of October 10, 2016, it was reported on "CBS Morning News" that both Coca-Cola and Pepsi were contributing to – endorsing – the activities of the American Heart Association and the American Diabetes Association. This is a direct conflict of interest – unless you understand that America, as I've stated before, "eats its young." People get sick and the system finds a way to profit from it. And in like manner, people want to escape these realities, turn to getting drunk and high, and the system gets "paid." And this doctrine extends through institutions throughout the American system.

Therefore, read and learn.

INTRODUCTION

> A thousand cowards cannot produce one brave man. A thousand
> fools cannot produce one wise man"
>
> - Adolf Hitler

The previous quote, though extracted from a fascist dictator, nevertheless rings true. And the purpose my quoting it is because Nebraska is failing because it has adopted the philosophy of quantity over quality. Their ranks at the state level are far too inflated, and the same can be said about each county and city jurisdiction as well. A classic case of "the blind leading the blind," Nebraska is sinking deeper and deeper into the mire of mediocrity. They are becoming increasingly dependent on poverty grants from the government, feeding off of rural and minority communities. Their tourism is a joke and their tax-inflated coffers are deteriorating like the last leaves of a painfully prolonged autumn.

In Nebraska, hicks hire hire, appoint, nominate and support their fellow hicks. In February of 2018, it was found that some fifty children had been abused while in the care of Nebraska agencies. Why would this be a surprise? Nebraska's Department of Human Services and its affiliates have been either under investigation or in violation of some major rule or regulation for decades. The state is intellectually and financially broke and busted. It is a running joke in national circles because all people have to do is look at the political representatives that it sends to Washington, DC. Begging for grant money is a survival tactic in a state that is so mentally bankrupt.

With that having been said, we find the motive for "booty snatching." In this case booty has nothing directly to deal with the street version of the term, which links it to sex and related issues. "Booty," for the purposes of this book, is denotatively defined as, "Plunder taken from an enemy in time of war" or "Goods or property seized by force or piracy." Nebraska's method of operation, when it comes to programs and revenue generation, fits both definitions like a glove.

On March 21, 2016, a Nebraska state senator spoke:

> Unless we are able to grow our state we will continually talk about how we are going to fix our tax situation….a strategic plan that will help us focus on a plan that will help us to grow … Growth will come from a focused strategic plan … I will ask for your green vote on LB 1083. (March 21, 2016).

Seriously problematic revenue streams appears to be the central problem – hence the need to "snatch booty" from wherever they can find it. In January of 2017 it was stated that by the year 2019, the state of Nebraska will be about $900 million in the hole. The solution smacks of desperation although they continue to spend money as if they don't have a care in the world. And why? And the formula is simple: since it is a rural state dependent on farmers, it is the farmers who receive priority. That means that whatever they receive comes at the expense of "urbanites," and Nebraska only has two real urban enclaves, which are located in Omaha and Lincoln; both low-income and minority communities.

This is where the booty snatchers come in.

Within those enclaves live suburban white taxpayers who the state dare not rile, so they have to locate minority "pockets of poverty." That means the Latinos in the western panhandle, the Native Americans on the reservations (who for the most part are inundated with alcohol and then fined by police and state troopers) and African-Americans in Omaha, as well as a growing Latino community located in the 68107 zip code on the south side.

Each time the state develops a "program," its aim is to foster dependency and in doing so, create jobs for its under-achieving white population members. I refer to this as the "Toys for Tots Syndrome" (akin to "Food for Families" and

"Coats for Kids"). The key is to use charity and social services to "service" the minority and low-income and increase their dependency because most of what is provided is consumable.

Once that's gone, new programs are needed therefore justifying more begging by the cities and counties for Federal dollars. This approach is preferred to simply providing jobs for the low-income and minority who would then be able to feed their own families, buy toys for their own kids and coats for their own children.

To put it mildly the state is not doing as well as it is claiming, and its largest university system – the Nebraska University system – as of December 2016 has a hiring freeze and is experiencing a near billion dollar financial problem. Since a disproportionate percentage of state allocations go into that system, then it is clear that the state has a tendency to throw good money after bad. As more young people leave Nebraska for a more "urban" experience, as businesses see the state's population for what it is and, in the era of diversity, refuse to accept racism and discrimination as a daily function of doing business, times are going to get worse.

That is why the "booty snatchers" are so important, and when you read the analyses that follow, you will see why.

In this important book I cover what I view are the primary institutional arrangements that bleed the state dry, exploit the black community in the name of grant dollars and as a combination of these two factors, force the state into a situation where it spends an inordinate amount of time and resources chasing after and leeching for free money from various governmental entities – grant money. They promise that they need the money for positive changes but once the check arrives, they never institute the changes. The state continues to hire one bad manager after another, piss away the money, and the state is left moribund.

As the largest city in Nebraska and the only one with a sizable (read: exploitable) African-American population, Omaha is a reflection and reinforcement of the pitiful state of administrative affairs that permeates state decision making bodies.

In this book I address a number of these institutional arrangements.

This report begins with information regarding the unicameral form of government that dictates policy for the entire state. In this section I address the "farmer orientation" of the entire state and the ruralized ideas (as opposed to sophisticated, modern urban approaches) that appear to dominate the thinking of the state's leadership.

As case studies I chose several former members of the Nebraska legislature and their "antics" as typical of the "hidden" foolishness that takes place behind closed doors. I chose Rex Haberman, the representative from Imperial, Nebraska (who State Senator Ernie Chambers used to refer to as "the Imperial wizard"), John

DeCamp, the state senator from Neligh, Nebraska and more recently Bill Kintner, the senator who represents Nebraska City and deems himself a "Reagan conservative" but was caught in a scandal regarding the use of state computers for "cybersex."

In a related section I address electoral politics which I view as the "ethnocentric foundation" for the greed that serves as the basis for the "invasion of the booty snatchers" motif that I explain throughout the report. Related sections that serve as keys to Nebraska's leadership style and its lack of vision are: the lack of creativity, originality and modernity, its poor management styles and vision as they relate to tax revenue shortages, and the problems that permeate the state's tourism department, which filters down into Omaha, the state's largest city.

Related and discussed in the area of tourism are issues of how Omaha is covered by the national media (usually a façade to hide its segregation and political problems), as well as general information about its tourism "philosophy." The recent termination of the director of Tourism following the abuse of hundreds of thousands of dollars of taxpayers' money in 2016 is then followed up with a proposal that could "fix" the problem, a proposed Nebraska Oversight and Visitors Association (NOVA).

The next segment of the report touches upon "entrepreneurship" and features a speech by a senior community development advisor, a young "negro" who hails from Omaha and is a self-proclaimed "expert" on business development. Moving on the issues of "tax relief" as a pacification method to keep citizens at bay is described and keeps many of them from leaving the state. In this section I also describe how the city of Omaha has used and continues to abuse tax increment financing even amid all of its tax and financial problems.

The report then turns to some of the ways that the state turns "booty snatcher" and exploits the poverty of blacks and low-income people in its ongoing quest to leech for as many free dollars as it can suck off of the government's teet.These approaches range from the use of police grants to gain more overtime pay to a discussion of how rampant and pervasive racial segregation generates additional grant money from the Federal government.

In the area of "community development," an explanation of Omaha's abuse of Urban Community Action Grants and more recently, of the Susie Buffett-run "Empowerment Network" continue to use the black community's status as a "pocket of poverty" to leech for Federal, State, County and City grant funding for various "projects" which maintain the poverty that, in turn, continues to quality the city of Omaha for future grant funding.

The report includes a section on "education," and shows how the current crop of educators, borrowing from past pseudo-educators, continue to make the same mistakes at the expense of minority students. A discussion of the "exodus" of students from Nebraska is addressed as is an overview of higher education and its generally mediocre status (with the exception of Creighton University). Stopgap and foolish attempts by the largest school district in the state, the Omaha Public Schools, is evident in the analysis of the ordering of 8,000 "cultural proficiency manuals" that were handed out to every single employee in the district and which did not change a single attitude or action as these relate to racial and ethnic understanding. The ecological fallacies that permeate the Journal are also explored.

After a discussion of property taxes and "land manipulation," a discussion of "the farmland crisis" shows how the state of Nebraska is in a financial downtown. As a result, sections of the report also reveal the ideological, social and financial problems of several Nebraska institutions: the Department of Corrections, the penal system and its abuse of "restrictive housing" and young males of color and its "social service" delivery system. As an example of a nonprofit steeped in greed, a case study of Goodwill Industries is also shared and analyzed.

THE NEBRASKA UNICAMERAL: HILLBILLY ORIGINS, TIME CONSUMING CONTROVERSIES

In addition to the plethora of problems outlined in this book, a key to the on-going continuity of the poor management, decision making, continual loss of population and revenue, dearth of creative approaches and the like is the people who Nebraskans elect.

As a hick state, their choices are usually between one rich farmer over the other. Since Omaha is the only city in the state with any size (under 500,000) and the second largest city is the capital city of Lincoln with just over 172,000 the pickin's, as the saying goes, are slim. For the past 35-plus years, a black man – State Senator Ernie Chambers – has dominated the legislature, mastering law and rules and improving their poorly worded and written state Constitution. There are forty nine (49) member of the Legislature and it is the only Unicameral in the nation. With all this going on and a black man dominating it (oftentimes overruled because the sheer numbers of these hillbillies), there are usually time consuming controversies , some of which I will document here.

I cannot capture or remember them all because, remember I didn't arrive in Omaha until 1977 and didn't receive my third Master's degree in Political Science until 2000. But there are several incidents that are worth of mention that show, once again, why the only option left for the state, the only option to keep it from hemorrhaging money, is to beg and leech for Federal grant funds and to tax and where possible, fine the hell out of its 1,700,000 total residents.

Here are some of the more controversial issues that impacted on black people directly and/or indirectly over the years. And when you read them you will see, as I have, that when it comes to racism, buffoonery, and in many cases outright stupidity, the Nebraska state legislature (with the exception of state senator Ernie Chambers) reigns without rival.

Some of the following controversies did not have a direct impact on the Nebraska economy, but did have an impact on the reputation of the state which, indirectly, impacts on the way that people view the state. As people view the state, so goes their decisions as to whether or not it is a state that they want to visit. Some of these controversies display racism, and black people are concerned about where their tourist dollars go; those visiting will well remember some of the incidents I am about to describe.

Nebraska Unicameral: Farmer Politics Personified

When I charge that Nebraska is dominated and directed by "farmer politics," I don't necessarily mean it as an insult. It is simply a statement of face: Nebraska is a rural state and its leading exports are cattle, soybeans and corn. Their nickname is "The Cornhusker State." What else can we conclude? They willingly, since their inception, felt pride in the fact that they were hicks. So be it. Hicks thou shalt be.

Politics, as I've learned over the years, is the art and science of using power. White people pushed natives off the land and then had the nerve to name the state "Nebraska," which according to one source is based on an Oto Indian word Nebrathka meaning "flat water" (referring to the Platte River, which is also an official symbol of Nebraska) (State Symbols USA, 2016). But ripping off the name, modifying it and then moving in was just the beginning:

> Indigenous peoples including Omaha, Missouria, Ponca, Pawnee, Otoe, and various branches of the Lakota (Sioux) tribes lived in the region of present-day Nebraska for thousands of years before European exploration. The state is crossed by many historic trails and was explored by the Lewis and Clark Expedition …. In the 1860s, after the US government forced many of the Native American tribes to cede their lands and settle on reservations, it opened large tracts of land to agricultural development by Europeans and Americans. Under the Homestead Act, thousands of settlers migrated into Nebraska to claim free land granted by the federal government … Nebraska became the 37th state on March 1, 1867, and the capital was moved from Omaha to the center at Lancaster, later renamed Lincoln after the recently assassinated President of the United States, Abraham Lincoln (Wikipedia, 2016).

The art and science of using power. Farmer politics included incursion, invasion, murder and relocation of the native Americans. In their schools they attempt to gloss over this "takeover" as much as possible, but the facts are right there for anyone who can read. They open up an area, invite their white brothers in after forcing the natives out, put the natives on reservations and then open up large tracks of land that they had just stolen. Today that land is, for the most part, the property of these same farmers who now dominate and direct the economy, policies and procedures of the Nebraska legislature. In other words, lawless men making laws for others to respect and obey.

These are the types of facts and foundations that set the stage for the "farmer politics" that permeated the state for decades. The only reason that the state has any respect or semblance of urbanity is due to a decision made by a white governor named Tiemann and a respected black man, Edward Danner, who was a butcher and vice president if the United Packinghouse Workers of America, which represented labor and meat packing industry.

Danner represented North Omaha as a senator beginning in 1963, representing the ghetto, and was also active in civil rights. But he died in office in 1970s and the governor appointed the conservative businessman George Althouse, to replace him. Althouse opened his mouth one day on the floor of the legislature and said something about God favoring the white man to rule or some shit like that and it made the local newspapers.

A young firebrand named Ernie Chambers got wind of it and decided to launch a campaign against Althouse, since the comments also peeved a large number of North Omaha residents. Althouse completed Danner's term, but when election time came around he had to face Ernie Chambers, a brilliant young man with a law degree from Creighton – and a black nationalist. Chambers obliterated him and has served since that time until today, with the exception of two years when he had to step down due to term limits, which the "farmer politicians" forced through directly for the purpose of getting Ernie out of the legislature.

With Chambers in their ranks the Nebraska Unicameral got more national and international attention than it ever got before. Chambers nearly single-handedly ushered these hicks into the 20th century and their "farmer politics" had to move over for more pressing issues like, civil rights, affirmative action, police-community relations, divesting in South Africa, racism in college sports (namely the University of Nebraska Lincoln football team) and so on.

The reason for the emphasis on "farmer politics" is because the rural mentality – which in many cases is inherently anti-black – paves the way for many of the problems that the state is now having and the exploitation of its minority populations which represents the on-going welfare checks (hence "booty") that the State applies for, receives, and then continually abuses.

The Rex Haberman controversy

Since this farmer type hailed from tiny Imperial, Nebraska (another farming community) Senator Chambers dubbed him "the Imperial Wizard" (as in Ku Klux Klan leadership) after he made comments about the breasts of South African women on a post card.

This was totally unnecessary and Haberman wasn't even in town when he mailed the post card. But Senator Chambers got hold of it and dogged him out. The hick later apologized, but I mention this incident to show you, the reader, how much bullshit takes place at the legislative level in the state of Nebraska and that this is what happens when the majority of your 49 members are either farmers or involved somehow in agribusiness.

The John DeCamp "black prostitutes" controversy

In February of 1978, a white State Senator, John DeCamp, used the word "nigger" on the floor of the Legislature, angering Senator Ernie Chambers. What took place after that included a poem from Chambers, written about DeCamp, which read, in part, that DeCamp [was],

> Shrieking in high, piercing nasal tones
> A voice that does shake and rattle the bones;
> Assaulting the air and punishing the ears,
> He seeks to shore up his wavering peers.

DeCamp responded that he felt the poem was a personal attack "that was as serious as using the word "nigger," which, he said, he would never use. Chambers objected and took several steps toward DeCamp before being called to order. He said the use of the word "nigger" was far more serious than a personal attack. The exchange ended several hours later when DeCamp took the floor to apologize (Omaha World Herald, 1978).

This is the kind of "farmer politics' foolishness that transpires on the floor of the Nebraska Legislature as each of these white senators does their best to "out-legislate" the only black man in the 49-person body, Senator Chambers. All they do in the final analysis is make total asses out of themselves.

But DeCamp knows that he lives in a hick state that is also racist, and as a result, he can get elected based on the following biographical claims which appear on his lie-filled website:

> During 16 years in office, former state senator John DeCamp was cited, even by his enemies at the World-Herald, as one of the most effective legislators in Nebraska history. A highly decorated Vietnam War veterans, in 1975 he initiated Operation Baby Lift, which evacuated 2,800 orphaned Vietnamese children. He practices law in Lincoln, Nebraska, is married, and is the father of four children.

Comparatively speaking DeCamp stood out. A fat, short white man in glasses who had a law degree was still a cut above the farm-oriented hicks that are a majority in the legislature. But next to Senator Ernie Chambers, he was just a nobody, which is why he took the shot at Ernie's district, a black community that he (DeCamp) wouldn't have the guts to take a step inside of.

The Bill Kintner "Cybersex" controversy (2016)

State Senator Bill Kintner of Papillion, a big mouthed Republican member of the Nebraska legislature got busted when he used a government computer to view sex videos. As it was reported on August 2, 2016, when State Senator Ernie Chambers called for Kintner's immediate suspension, he was defended by both the Republican governor and others. Both direct nepotism and what I call "racial nepotism" was again a part of the Nebraska formula for folly and failure. According to the aksarben.blogspot.com,

> Chambers criticized both Gov. Ricketts and Attorney General Doug Peterson for failing to act decisively in the year since evidence of this scandal emerged. He said Ricketts should have demanded to know whether Kintner had misused state resources and insisted that he resign if there was evidence of such misuse. "I believe there was a determination on the part of the governor and the attorney general which, in my opinion, seems to smack of the Republicans circling the wagons to protect a very loud member of their party," he said.

And this is what takes place in Nebraska politics, and here is where the "buddy system" comes in: Kintner, a Republican, is a key ally of Ricketts. Kintner also is married to Lauren Kintner, who leads Ricketts' policy research office. So they hire their friends and family m embers and then if something goes wrong, they rely on their fellow white pals from higher up to defend them, bend the law, do whatever has to be done. This has been going on in Nebraska for centuries, and continues to this day.

It was evident that Sen. Kintner misused state resources. But so what? That is what this book is about is it not? It's called "Invasion of the Booty Snatchers" because these white people have robbed the state of Nebraska blind and was make up for the shortfalls on the backs of the poor and minority. This is but one more example.

ELECTORAL POLITICS: THE FOUNDATION FOR ETHNOCENTRIC GREED IN NEBRASKA

Over the years the state has had slogans like, "Nebraska the Good Life" and "Nebraska Nice." As you can figure in a state of 1,700,000 residents that has only 50,000 black people in it, these sloganeers are speaking about white people for the most part. There may be a few token Asians thrown into the mix, but Nebraska is lily-white from top to bottom. And the key is that the state insists on remaining that way, refusing to change with the times and the demography, opting to allow in immigrants and refugees from other countries (who also represent revenue streams) instead of doing right by the black people in the North Omaha ghetto or the Latinos in the South Omaha barrio.

Nebraska's racism and ethnocentric behavior manifests itself in a plethora of areas, and that is especially evident in traditional politics. Whether Democrat or Republican, lily-whiteness is pervasive and is reflected in the decisions that are made, even at the caucus level.

For instance, the Nebraska Democratic Caucus, which is supposed to be more liberal and race conscious than the Republicans. In June of 2016 there were two incidents which showed that not only is Nebraska racist, but its younger version of the old boys' network is also apparently as discriminatory as the old farts are.

On July 23, 2016 the World Herald carried an article titled, "Sanders Supporters and Latinos Smooth Rift." According to the article,

> A cadre of young Bernie Sanders backers in Nebraska learned this week that it isn't right to play politics with Latinos. During last weekend's Democratic State convention, the Sanders group was accused of being "paternalistic" and exhibiting "white privilege" after it engineered the ouster of a long-time Latino leader in favor or a Sanders supporter as chairman of a Latino-centered caucus (Tysver, 2016).

Now left to their own devices, this would have been business as usual. Nebraska's "white power" message pervades every sphere of political life. After State Senator Ernie Chambers got district elections for the school board, the city council, and the county board, these white people nevertheless want to protect their system. Fortunately for them the representation of these largely black quadrants have been more selfish, greedy and immature than actual politicos. So in that whites are happy that they can use bribery and threats to nevertheless control issues in and around the black community.

In this case, the Latinos are still in a similar boat. Caucuses are nothing but people who round up votes and decide on issues that are going to make the white man's system more powerful. They think they are putting in work but as they end up seeing, their lives are no better off once the elections are over. This "Latino leader" who was eventually selected really "won" nothing: she is a good woman but she doesn't address racism the way she should. Besides, inclusion in these caucuses includes a section called "special interest caucuses" and, as can be expected, that's where the place the "niggas and the spics."

The article further explains that,

> Many of those in the Sanders group were young, white and male. And may of them apologized profusely during an emotional meeting Tuesday with Latino leaders in South Omaha. The meeting end with the Sanders supporter stepping down as chairman and allowing the leader of the Latino caucus to resume the health (Tysver, 2016).

They key words in the previous passage are, "young, white and male." The white man grooms his youth and always has a succession plan so he can keep the white supremacy system going. How else do you think a state as backwards as Nebraska could maintain its farmer-like, hillbilly image for a century? Unlike black people who want to get a position and hold on to it for eternity so that once they croak, the organization dies, white people think ahead. Even when they eventually die off, their system will still be intact to ensure that conscious and aware black and brown people remain at the bottom of the heap.

And it's not just Latinos.

During the same time period I received a series of "save us" emails from people in the black community. It seems that Luis Jimenez had convinced this black woman, Carlose Talkington to lobby me for help in the case of some "young man," Maurice Jones, who was being impeached and asked to resign from the board of the Black Caucus of the Democratic Party. I told them to kiss my ass because I had more important things to do than to buttress some white run political party and its "niggerologist" participants.

Here is the bullshit email I received from Talkington on July 18, 2016:

> On Mon, Jul 18, 2016 at 6:08 PM, Carlose Marie Talkington
> carlose.m.talkington@gmail.com> wrote:
>
> > Matthew, I can appreciate your views, but this young man needs
> support, the young man in question is an African American male,
> 17 years old, who is being impeached, because he wants to make
> sure African American's and the Black community from which he
> was raised , here in Omaha!! are being represented on the Black
> Caucus, which they are trying to slide a White woman in the
> position!! his name is Maurice Jones, a young Black man
> determined to make a difference!
> Carlose

After more than 45 years of working in defense and development of black people, I have seen various examples of how we, as a race, just don't get it. The code words in the email cited above are "a young Black man determined to make a difference." Aren't we all? But here's the difference between me and most: when I'm determined to do it, first of all I get it done. Secondly, I don't need any assistance to do what I think is right because most of the time the people I'm trying to help are more dedicated to maintaining the status quo than they are to actually "making a difference." And third, how can you "make a difference" if you're leeching to be a part of the system that doesn't want you to be a part of it? Who didn't want your ancestors to be a part of it? And who, to this day, work continually to keep you and yours from EVER being a part of it.

Two different issues in the more "liberal" of the two parties in the state of Nebraska. The Latinos and the Blacks scrounging to get their piece of the rock in a system that despises them. These twin incidents then, define the focus, fulcrum and foundation for race relations as related to the "traditional politics" of Nebraska as a state.

The "invasion of the booty snatchers" is secured ideologically and with a vision rooted in and reinforced by greed. Add to this childish obsession with wanting all the marbles, you have to also understand the equally childish lack of foresight and cultural intelligence that comes along with it. In the next section of this book I deal with the lack of creativity, modernity and originality and why Nebraska remains mired in mediocrity.

THE LACK OF CREATIVITY, ORIGINALITY AND MODERNITY

One reason why Nebraska in general and Omaha in particular continue to wallow in mediocrity and continue to be a "flyer over" state is because of its lack of creativity, and modernity. They can't even get together on a lie that promotes their own state. That "Nebraska Nice" bullshit is a direct theft of the "Wisconsin Nice" slogan that has existed for decades. And from there the dependency on outside consultants and ideas just keeps on coming.

These white people never change. They know what the problems are because they created them. Then, when enough damage has been done, here they come with "programs," "projects," and "organizations" that beg for free grant money to "take a stab" at the problem; never any guarantees, just the "attempt" to do something for "the negroes."

Moving on:

> The new group, Seventy Five North Revitalization Inc., is being advised by Purpose Built Communities of Atlanta and intends to coordinate its plans with the Omaha Public Schools and with Omaha government and private-sector improvement groups. "It's exciting," said Susan Buffett, who accompanied her father and other Omahans last week to Indianapolis to visit a redevelopment area that uses Purpose Built Communities' methods. "There is a lot of potential." Her Sherwood Foundation supports Seventy Five North (Jordon, 2011).

How much is being paid to Purpose Built Communities of Atlanta for its "advice"? Why are you going outside of Omaha (as is the tendency) for advice and tips on what to do with North Omaha when you've got an entire community of life-long residents who are never consulted on their own quality of life issues? An article I wrote 21 years ago – over two decades -- that appeared in the June 7, 1982 edition of the Omaha World Herald titled, "Minorities Can Help Build Omaha" drove home the point rather well. In part, I wrote:

> If we add up the monies spent on "outside consultants" since the year 1979, we can already see capital flowing outside of our city. For example, Adam Pinsker – a "consultant" from New York – has already received over $35,000 from our city's Chamber of Commerce, local businessmen, Creighton University and the Metropolitan Arts Council. In its quest for a "United Arts Fund," the chamber committee spent an additional $41,500 for a C.W. Shavers report (Stelly, 1982)

I continued:

The Department of Housing and Community Development gave
the Real Estate Research Corporation of Chicago $8,500 in 1980 to
do a study on the Garden Apartments. In 1981 this same research
group was given another $25,765 to do a market analysis of 24th and
Lake Streets. Between 1979 and 1981, the "North Omaha Plan" has
cost over $90,000. Again, outsiders – these from Berkeley, Calif. –
took the money and ran. These approximated figures (approximated
because they are underestimated) total $200,765 spent since 1979
alone (Stelly, 1982).

A man named Dan Karnish, white, responded to the article which received a
great deal of noticeable attention and kudos, and on June 12th, wrote a response to
the "Public Pulse" under the headline, 'Use Our Local Talent.' His name was Don
Karnish and he wrote,

Matthew Stelly's June 7 Another Point of View ("Minorities Can
Help Build Omaha") touched on many interesting points, especially
the ridiculous recruiting of consultants from New England and
California. The fact that more than $200,000 was spent on these
consultants is sickening. It seems that if a consultant is from the
West or East coast, everyone thinks he is some sort of superhuman
intellectual. We have an abundance of talented people in this city.
It's time we Omahans pulled our heads out of the sand and used our
own natural resources to build a better community.
Don Karnish

As you can see I have been documenting the city's "copycat tendencies" for
at least 34 years, although it has been much longer. They are sorely lacking in
anything remotely entertaining so they have to borrow what others have done. And
this is but the beginning.

POOR MANAGEMENT AND VISION LEADS TO TAX REVENUE SHORTAGES

There are tax revenue shortages because Nebraska has very high taxes.
According to Senator Jim Smith of Papillion, Nebraska has the eighth highest
property tax burden in the nation and is 14th in the nation in income tax. Despite
this, the state is still a loser. Why is this the case? Who gets hurt in order to
scrounge up the money needed? This section hopes to answer these questions.

Newspaper headlines are written to generate interest. When Nebraska's
government is in financial trouble – and it usually is – the tendency is to downplay
the problem with vague and nebulous claims of what might take place.

Such is the case in the area of tax related issues. For instance, on April 2, 2015, the World-Herald's Martha Stoddard, one of its top reporters, wrote an article that the newspaper headlined, "Nebraska's Property Tax Credit Fund May Grow to $200 Per Year." The key word in that headline is the word "may." In other words there is nothing definite so one has to ask why the article appeared in the first place. It appeared to quell any fears that Nebraskans might rightfully have about the piss-pot pour management taking place by and in its state government

Now, fast forward to the following article by the same reporter that appeared in the July 15, 2016 issues of the same newspaper. Only fourteen months later and now the headline reads, "Nebraska Ended Last Fiscal Year with $95M Less Revenue than Expected; Rickets Orders Agencies to Tighten Belts."

The key words in that headline are "less than expected." But this wasn't the first time. Stoddard (2016) reminds us that, "In April, legislative fiscal staff projected that state revenues would fall $234 million short of expected state spending during the period beginning July 1, 2017. So the people charged with the economic fate of the State continue to make error after error. And even in that they still have the gall to provide updates "on those projections when a committee of key lawmakers and the Tax Commissioner meet later this month." The dumb keep on leading the way and the blind continue to lead the blind.

In my view what this adds up to is the fact that there appear to be people who are making projections, aimed at again subduing any concerns about mismanagement at the government level. So they give these bullshit projections to bamboozle the public and keep concerned citizens at bay. In other words, the projections were guesses – they were estimates. And so it goes in Nebraska. Realizing they have a largely hick and uneducated population, the media carries water for the political entities who continue screwing up the money and not doing their jobs. As a result, revenue shortfalls are inevitable.

Let's take a look at key parts of the article of July 15, 2016 – headlined, ""Nebraska Ended Last Fiscal Year with $95M Less Revenue than Expected; Rickets Orders Agencies to Tighten Belts." and see why "the invasion of the booty snatchers" is a tactic that is a financial imperative in a state that is experiencing shortfall after shortfall.

According to the World Herald piece,

> Nebraska ended its last fiscal year with $95 million less tax
> revenue than expected, according to a state report released
> Thursday. In response, Gov. Pete Ricketts ordered state agencies to
> tighten their belts and watch their pennies during the fiscal year
> that began July 1. But he said there is no need to call the State
> Legislature back to Lincoln for a special budget-cutting session
> (Stoddard, 2016).

Why was all that money "expected"? Because of previous fuckups by those who are in charge of making budget projections. And who were they hired by? Other people in Nebraska, mostly in the human resources department, who are entrusted to make sure that they bring credible people on board. If not that, then these people are "appointed" by the old boy's network. In any case, it is a clear cut case of one hand washes the other and the result is the kind of mistake-riddled financial realities that you read about in the previous paragraph.

> Nor has he given up hopes of cutting taxes during the next two-
> year state budget period, which will start on July 1, 2017. "This is
> not a crisis," Ricketts said. "This is what we get paid to do, to
> manage our budgets." (Stoddard, 2016).

These Nebraska politicians have been running the "long con" on residents for decades. Here you see the governor, a millionaire, pledging to cut taxes in a state that is hemorrhaging money. Then he has the gall to add that "this is what we get paid to do, to manage our budgets." So since such management has been an abysmal failure for the past several decades, aren't those failures tantamount to non-feasance? Haven't they violated the oath they swore to when they took office? Why do they keep screwing up and then getting away with it? You know why: because the majority of their constituents are hicks, hillbillies and farmer-types. That's why.

The July 2016 article on Ricketts "ordering agencies to tighten belts" continues:

> The governor directed all agencies under the control of his office
> to take such steps as reviewing all hiring, limiting travel to
> essential services, coordinating technology and other purchases,
> and working with fellow agencies to find efficiencies. He also
> warned them not to expect that they can carry over unspent funds
> from the fiscal year that ended June 30. (Stoddard, 2016).

What Ricketts was outlining could have been found in any introductory book on budgeting. In fact, what he is "proposing" is what should have been done all along. And the fact that it wasn't done, or was done in an inadequate way, is the reason for Nebraska's on-going budget crises and why the "invasion of the booty snatchers" is a strategy that relies on the exploitation of the poor and gullible; those in power are simply not passing muster. No state is more than the sum total of the people who vote for its leadership: in simpler terms "stupid is as stupid does."

Continuing:

> The governor requested similar actions from noncode agencies, those administered by independent boards and commissions. In memos to both groups, Ricketts said he had instructed the state budget office to cut quarterly allotments to state agencies by 1 percent every three months. He said the move aims to encourage fiscal responsibility. (Stoddard, 2016).

Playing catch up. I lay this at the feet of the personnel/human resources directors. They are the ones hiring these idiots to run various departments and after the hiring is done, there is no supervision or monitoring. Once hundreds of thousands are stolen or mis-managed, it is only *then* that people like Ricketts pretend to want to "take charge" and make chances. And yet what does the silly governor conclude? He tells the World-Herald, "That's a way to send a message we need to be watching our dollars, tightening our belts and making sure we're doing a good job for the taxpayers," he said. (Stoddard, 2016).

And it's only going to get worse as more and more people are jumping ship after they college their huge salaries and benefits. Already gone are the chancellor of the University of Nebraska at Omaha, John Christensen and in early October of 2016, the superintendent of the state's largest school district, Mark Evans, also decided to call it quits. Without real leadership Nebraska is only going to find itself spiraling deeper into an abyss of depression. But they have always been good about covering up the decadence and buffoonery with statements akin to the ones that follow:

> The reduction in allotments will affect all state agencies, not just those under the governor's control. Neither the governor nor Tax Commissioner Tony Fulton would predict whether Nebraska is headed for a deeper shortfall of tax revenues in the coming months and years. "We don't make any predictions about where this is going," Ricketts said. (Stoddard, 2016).

You don't have to be able to "predict" if Nebraska is "headed for a deeper shortfall of tax revenues." Just read this book! I've been on these buttheads for decades, documenting their on-going and costly instances of graft, greed, financial abuse, mistakes and so on. They simply cannot cut muster because they want to leave hiring decisions to people who hire based on race, not merit; based on ethnic kinship, not qualifications. And when they do that, they end up hiring people who are as duplicitous and disingenuous as they are. In other words, it's a very vicious cycle. Therefore "where is this going"? To hell in a hand basket, that's where.

Some sober minds prevail such as those of State Senator Ernie Chambers and another senator with a functioning brain stem, Heath Mello:

But Omaha State Sen. Heath Mello, the Appropriations Committee
chairman, said state agencies need to prepare for the likelihood of
seeing minimal growth in funding for the next state budget period.
"I think it's prudent for the governor to begin the process of asking
agencies to restrain their spending," he said. Mello noted that the
state budget office has instructed agencies to identify potential cuts
equal to 8 percent of their current budgets. The lists of possible
cuts are to be submitted to the governor by Sept. 15, along with
agency budget requests. (Stoddard, 2016).

What Mello is calling "minimal growth in funding" is a compliment. The
state deserves NO growth, NO revenue and NO budgeting increases until it can
first of all show that its hiring decisions reflect bringing people on board who can
think, plan, project long-term revenue and who are not a part of the old boys'
network.

Mello is again most generous when he says, ""I think it's prudent for the
governor to begin the process of asking agencies to restrain their spending," The
governor can't "lead where he won't go." Nor can he "teach what he doesn't
know." This idiot made his money because of his father, much like Donald Trump
did. He has already broken the law and ordered an illegal drug that is geared
toward a legal injection/death penalty law that is not even in effect! That should
tell you something right there. How can you trust an idiot to lead and provide
direction. But then again, "on the island of the blind, the one-eyed man is king."

And in my view it will get worse before it gets better:

The board will meet this fall to revise its projections for the 2016-
17 fiscal year and issue its first forecast of tax revenues for the
2017-19 budget period. (Stoddard, 2016).

Where are the revenue streams that can make up for these projected
shortfalls and losses? Nowhere to be found, and why? Because the other
departments and divisions around the state are screwing up as well. From
corrections to tourism, they're all having a ball with taxpayer's money. And
speaking of tourism, let's take a look at how millions were bilked out of that area
for the pleasure of some white woman, her family and her favorites.

PROBLEMS IN NEBRASKA TOURISM

On September 25, 1997 – nearly two decades ago -- a man named Tony
Dworak contacted me about my organization, the Triple One Neighborhood
Association. Along with Robert Bauldwin, the associate director of TONA, we met

with him on the campus of the University of Nebraska at Omaha. He introduced himself and stated that he was an official with the State of Nebraska Department for Economic Development Office of Tourism. Robert and I used his ass all the way up. What he wanted and needed was a tour of and insights about North Omaha for a tourism booklet he was preparing. So we obliged him and for the next several hours, provided him a tour of the boulevards, the housing and organizations, and told him about the racism and segregation that made the community as compartmentalized as it was.

He dropped us off and then on September 25, 1997 – that evening in fact – he sent the following email that I picked up on my UNO computer:

> Thanks for the good word, Mr. Stelly
>
> October 7 is real tight, but I forwarded this to Shirley. I will also give her your UNO number and ask her to speak with you directly. If it is too late for this project, don't let that stop you from trying a different one. But for some reason, I don't think you are the kind of guy who let's things stop him, so I won't worry about that!!
>
> I will send you another TARGET application. We will need to meet again where we can sit down and design the actual workings of the study ... not to mention decide on when to do it.
>
> Take 'er easy and thanks for the "North Omaha 101" course you gave me this morning. It was an eye-opener, and it made me interested in further study of the area.
> Tony Dworak, NE Tourism

The book on North Omaha came out early the following year and Dworak wisely put my name in it as a major consultant. This document would come in handy in my future work to promote tourism in North Omaha and to show that indeed, I was on the cutting edge of promoting it. That includes a proposal in around 1994 at a time when Jay Baum was heading the Omaha office of Tourism. I created an organization called NOVA – North Omaha Visitors Association and submitted it for funding. The gist of and budget for that organization is enclosed at the end of this proposal. Nothing was ever done.

FLASHBACK TO 1991: OMAHA TOURISM AND "GOOD MORNING AMERICA"

On my June 1, 1991 program, I got a chance to dog out both Milwaukee and Omaha. Earlier, the TV show "Good Morning America" had launched what they called their "Heart of America Tour" and one of the cities that they visited was Omaha. They did a piss-pot pour job, interviewed a few Uncle Toms like Eddie Staton, and talked about the Strategic Air Command as if it were in Omaha (it's in Bellevue).

When ABC's "Good Morning America" came to Milwaukee, after leaving Omaha, McGee and some of his flunkies rushed the stage in an attempt to bogart the microphones. They got a little play out of it but what they mostly did was make asses out of themselves. Constantly hungry for attention, McGee had a real mental problem, but since the average Milwaukee black was also from the Deep South and as stupid as McGee, he had a built-in following.

I decided to review the program and also compare Omaha and Milwaukee in regard to their respective black communities. Following is my essay, "The Heart of America Tour: Regional Politics versus Public Relations," which appeared in the Milwaukee Courier:

> On Tuesday, May 14th, The Good Morning America team visited Milwaukee. On May 16th, hosts Joan Lunden and Charles Gibson visited Omaha, Nebraska. All of this was part of what was called "The Heart of America Bus Tour," and also included Kansas City and Jefferson, Missouri, as well as Minneapolis, Minnesota. The Heartland, as we all well know, is one of those areas of the country where blacks are not in large numbers, and if more evidence of this is needed, one need merely take a look at the way Lunden and Gibson skipped from city to city, skimming over important issues and instead, used the awesome power of ABC as nothing more than a public relations tool for a part of the country that obviously can't compete with the tourism numbers on the west and east coasts.
>
> In Milwaukee, the interviews took place on the lakefront. Bo Black, the director of Summerfest and public relations magnate Ben Barkin, were on the television smiling and acting as if Milwaukee was utopia. While Barkin name-dropped on the air, restaurants were mentioned and Channel 12's Jerry Taff presented a short clip on how wonderful Milwaukee is. In Omaha, Good Morning America did the same thing. The Central Park Mall is the city's crown jewel, and like the lakefront, was built to add something urbane to a rapidly growing downtown area. Milwaukee has its Old World Third Street and Omaha has its Old Market area. Both of them white ethnic reminders of the way things used to be, complete with cobblestone streets, décor and of course, no black or Latino businesses.
>
> In Omaha, Taff's counterpart from KETV Channel 7 is Carole Shrader. She begged and pleaded for money to save the Omaha Royals minor league baseball team. And Charles Gibson even went

so far as to ask millionaire Warren Buffett to kick in some money to save the team. In comparison, we all know the role that the local media here in Milwaukee has played in leeching for and receiving, more than $300 million to build the Brewers a stadium right here, another similarity.

While in Omaha, Lunden and Gibson gave a great deal of attention to Criss Rexall Drug Store, a place where original soda fountains, dating back to the '50s, still exist, and still attract tourists from all over the region to sit and have the traditional ice cream soda of their choice. Again, more pristine nostalgia in an attempt to paint a picture of "goodness" for the city of Omaha.

But the Criss family played a big role in the founding of Creighton University, as well as Mutual of Omaha Insurance Company. And along with Richard Anderson at the Omaha World Herald, these powers control most of the city, and dominate the entire black community. Just as the Greater Milwaukee Committee does in Milwaukee, the Criss family, V.J. Skutt (president of Mutual of Omaha), Boys Town and a new mayor P.J. Morgan (a real estate tycoon), help bolster the image of "the good life' in a city where the median income for a black family of four is $7,500 a year, more than $2,000 less than in Milwaukee.

The duo was willing to refer to Omaha as 'a city full of suprises.' But what would have been the real surprise would have been to tell viewers that this city of 600,000 (an exaggerated figure) has 50,000 black people who just had a freeway rammed down the heart of the black community; who have an unemployment rate of over 25 percent in a city and a state that always ranks near the top in overall lowest unemployment, and an infant mortality rate that is three times that of the city's whites. The nation would have been surprised to know that Omaha is the birth place of one of the world's leading black nationalists, Malcolm X. They would have been even more surprised that there is a black state senator from Omaha, Ernest Chambers who, like Malcolm, is one of the most articulate spokesmen for black people in this country.

The team decided that it was important to give Oakland, Nebraska a chance to boast about being the Swedish capital of Nebraska, and even went so far as to give viewers a trip through Alliance, Broken Bow, Comstock, Kearney and so on – as if these hick towns are suburbs of Omaha. They are not! Obviously, Lunden and Gibson ran out of things to talk about and decided to give some of the smaller towns in the Cornhusker state some free publicity.

The nation would have been interested in knowing how greedy Boys Town really is. Flashbacks on the Mickey Rooney-Spencer Tracey movie was anticipated, and administrators boasted that

Boys Town "helped more than 16,000 troubled youth over the years" and has even gone co-ed. But all is not kosher in Boys Town, and serious investigative reporting or interviews with people of color would have revealed that.

For instance, Boys Town has a nationwide begging campaign and even though they don't need money, they have one of the biggest stockpiles in the entire region. Furthermore, the money is so plentiful that they built a school – Father Flanagan High School – right in the heart of Omaha's inner city so that they can continue to use the grant money approach to exploit more of the city's poor.

In Milwaukee, the featured band was the Bodeans. In Omaha, it was the Strategic Air Command band playing "Stars and Stripes," even though the SAC base is actually located in Bellevue, not Omaha. Furthermore who chose the Bodeans when there is the Eddie Butts Band and other more talented groups? Why not give an unknown band some attention instead of always focusing on white groups? And Omaha boasts renowned jazz saxophonist Preston Love! There can be but one explanation: both cities have a lily-white image and they want to keep it that way.

While Bo Black was at least conscious enough to mention African World Festival during their presentation on fht city's festivals, why wasn't Good Morning America informed of the fact that one of Omaha's biggest celebrations during the summer is the July 4th "Stone Soul Picnic," which is African-American oriented?

Alderman Michael McGee had the right idea by making it known that Milwaukee has racial problems, problems that both Gibson and Lunden had to have known about, and had they had their way, would have rather evaded and avoided. Omahans obviously don't have that much dignity. They let Good Morning America paint a rosy picture of a city that is blatantly segregated: 95% of blacks in Omaha live in an eight-square mile area in the northeast sector of the city. And racist. They ignored the celebrated Senator Chambers, the state's leading black spokesman. Can we consider these accidents?

Not when these same morning show hosts can dig up unknown cities, visit secret areas and talk to individuals who are not even known on their own block, let alone statewide.

Boys Town had no way of knowing that the author of the preceding article – me – hailed from Omaha and had an extensive file on Boys Town's antics in and around the black community of Omaha. They had no idea that Matthew Stelly had been active in the controversy surrounding the North Freeway's incursion into North Omaha and how Dominican High School played a role in that. Elsewhere in this paper you will find a speech by Nebraska State Senator Ernie Chambers that clearly documents the damage that Dominican and Father Flanagan High School did to the residents of Omaha's black community

At any rate, in response to the preceding article, which also appeared in the June 1, 1991 issue of the Milwaukee Courier, Boys Town wrote a rather bellicose letter in response. Since my by-line was not on the article, Boys Town addressed the letter to the Managing Editor – my friend, Joni Alston -- who then forwarded it to me. Dated July 26, 1991, take note of how this "charitable" and "Christian" organization lashes out at those who have information that runs counter to the way they expect America to think and feel:

> Ms. Joni Alston, Managing Editor
> The Milwaukee Courier
> 2431 West Hopkins
> Milwaukee, WI 53206-1251
>
> Dear Ms. Alston:
>
> Frankly, we here at Boys Town in Nebraska are very surprised at the misdirected vehemency shown toward our organization in your June 1, 1991 article on the "Heart of America Tour."
>
> While we are supportive of your newspaper promoting Black causes, directing anger at Boys Town is off base. Phrases in the article show a lack of knowledge about Boys Town's operation and an even greater lack of understanding that Boys Town is one of the most helpful and supportive organizations to the Black community, not only in Omaha, but around the country.
>
> For example, Father Flanagan High School is a comprehensive, alternative-education school which is unique in providing opportunities to 300 inner-city youth every year, most of whom are Black youngsters from poverty-stricken backgrounds or who are threatened by the gang problem in the area. The "grant money" you speak of is practically non-existent, totaling only $88,310 last year for hot lunch and child care programs. This is the same any public or parochial school would receive to support children of poverty. That amount is nothing compared to the more than $2.5 million which Boys Town contributes to run Father Flanagan High School each and every year for the direct benefit of the community and the improved prospects of its students. Would you spend $2.5 million in order to receive $88,310 in grants?
>
> To suggest Boys Town is greedy also shows a severe lack of insight. While Boys Town does have an endowment fund, it does not begin to cover our annual operating costs. This year Boys Town will directly assist more than 15,000 abused, abandoned, or handicapped children of all races, creeds and colors. The type of care and treatment we provide is expensive and requires fund-raising activities. To imply Boys Town is needlessly "begging" is

not only inaccurate, but downright damaging to our good
reputation.

 We have no idea to whom you are referring in saying that
interviews with people of color would have revealed problems.
Our relationships with the Black communities in Omaha and our
many other cities around the country are more than just solid and
rewarding, they are excellent. To let your news columns be
poisoned by the misguided thoughts of a few individuals on the
fringe is unfair and totally uncalled for.

 I would like to see your erroneous reporting corrected. We will
be happy to assist in any further information you need to correct
this outrageous diatribe against Boys Town. I'll look forward to
receiving the clip of the story that corrects your gross inaccuracies.

Sincerely,
Randal R. Blauvelt, APR
Director, Public Relations

 I wasn't apologizing for shit. Not to those assholes who over the years have been involved in pedophile-related behavior and got busted for it back during the expose done on the Franklin Credit Union of Omaha. Boys Town and the rest of them were the racists behind the construction and then closure of Father Flanagan High School in the Omaha black community, a controversy that I was in the middle of. And I learned, directly, that Boys Town doesn't give a shit about black people unless it can recruit them, bring them in, and then use their sob stories to generate free social service-related grant money.

 And do you know what else they do? They publish dozens of "studies" about those same low-income and minority kids. They use those kids in surveys and studies and then get their names plastered all over these scholarly journals that supposedly "teach" people about how to "handle" what they call "at-risk" kids. At no point do I see, in any of these journals or hear from any of these scholars any mention of the source that puts so many kids "at risk":

 White folks. One more piece of evidence that "the invasion of the booty snatchers" is no myth, but is alive and well and living right there in west Omaha, under the stature of Father Flanagan with some kid on hi s back over the inscription, "He ain't heavy – he's my brother."

ABOUT TOURISM IN NEBRASKA AND OMAHA

 When I first arrived in Omaha in June of 1977, I immediately took note of the tourism-related slogan of Omaha, Nebraska, which was, "Omaha: America's Best Kept Secret." After living here for several months, I immediately began to notice why. And from what I have gleaned having written its history (as well as the history of North Omaha, the UNO Black Studies Department, and the history of the Minority Affairs Departments on NU campuses) I can now see why: if I had a racist and tradition as nonproductive and Neanderthal as Omaha's I would keep it a secret, too.

Apparently, I am not the only person who sees the Nebraska situation this way. Why else would a tourism department have a budget of $6 million, an increase of about $1.6 million from three years ago? The fact is the average U.S. state tourism budget in 2013 was an estimated $14.9 million (Skankman, 2013).

So even though Nebraska's budget is far less than other states, one can question if Nebraska has much more to offer than other similarly sized states. Other than the rural "come visit the cowboys" veneer, what can really be said about the Cornhusker State? In recent years even its football team has faltered, reminding me of an oft-heard joke told by people in regard to Nebraska's football team and the fact that the stadium is packed every Saturday:

> Q: Why did the Nebraska Board of Regents decide to cover
> Memorial Stadium in cardboard?
> A: Because the Huskers always look better on paper.

Without tourism dollars, Nebraska is going to wither away like the last leaves of a painfully prolonged autumn. I believe that the leadership can see it coming, which is why, in acts of desperation, you read more stories about outright thefts of public dollars as if those who commit these acts are making a last-ditch effort to "run fer the hills"! This appears to me to be what was revealed when Nebraska's auditor performed a recent audit of the Tourism Department. This brief paper is a response to that article and an offer of a "change" in the Department that would be able to save dollars, increase tourism and change the corn pone-like image of the state.

TOURISM MALFEASANCE AT THE STATE LEVEL, 2016

On April 30, 2016 an article appeared in the *Omaha World Herald* under the headline," Auditor: State Tourism Commission 'Took Advantage of the Nebraska Taxpayers'. The article, written by Paul Hammel, was detailed and outlined yet one more example of how racial nepotism in the hiring policies of Nebraska leads to managers, supervisors and other decision makers who simply are not qualified for the positions they hold. This is true of the Banking and Finance Department, the Department of Health and Human Services, Correctional Service, State Patrol, Education, Economic Development and the rest. This is important to know because all of these have experienced highly publicized failures and as a result, the entire state has a buffoonish reputation. This, in turn impacts of businesses that have to think about relocating here and as such, also impacts on people who want to come here with their families to raise children.

Following is my analysis of the contents of that World-Herald article with emphasis on history, tradition, tourism principles and business protocols and logic.

The article begins, thusly:

> LINCOLN — A new state audit has slammed the Nebraska
> Tourism Commission for excessive spending on conference
> speakers and photo shoots, improperly reimbursing a contractor for
> alcohol and cigarettes, and using the executive director's daughter
> in a state tourism advertising campaign.

This is the same thing that the Federal government busted the Department of health and Social Services for about eight years ago. This is a similar thing that the Department of Corrections continues to get busted for. All of these atrocities revolve around a single issue: mismanagement. And the reason for that is that these Nebraskans get their jobs through appointments and hirings made by idiotic personnel department managers. Not only that, but what the article refers to as hiring of a relative (nepotism) is worse than that: if you include hirings based on race, then that nepotism becomes ethnocentric decision making, also known as "discrimination." And everyone in the state knows that Nebraska is guilty of *that!*

Continuing:

> The commission, which became an independent agency four years
> ago, also was criticized for getting dozens of free meals from its
> advertising firm, Bailey Lauerman, and for allowing the firm's ad
> contract to go over budget by $4.4 million in the past three years.

This is how it's done in Nebraska. You have to understand that State Senator Ernie Chambers has accused them time and time again of mooching. The state legislature is guilty of it as Chambers as pointed out, and it's contagious. Put simply, these are hicks in suits; these are hillbillies in high heels. You can take people out of the country but you can't take the country out of these people. They have the power to hire and they do it based on race, how many years you've been in Nebraska (whether or not you're what they call "home grown") and similar subjective variables. After being hired, if they find out you're a pedophile or a pervert, these Nebraskans will protect you (read: late *Omaha World Herald* publisher Harold Anderson, former Nebraska University system president Ronald Roskens, etc.).

And you wonder why tourism, like the character and morality of the people who run it, is declining? The article adds that,

> The audit also cited as excessive $18,000 in moving expenses that were paid to an employee who relocated from Sidney to Kearney and a $44,000 fee for a 90-minute speech at the commission's annual conference.

Relocating from hick-ass Sidney Nebraska to Kearney? That's like moving from one hillbilly location to another! It cost eighteen grand? Sidney has a population of 6,914 and Kearney has a total of 32,469. In Nebraska terms, the latter is a "big city," but here's the point I'm making about the expensive relocation costs: its 218 miles from Sidney to Kearney. What in the FUCK was this person moving that came to eighteen grand? And if the person was already an employee, why didn't he/she bear some of his/her own costs? And of what value was this person that merited paying all this money? And what has been produced by this person, since the relocation, that justified the sacrifice of time, energy and money to bring that person to Kearney?

These are the types of questions that should have been asked when the act was being committed, and surely there are some pissed off employees who knew about it but said nothing because they feared for the loss of their own jobs.

Then there's the $44,000 for a speech that lasted an hour and a half. Are you kidding me? Just recently in Omaha a black doctor from the University of Nebraska Medical Center figured she'd have a "discussion on race" and paid this nutty white woman some money to come to Omaha and speak for ten minutes. I don't know how much was paid, but you remember Rachel Dolezal – the crazy white woman who believed she was black?

These monies have to be refunded, plain and simple. These white people are wondering why they have the reputation of being a "flyover state," meaning that people only come here or fly over here to get somewhere else. That is because the "somewhere else" they are heading doesn't have the plethora of problems that this state has! And rather than admit that it's their own buffoonery and ineptitude, they blame it on the sun or on the economy or on Obama.

The article documents a comment by the auditor:

> "We had heard some rumblings that Tourism was operating as a rogue agency without any oversight," said State Auditor Charlie Janssen. "It appears that was the case. They kind of took advantage of the Nebraska taxpayers."

How long were those "rumblings" heard before the auditor decided to act? And the fact is, if those rumblings were coming from a black person or a black agency, they would not have gone on for long! The rumblings were heard because the auditor and the people committing the acts of malfeasance are of the same race! The Auditor should be fired; his after-the-fact, day-late-dollar-shot "discovery" is evidence that he has selective decision making approaches: he's supposed to be an on-going monitor of expenditures; he's not supposed to sit around and allow his brothers and sisters who are as pale as he is to abuse taxpayers' money and then, because he didn't get some pussy the night before, come to work angry and then call the World-Herald and "spill the beans"!

And what is this shit, "They kind of took advantage of the Nebraska taxpayers"? That's akin to these white cops talking about "we kind of thought that the unarmed black youth was a threat" or the white firemen claiming, "we kind of thought that the house couldn't be saved, anyway." This is delayed thinking and as a result, on-going delayed applications of what is being thought about. These kinds of actions would counter to the "time is money" ethic that America runs on. The act was so egregious that the major newspaper, a conservative rag if there ever was one, used the excuse in its headline: "). Auditor: State Tourism Commission 'Took Advantage of the Nebraska Taxpayers'."

So the headline is more definitive than the response that the auditor gave to Paul Hammel. If what was written wasn't true, there would be grounds for a libel suit. And the headline itself is grounds for the termination of the auditor! He is supposed to be a watchdog over the money – if someone took advantage of taxpayers, then he should have known about it and acted with all deliberate speed!

But instead, in vintage Nebraska fashion, they want to sit down and write reports. I've read enough of these reports to know that they can't write worth a shit and secondly, the reports are as flawed and fluffed up as the thinking of the people who put them together. Their aim is not to hurt anyone's feelings instead of just telling the truth and letting the flak fall where it may. That is, if the victim or perpetrator is white; if it's a black man, woman or child, then all's fair, and lies and manipulations are readily printed. I've got reams of essays documenting the World-Herald's fuckups to justify this latter point.

But back to the "report":

> The 79-page audit was released late Friday. The Tourism Commission, in its official response to the audit, acknowledged that some expenses and reimbursements were not properly tracked, and pledged to work with the Nebraska Department of Administrative Services to tighten procedures.

What? Take note of the illogical progression: auditor discovers improprieties and decides they are serious enough to document in writing; ignoring the seriousness, he sits around and writes a 79-page document at a time when one sentence would have sufficed. That sentence should have been: "The Department of Tourism has fucked up taxpayers money"! It's very simple.

But by taking all that time with the audit's volume (rather than validity), they stall time for the perpetrators to get together and come up with lies to back up their actions. And as I say, I've seen and read their vaunted "studies," "reports" and "strategic plans." And when all is said and done, none of them, to date, have made a lick of damn sense.

"Tighten procedures"? This is the same thing that DHHS, the Department of Corrections and the other Departments claim when they get caught with their hands in the cookie jar! But what about the people who wrote the procedures? What about the committee that read the procedures and then green-lighted them? And what about the people who were victimized during the time when these procedures were proven to be inadequate? *So they blame the written word and a booklet rather than the idiots who were the authors of both.*

Were it not for Senator Chambers (the lone black man in the legislature), it is doubtful if this discovery of misfeasance would have ever been made:

> This spring, as part of the state budget bill, lawmakers required the tourism office to contract with Administrative Services to provide oversight on its spending.

You have to remember that the members of the Legislature are the same hicks who think that Nebraska football is some kind of godsend. They worship that mediocre team because it is literally the only game in town. These Nebraska hicks have nothing else to look forward to all year long. Tourism is important because it generates revenue. But I am sure that not everyone who works in the Tourism Division is a total idiot: they have to know that Nebraska is a dead-end state. They have to know that the people are borderline morons because they are married to them and live next door to them.

Therefore, the lack of competency starts at the top and filters down. Senator Chambers is the lone legislator who knows the law and who challenges the racism that permeates the State of Nebraska's various departments and programs. Whatever was gotten away with during this monetary rip-off was known about long before. But these white people look out for one another, and this article in the World Herald is an indicator of that. In fact, the World Herald often buttresses and lies and manipulated manifestations of reality that the State of Nebraska and the

City of Omaha use on a regular basis. I've proven that in past articles and manuscripts.

Casting blame is another tactics that the poorly trained administrators tend to use when they are busted. Check it out:

> State Tourism Director Kathy McKillip said Saturday that many of the problems were related to the lack of a policy and procedures manual for the newly independent agency. A manual is now being drawn up for approval by the commission in August. "Where there are weaknesses, then we need to learn from them … and move forward," McKillip said. The agency, in its official response, defended some of the spending as necessary to promote the state and, in some cases, an effort to save money.

See? Such excuses remind me of some lyrics from Stevie Wonder's 1972 song, "I'll Blame It On the Sun":

> But I'll blame it on the sun,
> The sun that didn't shine,
> I'll blame it on the wind and the trees.
>
> I'll blame it on the time that never was enough,
> I'll blame it on the tide and the sea,
> But, my heart blames it on me.

If the agency was "newly independent," that didn't mean they had to start from scratch. They still had basic rules in place, especially when it came to organizational expenditures. To stall more time and attempt to bullshit the press, she talks about a manual "being drawn up for approval by the commission in August." Now this article appeared in April – that gives these nincompoops four months to bullshit, accumulate a bunch of charts and graphs and then had in a voluminous document that will take fellow commission idiots months to read.

And they wonder why the state is losing population? I'll tell you why: even these farmers and farm girls get tired of hearing general truisms being pawned off as strategy. Check out where McKillup posits, ""Where there are weaknesses, then we need to learn from them … and move forward." Say what?? You learn from weaknesses, learn and them move forward? What about correcting the weaknesses? Her own words indict her and clearly establish that she's an imbecile. You read it here first.

More evidence of McKillip's complicity in the rip-off can be seen in the following excerpt:

> One case involved the hiring of McKillip's daughter as part of a
> group of college-age "talent" used for a nine-day photo shoot
> across the state last summer. The shoot was organized by Omaha-
> based Bailey Lauerman to produce video and photographs for state
> tourism advertising at attractions and parks across the state.
> The daughter, Emma, was featured on the cover of the 2016 State
> Tourism Guide, the major annual publication of the Tourism
> Commission.

So what do we have? First of all, nepotism. Secondly, as a consequence of that choice, other students (perhaps more qualified) were bypassed. So that's a form of discrimination on another level. Then, the people who organized the shoot were the same ones that it would later be found to be giving money to her organization. In other words, payola – which is, of course against the law. Then, they feature McKillip's daughter on the cover of a 2016 Tourism Guide – and you don't think that the placement of that picture was the result of money changing hands? There are beautiful women from all over the nation who would give an eye tooth for a cover placement!

All of these acts are grounds for termination. The fact that these acts are now documenting in a monopoly newspaper that owns almost every newspaper in the state. Even if it doesn't its influence is region wide. According to a Wikipedia website,

> The Omaha World-Herald is the primary daily newspaper of
> Nebraska and portions of southwest Iowa. It is based in Omaha,
> Nebraska. For decades it circulated daily throughout Nebraska and
> in parts of Kansas, South Dakota, Missouri, Colorado and
> Wyoming. In 2008, distribution was reduced to the eastern third of
> Nebraska and western Iowa.

So then, the young Ms. McKillip is getting publicity because of the article and statewide publicity because of the tourism magazine. It's more racial nepotism as the following passage implies:

> McKillip, as well as a Bailey Lauerman official, said the daughter
> was hired by the ad agency — not McKillip — and was paid the
> same rate, $550 plus expenses, as others on the shoot June 2
> through 10.

This is bullshit. She may have been paid $550, but the "plus expenses" can mean anything. And remember how much was paid to some no-name simply to relocate from Sidney to Kearney with no publicity involved! These people have projections and information that shows that Nebraska, as a state, is going down the tubes. If the farmers don't hurry up and market their genetically engineered poison to the people all over the world, Nebraska is going to be a thing of the past. So since they have to know that, the leadership has literally decided to "take the money and run."

Laws made by lawless men – a Nebraska tradition. If you don't believe it, check out the following:

> The audit said the daughter's hiring probably didn't violate the state's nepotism laws because she was not a state employee. But the audit expressed concerns that either her mother had violated a state law barring public officials from obtaining financial gain for themselves or family members, or the ad agency — which was paid $3.6 million last year by the tourism agency — had violated a law prohibiting the offering of something of value to influence a public official. Both are misdemeanors, punishable by up to three months in jail, a $500 fine or both.

The article claims that according to the audit, "… the daughter's hiring probably didn't violate the state's nepotism laws because she was not a state employee." Bullshit. It's not the status of the daughter at the time of the hiring – it's the act itself. The article explains that the audit "expressed concerns" about the mother and/or family obtaining financial gain or that the ad agency had influenced a public official. Why don't they call it what it is? It's bribery, plain and simple. And McKillip benefited from it and when she took the check home she purchased food that her family ate, she paid her mortgage and car note. That is no misdemeanor: that is grand larceny!

Passing the buck, the auditor wants a "legal opinion" on what is clearly what I just said it was:

> Janssen said his audit would be forwarded to the Nebraska Attorney General's Office to determine if a law had been violated, as is the case with all audits. "It's very questionable," the auditor said of the hiring. McKillip said no laws had been broken. "That could be perceived that way. It wasn't the case here," she said.

When it comes to white people, the perception IS the reality, whether it is valid or not. It's called discretion, and they have it in volumes, including judges, cops, educators and others. Their reality is the only one that matters, regardless of how limited, parochial or myopic it is. Their criminals don't go to jail because the decision makers have a low regard for the Nebraska taxpayer – that is the only logical way to explain it. If they gave a shit, they wouldn't be continuing to rip them off and then say, "Oops, I did it again." So stupid are Nebraskans that Con-Agra got fed up and moved most of its offices to Chicago.

Simply put, Nebraska tourism failures are due to its own cultural arrogance, collective ignorance and on-going abuse of funding. More on these points later in this paper.

Moving right along:

> The Tourism Commission, according to McKillip, used "local talent" rather than hiring professional models as a way to save money. She said past Tourism Commission interns and volunteers, along with fraternity and sorority members from the University of Nebraska-Lincoln, were asked to apply. By using them, professional fees of up to $2,500 to $5,000 per day were avoided, the agency said in the audit.

There's a reason why people select professionals over "local talent," especially when that local talent hails from a hick area like Nebraska. And why does the selection of that local talent not come from a beauty school or a talent agency, but her own daughter? What qualifies her daughter other than the fact that she might be nice looking? Other people from sororities and fraternities (?) were asked to apply for the cover photo? And this was done to save money even though the magazine was going to be regionally circulated?

This spate of bad decisions is more than enough evidence to have McKillip "banned and disbarred" to use lawyer talk. Of course she's not an attorney and apparently knows nothing about the law. But she had to know the rules of her agency and she surely violated those because she felt she could get away with what she was doing. Once busted, she blames the policies. When she can't explain her actions of nepotism and greed, check outlines what her "goal" was:

> "The goal of ... (the) photo shoot was to be as cost effective and time efficient as possible while covering hundreds of miles supporting Nebraska's diverse activities and attractions," the agency's response said.

After spending all that money to relocate a local hick from one small town to another? After spending all that taxpayers' dough on a 90-minute speech (which comes out to about to about $488 per minute! And she has the gall to talk about expenditures being "cost-effective"?

Apparently, the buffoonery gets worse:

> The Tourism Commission also stated that it was "challenging" to find talent in the 18- to 26-year-old age range willing to leave a

> summer job for more than a week, work up to 12 hours a day and
> "camp out as needed." McKillip said only seven people applied.
> Janssen said he found it hard to believe it was difficult to find
> young people to "basically have a free vacation and get paid for
> it.""But the (Tourism) publication is very professional and very
> nice," he said.

So a publication that features novices nevertheless turned out to be "very professional and very nice." So that raises a question: of what use are real professionals?! Why bother? All you have to do is have a daughter who needs some money, hire her and to be damned with the likes of top modeling agencies like Elite, Ford, Storm, Q model, or L.A. Model? Why not just do away with professional modeling agencies in New York, Los Angeles and Chicago and use tourism money to announce the newly formed Cornhusker Modeling Agency replete with the slogan, "We may be corn-fed, but we're cute"!?

Making the Tourism Department an independent agency was the result of the votes of hillbilly senators from small towns who, for the most part, don't know their asses from a hole in the ground. As it was explained in the article,

> Janssen said he was among the senators who voted to make
> Tourism an independent agency in 2012. Prior to that it had been a
> division of the Nebraska Department of Economic Development
> and was overseen by that agency's director.

As you can see in this paper, it was in their previous status that I assisted Tony Dworak by educating him about North Omaha. But white organizational "independence" usually results in maverick-type behavior, which is why they had oversight in the first place. It seems that the hiring/appointment of McKillip led to the problems that were outlined by the auditor, and when combined with the auditor's own poor monitoring skills, the result was predictable. The staff of the "new" tourism office appears to be yet another waste of taxpayer dollars if we go by outcomes and results. Again, the article explains:

> Currently the tourism office has a staff of 11 and a yearly budget
> of about $6 million, an increase of about $1.6 million from three
> years ago. It is overseen by a nine-member board that represents
> different segments of the state's tourism industry, from tourism
> attractions to lodging facilities, the State Game and Parks
> Commission and Nebraska Travel Association. The members, who
> are selected by the governor, hired the executive director.

Why does this office receive an increase in funding? Is that raise commensurate with the level of desperation that these Nebraskans are feeling as they attempt to pawn their hick state off as a "destination state"? It has one city that claims to have half a million people, but that's probably exaggerated; I've lived in two cities that alone have doubled that number (Chicago, Dallas). Their offerings are slim and limited to restaurants and their concerts revolve around country and western and white groups that attempt to have "soul." The young people see all this and can't wait to leave – what the state refers to as a "brain drain."

Brain drain, and the fear of it. And this has been the reality for a long time, points made by both the Urban league and the Omaha World Herald back in 1984. Check out the following excerpt. As I documented in my "State of Black Nebraska 2000: A Critical Analysis in 2003:

> Do blacks think that younger residents tend to stay here after completing high school? Let me reiterate that the data already shows that black and white kids are trying as hard as they can to leave Nebraska when they graduate. In fact, research unveils that the Urban League's own 1984 report, conducted by the Center for Applied Urban Research, proved as much. (p. 25).

And,

> A December 18, 1984 article about the report's findings appeared in the Omaha World Herald, and here were the key points regarding young residents: "Omaha could lose many talented black youths if the quality of life for black Omahans does not improve, said Rodney Wead, director of United Methodist Community Centers. Wead was asked to comment on the Urban League of Nebraska's 1984 report on the "State of Black Omaha" …Wead said with the picture of Omaha presented by the report, black graduates might not want to stay in the city if steps are not taken to provide better educational and economic opportunities for the minority population. "When talented young people are not able to present their gifts to the city, everyone loses, both blacks and whites," he said (Omaha World Herald, December 18, 1984).

So tourism-fed lies are aimed at duping young people into remaining in Nebraska, regardless of their negligible life-chances. They want to leave and they have to be replaced with tourism promotions, akin to the lies constantly written by the Omaha World Herald's Michael Kelly as he finds off-the-wall "tourism experts" who lie and claim that Omaha is number three in tourism in the nation. Such bullshit feeds into the offsetting of the prospective losses of young people who grow sick of Nebraska and feeds into the revenue stream by bringing in tourists who, of course, pay for amenities, hotel rooms and so on.

So where does Tourism show that it merits an increase in its budget? The governor is the key, and the past several state leaders they've had appear to have low intelligence. They are all millionaires who get in office and then live off the government dole themselves. Where is the improvement, the uplift and progress? How can a state grow when all it has to fall back on is genetically engineered crops and farm animals? The budget of over six million is a waste of taxpayers' money. I hope that the article by Paul Hammel and my own profoundly deep response to it, prove this to be the case.

Then, to add insult to financial injury, check out the following:

> When Janssen was asked if he still supports having Tourism as an
> independent agency, he said yes, but added that he expects the
> board members to take a more active role in managing the agency.

The problem is with the board members and the entire selection and appointment process. Don't they get it? The board members were all there and signed off on the antics of McKillip. The governor sat back and did nothing to oversee what was taking place. The legislature allowed this ragtag group of "tourism planners" to become independent and they abused it. What else is there to do but to abolish it and replace it with the kind of tourism setup that I have proposed later in this paper. Anything short of that is nothing short of repeating that which has proven to be played out.

Again, Janssen:

> "I'm hopeful that they just weren't aware of the jobs they were
> supposed to be performing, the director included," the auditor said.
> "But if you look at their replies, they seem to be somewhat
> defensive and say they were operating OK, which was not the
> case."Clearly there's been quite a lack of oversight on that
> agency," Janssen said.

"Just weren't aware"? Then why were they hired? Who hired them? What took place during the interviews? The oversight that Janssen charges the agency with lacking is his fault! Who else is to blame? McKillip rightfully felt she had a clean slate and acted as if there were no checks and balances. This is the prototypical example of an organization that is out of control. Again, it should be condemned, and then corrected with the introduction and establishment of its opposite.

Continuing:

> A member of the Tourism board, Jeff Boeka, a North Platte
> manager of motels, said the audit was disappointing. He said the

> board will be forming a committee at its meeting Tuesday in
> Omaha to draft tighter rules and procedures. When asked if the
> director's job might be in jeopardy, Boeka said he couldn't speak
> for the nine-member board."I think Kathy has done a great job of
> raising awareness of Nebraska tourism, but there are things that
> need to be fixed," he said.

It appears that Boeka doesn't know his ass from a hole in the ground, either. It's not the purpose of the tourism board to "Raise awareness of Nebraska tourism." It is the purpose to promote Nebraska as a state and, in fact, some would argue that the existence of the tourism vehicle should be low key or negligible. This guy manages (not owns) motels, not hotels. His clients are low income people traveling across the state, probably trying to get the hell out of Dodge. And he's on the board? Based on what? What are his qualifications?

One hand continues to wash the other, and all of the hands are pale. Take note:

> The Legislature's Appropriations Committee, in a Feb. 29 letter
> included in the audit, also expressed concerns about oversight and
> governance at the Tourism Commission. State Sen. Heath Mello,
> chairman of the committee, said Saturday that he thinks the new
> oversight requirements added by senators should address most of
> the problems identified in the audit.

Mello is, on most occasions, aware of what is going on. But as you can see in his previous comments, he is as blind as the rest of them. Oversight requirements in the hands of idiots are like putting knives in the hands of someone with cerebral palsy. The first step is cleaning house and replacing the rule breakers with people who are taking the job seriously and who have a plan and a vision. If you do that, then you give the people in charge the power to bring on others who they will be responsible for. Then, when heads roll, everybody's rolls and there won't be any finger pointing once things get hot. This is called a plan, and it is superior to the band-aid approach that Sen. Mello, the Nebraska legislature and the governor have used to date.

The article continues:

> In the February letter the committee faulted McKillip for not
> seeking approval from the nine-member board before asking the
> Legislature for additional spending authority of about $750,000,
> and for spending about $293,000 more money than the state
> received last year in lodging taxes — the primary source of funds
> for the tourism agency.

Lodging taxes? Asking for money without the approval of the board? What kind of agency is this? If Warren Buffett loves Nebraska so much, why don't he and/or daughter Susie kick in a few million so that this tourism can begin with some real independence and then be forced to generate funds on its own? In that way, they can stop leeching off the legislature which foolishly gives them the money *sans* track record! The problems are from the top to the bottom and it's time for an overhaul; it's not like the tourism plan – whatever that is – is breaking any major records. Even its largest city, Omaha, is barely scraping by with its silly logos, outlandish slogans and nearly total lack of anything resembling urbanity!

And,

> The agency, the letter said, cannot spend more than has been authorized by the Legislature. McKillip said commissioners were aware that she was seeking more funds, there just hadn't been a formal vote to approve it. Lodging tax receipts are increasing about 8 percent a year, so the funds are available, she said. "The concept is, if the money is there, to utilize it," McKillip said. "Our job as a commission being new is to be assertive in marketing Nebraska."

What? Ass-backwards thinking leads to ass-backwards results. She says that "the concept is, if the money is there, to utilize it." No, that's not quite the entire formula. The concept is, "if the money is there, budget it and then use it *appropriately.*" She further claims that their job as a "new commission being new is to be assertive in marketing Nebraska." Again, she is in error.

First of all, they are not a "new commission;" they are a twisted and tawdry extension of that which already existed. Secondly, it's therefore not "new" because it is under the same rules and protocols as it was when it was under the auspices of the Economic Development Department. And third, being "assertive in marketing Nebraska" implies that there is something worth marketing! You can be assertive in marketing a turd, but it is doubtful if there will be any interest!

If you want to promote rural environments, back-to-nature, fishing and hunting, then that's fine. But do it in a way where people of color – rapidly becoming the majority all over the nation – are going to want to get involved as well. The lily-white immediate primary markets consist of South Dakota, Kansas, Iowa and Wyoming. Is there any wonder why this vanilla orientation produces vanilla results? You need to literally and figuratively "add some color" to the plan if you are going to get some results that smack of diversity, inclusion and warmth!

According to the article, "The audit cited dozens of examples of questionable Tourism spending and accounting practices," and listed some of them. And before going through them one-by-one, let me say this: How much more taxpayers' money is going to have to be mis-spent before these white people move past defining such actions as "questionable" and start pressing some damn charges against these masters of misappropriation?

Now for the "questionable" practices:

> » Spending $18,000 to move one employee from Sidney to
> Kearney, a distance of 217 miles. The expense seemed excessive,
> the audit said, and included paying $8,000 to a Realtor as a
> commission for selling the employee's house. Tourism responded
> that paying moving expenses is allowed, and that moving the 10-
> year employee to a more central location in the state prevented the
> need to hire another full-time employee.

Such bullshit, and although I addressed this decision earlier, I omitted expressing concerns about the realtor who sold the employees house. So then, that person not only got money for moving but also pocketed funds from the sale of the house without having to pay a percentage of that money to the realtor! This is outright thievery of taxpayers' money! How important was this employee? Why don't' they give the names they would do if the person was black and from North Omaha? Why are they protecting the culprits who benefited from the theft of taxpayers' money and the malfeasant behavior by McKillip?

There's more:

> » Providing complimentary massages and paying one speaker a
> $44,000 fee for a 90-minute speech for the 2015 state tourism
> conference in Columbus. Three other speakers were paid more
> than $9,000 each. Overall, the cost of the 2015 event exceeded
> sponsorships and other conference revenue by about $84,000,
> which had to be covered by other Tourism funds.
> The commission said it received suggestions to bring in nationally
> recognized speakers, and the keynote speaker, Shawn Achor, a co-
> founder of GoodThink Inc., fit that description. "Not all
> conferences break even," the agency said, adding that many
> national speakers won't come to Nebraska because of flight
> limitations and ground travel required.

Say what??? Covering a convention with Tourism funds? What came of it? Is there a publication or a video? How in the FUCK does jacking off some white boys at a convention benefit the numbers of people who are being contacted to come to Nebraska in the name of "tourism"? But remember: these are the same people that hired a pedophile to run their university system and serve as the chancellor of UNO; these are the same people who had, as the publisher of their leading newspaper, another pedophile who approved the on-going degradation and stigmatizing of the black community but who covered his own ass (no pun intended) when it came to fessing up to what he had done. (And another editor of the World-Herald, John Gottschalk, purchased a fitness center and put it in the name of his 7-year old daughter – and got away with it).

In other words, lack of character is par for the course when it comes to Nebraska leadership and decision makers. Is it therefore any wonder that their employees and other subordinates follow suit?

The same lies are told when it comes to justifying their expenditures on speakers. They spend all this money because they are a hick state that is known for being gullible. They are a state so gullible and behind in the times that they can be easily bilked and bamboozled when told that the speaker will "make things happen." And they fall for it.

Evidence can be found in the previous excerpt where it states, "The commission said it received suggestions to bring in nationally recognized speakers, and the keynote speaker, Shawn Achor, a co-founder of GoodThink Inc., fit that description. "Not all conferences break even," the agency said, adding that many national speakers won't come to Nebraska because of flight limitations and ground travel required." Bullshit. It's called scheduling or booking. Discounts can be found and arrangements can be made. A number of the speakers that come to Nebraska have relatives or friends who are already here. Why pay for a hotel suite when these hicks can crash out in the barn or on some firewood out back?

These hillbillies are quick to spend money when it doesn't come out of their own pockets. And then as they squander, they squabble to the legislature about needing more, wanting more. These are the actions of children who continue to beg for an increase in their allowance even while not doing a damn thing to earn it! This would be a joke were it not so pitiable.

The violations continue:

> » Lacking procedures for tracking purchase orders against the
> agency's contracts; thus, Tourism couldn't tell if spending was
> within established budgets. Expenditures under two Bailey
> Lauerman contracts went over budget by $4.4 million between
> August 2013 and February 2016.
> The Tourism Commission acknowledged that the contracts went
> over budget, but said that was being corrected by working with
> Administrative Services, the state agency that handles most state
> contracts.

This is straight up misfeasance and malfeasance combined! The budget is the most important thing that a director has to manage; it is what determines an organizations purpose, identity and direction! You can't let the neglect or oversight of the budget off as a simple "faux pas"! Nine words say it all: "Tourism couldn't tell if spending was within established budgets." This is the most important reason for dissolution of this corporation, for dismantling of this agency, for termination of anyone who is even remotely associated with buffoonery of this magnitude.

McKillips' greed and gargantuan gluttony appears to have no bounds:

> » Reimbursing McKillip $1,318 for more than 2,200 miles put on her daughter's convertible during the photo shoot, even though the Tourism Commission also paid for some gas for the vehicle. That double reimbursement, the audit stated, raised questions of "possible abuse, if not actual fraud."The agency responded that McKillip was unaware the daughter's fuel was being paid for, but said the car was used in the photo shoots.

What is it that the cops tell the grandmother or the young mom whose son has been busted for drug abuse while living in the house of one of these women? "Ignorance of the law is no excuse"? Well guess what: the same applies to McKillip. She didn't know that her daughter's fuel was being paid for? Who cares if the car was used in the photos or not? The daughter got paid, McKillip was already on the dole, the gas was paid for twice. How much more flaunting does this woman have to do before she gets her pink slip? If there was every any doubt that white privilege was real, then just read about what Mckillip got away with, and you'll be convinced.

Moving right along:

> » Reimbursing Bailey Lauerman for $350 in alcohol and cigarettes purchased during the photo shoot, a violation of state policies. The audit stated that because a number of receipts were missing or illegible, it could not be determined how $5,200 in expenses for the shoot were spent, but that it was "highly probable" that more was spent on alcohol.
> "... There did not appear to be any shortage of alcohol, food and other meals being consumed" on the photo shoot, said the audit, which questioned the cost of some meals and tips. The Tourism Commission said it was unaware reimbursement was being sought for alcohol, and it agreed with the state ban on such reimbursement. The agency said that some meals were purchased for photographing.

If state policies were violated, then what and where are the penalties? According to the audit, "it could not be determined how $5,200 in expenses for the shoot were spent, but that it was "highly probable" that more was spent on alcohol." And as such, are these not grounds for termination at most and at very least a long-term suspension? These are not only violations of the rules, these are violations of corporate protocol on every single level. This is an agency that is supposed to be charged with promoting the state and what is it promoting when it charges expensive dinners, gets its guests as drunk as skunks and then receives very little in return? The message is that Nebraska is "easy pickins" and that if you want to make a lot of money, these are the hillbillies that you can take advantage of.

Moreover, additional race-related (translation: white makes such violations "alright") conclusions can be drawn when it is written that, "The Tourism Commission said it was unaware reimbursement was being sought for alcohol, and it agreed with the state ban on such reimbursement." It "agrees" with the state? Well isn't that "mighty white" of them! That's like the janitor at the White House saying that he "agrees with" what Obama is saying in terms of legislation! These people can get away with this kind of bullshit because it is the norm; because it is par for the course. I have well documented the on-going travesties committed by Nebraska at the state level and in its largest city, Omaha. They are a breed unto themselves, and three things bind them together: (1) they are hicks; (2) they all despise black people and (3) they think "Go Big Red" football is the best thing since sliced bread.

Additional atrocities are documented as,

> » Spending $2,775 for the state airplane to fly a Tourism employee from Lincoln to Valentine for the photo shoot, then flying a Bailey Lauerman staffer and one of the student participants back to Lincoln. The return flight was diverted by bad weather, which resulted in food and overnight lodging expenses of $292 in Kearney.
> The agency said that it had used the state plane only twice in the past five years, but that using it saved time in getting people to remote locations. The weather delay was unforeseen, the Tourism Commission said.

What is it going to take for this auditor to submit a letter to the governor to terminate this agency? What is it going to take to have the people who work for Tourism suspended without pay for at least a month? It's not like they'd lose anything during their absence. If this were a movie, it would be a comedy. But in Nebraska even a well-documented article like the one written by Paul Hammel will do no good: it all falls on deaf ears because Nebraskans are the sum total of what their school system has made them. And if the small districts are even remotely anything like the Omaha Public Schools, then those who graduate should not even be allowed to carry sharp instruments, let alone proceed into the outside world of reality!

State Sen. Ernie Chambers continually accuses his colleagues in the Nebraska Legislature about their continual "mooching" off of the lobbyists (e.g., free lunches, free tickets to various college games, etc.). But it's not just the legislature: it appears to be a Nebraska *modus vivendi*:

> » Accepting gifts of meals and drinks from Bailey Lauerman and Swanson Russell, the state's public relations firm. Bailey Lauerman spent more than $2,500 on more than 35 occasions, including for the spouses of McKillip and a commissioner. Included was a $255 dinner for the director and a Bailey Lauerman employee at a restaurant in Austin, Texas, and a $109 lunch earlier in the day.
> "In general, employees who negotiate and sign government contracts or grant awards involving large sums of public funds ought not to receive gifts ... from vendors; likewise, vendors ought not to make valuable bestowals" to public employees, the audit stated, citing a state law prohibiting influence peddling.

These people were having a ball, and not only did McKillip have her daughter getting paid and getting her picture plastered all over the state, but her husband was on the dole as well. It was a family affair in the microcosm and when you add in the variable of race, it's one big ethnocentric family affair. Meanwhile, black people in North Omaha are ranked number one in the nation in black child poverty, the black unemployment rate among youth is the highest in the state, and black people have the highest population density in the state. This sounds like grounds for a major lawsuit if you ask me. They want to promote tourism to places that are overwhelmingly white and rural while its largest city, Omaha, treats black people like shit.

Not only do white people get a chance to cheat and steal, but other white people who are supposed to be in charge turn a blind eye and a deaf ear to the pilfering, pandering and plundering that it taking place right in front of them. For instance, take note that,

> The audit stated that it found no credible evidence that acceptance of the free dinners had influenced state employees, but it recommended that Tourism staff and commissioners start filing reports of gifts, as is required of other state officials.

No credible evidence? Let me establish some evidence using syllogistic reasoning. State employees have to eat dinner and are gluttons. The dinners are free. Therefore, these gluttons ate the dinners. And we all know that, "the hand that feeds, controls." And you expect people to believe that there was "no credible evidence" that these pigs weren't influenced by free food? Why else then, would the food be offered? Why didn't they pick up their own tab? Why weren't reports of the dinners and expenditures associated with the dinners filed per state official requirements?

After all the lies that have been told, McKillip continues her prevarications as do those associated with her. Therefore it is no surprise when the World-Herald article concludes as follows:

> McKillip said the Bailey Lauerman records were incorrect and her husband never received any meals.
> But she that, overall, lessons were learned through the audit.
> "Bottom line is that we need a policies and procedures manual," she said. An official with Bailey Lauerman, Mary Palu, said that while entertaining clients is a normal business practice, the agency was unaware of the restrictions on gifts to Tourism officials. She said those errors will be corrected.

Who is McKillip to tell someone what "the bottom line" is? She's already walked over every line that existed! She flaunts any line that gets in the way of her bilking taxpayers and getting paid! By her claiming that "lessons were learned" through the audit is an admission of guilt because it implies that she didn't understand – and therefore could not possibly obey – the lessons before the audit!

I don't know why Paul Hammel interviewed this Mary Palu chick, but she's a liar as well. Don't forget she works for the organization that got paid and also paid out some bucks – it was quid pro quo. And yet she makes the claim that while entertaining clients is a normal business practice, the agency was unaware of the restrictions on gifts to Tourism officials." Bullshit. When in doubt, err on the side of caution. These people are traveling as couples, as families, are getting drunk as skunks, eating the most expensive thing on the menu and if you ask me, probably fuckin' on the government's dime as well.

And they got away with it.

John Ricks, former associate director of the Colorado Tourism Office, has been offered the job six months after Kathy McKillip was canned. The big deal was that Rick was selected over more than fifty other applicants, two of whom were from Nebraska. It is therefore clear that these rednecks are beginning to see that to hire from within is a major mistake.

In vintage apologetic manner, the major newspaper posted an editorial on November 23, 2016 titled, "Editorial: Work Can help Tourism Commission Earn Public's Trust." Following are the highlights and my analyses:

> Nebraska wants more people to visit from beyond its borders and more Nebraskans to explore their own state. That's the bottom line

> for the state's growing, $650 million-a-year tourism industry.
> There's plenty of work awaiting the new executive director of the
> Nebraska Tourism Commission, selected last week from 54
> applicants. (Omaha World Herald, 2016)

Sheer fluff. The state's tourism industry can't grow unless the state does some "maturing" as far as its reputation, attitudes and traditions go. You can't expect people to visit the only large city in a state – Omaha – and be impressed when they hear racist jokes and sexist humor. And if white people can't stand it and then head back to their homes and share their experiences, then what do you think people of color who visit are going to feel?

Nebraska's reputation precedes it. You can't undo a century of relocating and killing off Indians when there are movies out there that boast about doing it. And when you offer up these "landmarks", many of them located in cities named after Native Americans, and then you don't see any Native Americans anywhere except on an occasional reservation, the kids are going to ask questions. And when they ask those questions, the tour guides are going to have to lie to them because if they tell the truth the word "genocide" is going to come up. Unless you visit one of the Holocaust prison camps or an old slave plantation in the South, who in the hell wants to go on a vacation in a state that is known for slaughtering and then "ghettoizing" the indigenous population?

The article continues:

> Job No. 1 for John Ricks and the tourism board is to restore the
> public's trust in the 11-employee state agency. The Tourism
> Commission spends about $6 million a year, primarily from hotel
> and motel lodging taxes, to promote tourism statewide. The
> agency's actions under previous director Kathy McKillip sullied its
> reputation. She was fired after an audit found numerous problems
> with the commission's financial oversight and accountability. The
> board, according to the audit, failed to provide needed oversight.
> (Omaha World Herald, 2016).

If indeed the tourism board "failed to provide needed oversight," then that means that McKillip didn't "sully" the reputation of the Tourism Commission by herself. The board aided and abetted her in her crimes just like the board or accountants at a bank are complicit when an act of embezzlement by a bank employee takes place. In other words, the tourism division is rife with crooks and those who look the other way. That is what the newly hired Ricks should be looking out for. It was not a case of one bad apple spoiling the whole bunch; it was a case of the whole bunch being rotten from the get-go.

The World-Herald editorial continues:

Ricks would do well to publicly discuss his plans to improve the agency's spending controls, just as the board should publicly express its expectations. It's vital that the agency demonstrate prudence with taxpayer funds and improve transparency about the agency's activities and finances. Another important job is repairing the agency's relationships with regional tourism industry leaders, who raised questions about McKillip's management and actions. Much of the work to rebuild those relationships has already begun under the capable interim leadership of Heather Hogue, the commission's deputy director, who stepped up when needed this spring. (Omaha World Herald, 2016).

Before getting into analyzing the previous excerpt, let me pose a question: who is the World Herald to give out tips on how to rectify a crooked organization? These are people who have been complicit in behind-the-scenes unethical and illegal activity for over a century. They have a lily-white staff and then they assign white women to cover news in the same black community that they also claim is so violent and filled with deviance. They attempt to determine who should be elected, usually individuals who are conservative and black people who have no proven track record of working to help those who need help the most. I have written extensively on the World-Herald's lack of ethics, so take what they write on these pages with a grain of salt. Their editorial board reflects the racist atmosphere of the newspaper.

Now, back to the previous passage where the claim is made that, ". It's vital that the agency demonstrate prudence with taxpayer funds and improve transparency about the agency's activities and finances." Improve transparency? That suggestion runs counter to the Nebraska tradition! State Senator Ernie Chambers has produced reams of documents over the decades that shows how these white people hide what they do, lie about it when caught, and simply replace one "bad egg" with another one because of their inept and race-based hiring practices. Transparency? As I've written and proven elsewhere, even the Business Ethics Alliance in Omaha, which lists some 260 major corporations and businesses, is "unethical"!

Next comes the "suggestion" that, "Another important job is repairing the agency's relationships with regional tourism industry leaders, who raised questions about McKillip's management and actions. Much of the work to rebuild those relationships has already begun under the capable interim leadership of Heather Hogue, the commission's deputy director, who stepped up when needed this spring." My question is where was Hogue when McKillip was making off with the money, spending it on alcohol and hotel rooms? Where was she at when they were relocating people on the taxpayers dime? She was right there. So how is she going to be deemed some kind of savior when she was riding along with the James gang all along?

> Ricks has served as an assistant director of tourism in Colorado, which has done an impressive job selling its mountains and hiking and rural and urban experiences to surrounding states. His previous work in Wyoming, too, is promising. Both states have a unique blend of attractions. So does Nebraska. From the Henry Doorly Zoo in Omaha to Chimney Rock in Bayard, the state offers day-trippers and vacationers a lot. (Omaha World Herald, 2016).

How are you going to compare scenic Colorado with ride 'em cowboy-oriented Nebraska? How are you going to compare progressive skiers and others in the Centennial State with farmers in the Cornhusker state? Ricks can't perform miracles! People leave Nebraska to tour Colorado, not the opposite! Like those before him he's taking a job with a large salary and claiming he'll do things that he will inevitably get burned out on once he realizes he can't do it!

The claim that "both states have a unique blend of attractions." Say what??? Colorado has three cities with over 300,000 population: Denver (682,545), Colorado Springs (456,568) and Aurora (355,407). Nebraska has one city that barely has 400,000 but claims to have a population of half a million. The second city in population is the capital city with about 175,000. Do you call that a fair comparison? And then, when you add the concept of attractions, Nebraska boasts a zoo and a giant rock. Denver alone dwarfs that, and we can then add professional sports teams and the statement that attempts to make Colorado and Nebraska appear to have a basis for equal comparison is totally absurd! In social research terms, it is an "ecological fallacy"!

The editorial continues:

> Ricks inherits an agency that, despite its financial shortcomings, has laid a lot of groundwork for branding Nebraska as a place worth visiting. But neither he nor the agency has a lot of time to show state leaders why the agency should remain independent. The Legislature made tourism an independent agency in 2012, aiming to encourage a coordinated, statewide strategy. Gov. Pete Ricketts, after the audit's findings became public, said he wanted to bring the agency back under his control. (Omaha World Herald, 2016).

Now come more contradictions that the World Herald doesn't expect it's eight-grade reading level followers to catch. But those of us with active brain stems can see right through the bullshit.

First of all the claim that Ricks inherits an agency that, "despite its financial shortcomings, has laid a lot of groundwork for branding Nebraska as a place worth visiting." You can't achieve external greatness if you're screwed up internally. How are you going to have "financial shortcoming" and then at the same time boast about having the power or potential to "brand" anything? Branding takes money for promotions, marketing, trademarks and outreach. As Booker T. Washington would suggest, "cast down your bucket where you are," Nebraska. Take care of your spend-happy traditions and tendencies, first. Get the budget together and then bring some people of color on board who have ideas about attracting visitors. That pro-Anglo, vanilla on top of mayonnaise approach ain't cuttin' it!

And as for making the tourism agency independent, you can plainly see what happened when that bright idea was implemented. But like a child that has been independent, if you bring it back under the roof with parents who are derelict, then that child is even WORSE off! Who is governor Ricketts to oversee the tourism division when he cannot even obey his own laws? When he insisted on bringing illegal death penalty drugs into the state at a time when the death penalty had been ruled unconstitutional? In other words, how can the blind lead the blind?

Moving on;

> Perhaps new leadership and a tourism board that is publicly committed to proper oversight can persuade lawmakers to wait a year, to give the agency time to prove independence can work. The commission can't afford more allegations of mismanaged spending, vendor favoritism or nepotism. The board should make plain that it won't let another executive director dodge its financial questions. (Omaha World Herald, 2016).

The key word in the fluff piece is the word "perhaps." Even the World Herald has to see the writing on the wall. After all, they were the ones who got their hands on the audit that led to the expose on McKillip. And that means that they would have to realize that the problem was much deeper than that particular overweight blonde. And yet they have the gall to write, "The commission can't afford more allegations of mismanaged spending, vendor favoritism or nepotism." They couldn't "afford" it before, but they did it! With no penalties in place, what's going to prevent Ricks from seeing the challenge ahead, collect a few years worth of paychecks and then cut out like other administrators across the state have done?

The editorial mercifully concludes with the following:

> The sooner the agency repairs its reputation, the sooner it can get back to the business of luring visitors to the state's many and varied attractions — from Lake McConaughy to the Niobrara

River, from Ashfall Fossil Beds to the Nebraska National Forest, from Arbor Lodge to the Stuhr Museum, and everything in between. (Omaha World Herald, 2016)

Interesting use of the word "lure" when it comes to getting visitors to come to the state. The term "lure" means, "to tempt (a person or an animal) to do something or to go somewhere, especially by offering some form of reward." In my book the term should be to "convince" people to come to Nebraska. To "lure" them seems to imply some kind of trickery or lies to get them to come. Does it not? This is the same method of operation employed by the World Herald to get people to read the jejune content of its newspaper!

For the reasons cited in the previous section, I hereby offer up a viable alternative ("Never take away what you can't replace or improve"). This document is going to be a part of a major lawsuit that I am going to file against the state of Nebraska for its on-going bilking of the Federal government at a time when the economy is teetering on edge. If black people have to go hungry and bleed, *I'm going to do all I can to make sure that the bleeding is reciprocal.*

NEBRASKA OVERSIGHT AND VISITORS' ASSOCIATION

Back in 1994, I submitted a proposal to the Omaha Visitors and Tourism Division a proposal that would have promoted North Omaha back then in a way that the city is claiming it wants to do now, some w22 years later.

I handed it to Jay Baum, who was then the director, and to Richard Paris, his assistant, a proposal for the creation of a "North Omaha Visitors Association" (NOVA). It was a call for and commitment to enhancing tourism in North Omaha by focusing on the boulevards, the historically incredible housing, and the 2th and Lake Street area which I then dubbed "the Cultureplex."

That idea also included a component called "MATES," which stood for the Metro Area Tourist Escort Service." No, it's not soft porn, but providing jobs for young people to serve as guides for out-of-town visitors and others who might, for some reason, "fear" the black community.

As outlined earlier, I had already assisted the Nebraska Economic Council on producing a booklet on North Omaha back in 1994, assisting Tony Dworak in doing his job.

This is an idea that Omaha is just now getting around to. Instead of suppressing my idea back in that day, they could have now benefitted from what is now costing them hundreds of thousands of dollars to do in consultant payments, advisors and the hiring of outside folk.

For the sake of this proposal, I take my NOVA concept that I originally wrote for North Omaha and re-name it and herein dub it, "The Nebraska Oversight and Visitors Association." Following are some concepts and characteristics.

The name says it all. There is a definite need for "oversight" when it comes to the inane and buffoonish expenditures that were well documented by Paul Hammel and the Omaha World Herald. Oversight is defined as "watchful care or management, supervision (Merriam-Webster College Dictionary, 2016). Following is a preliminary budget that represents savings to the state as well as recommended personnel who can do a much better job than the corporate incest-committed folk who now operate the Nebraska Division of Tourism.

All of the people listed for personnel are people with the kind of outreach and reputations that would, again, represent a major savings to the state. They are not of the "desperado ilk" that these mooching leeches seem to hail from, and that has been documented.

DEVELOPMENT BUDGET

CBDG	Budget – (1-year)	Requested from	Ideal Development
Personnel			
Executive Director		$75,000	$50,000
Associate Director		65,000	40,000
Program Director		55,500	35,000
Development Officer		50,000	------
Secretary/Receptionist		+40,000	28,000
Travel and Per Diem @ $200 per			
Mo x 12 months		2400	10,000*
Communication			
Telephone @ $100 per mo. x			
12 months		1200	2,000
Printing @ $350 per mo. x			
12 months		4200	5,200
Postage @ $200 per mo. x			
12 months		2400	4,000
Publicity @ $300 per mo. x			

12 months	3600	5,000

Supplies

Office
Equipment: printer @ $3000
Space Rental (including utilities
    Insurance, grounds and
    Maintenance @ $400 per
    Mo. x 12 months — 4800 — ------------

TOTAL REQUESTED: $303,600   **$179,200**

SUGGESTED PERSONNEL

Name and Title	Experience/Background/Rank

John Beasley	John Beasley Theatre, Omaha
	Nationally known actor
	Major films to credit (partial):
	    Sinister 2
	    The Purge: Anarchy
	    Walking Tall
	    The Sum of All Fears
	    The General's Daughter
	    Rudy

Frank LaMere	Winnebago Tribe South Sioux City, Nebraska
Aida Olivas	Hastings Nebraska Latino American Commission
Susan Buffett	International contacts Sherwood Foundation
Senator Deb Fisher	Washington and statewide contacts
Juanita "Jina" Red Nest	Scottsbluff WIA site director

	Suicide prevention
Hal Daub	Former Nebraska Congressman NU Board of Regents
Peggy Jones	Univ. of Nebraska at Omaha Associate Professor, Women and Gender Studies, UNO
Leticia Rodriguez	Madison, Nebraska Latino American Commission
Akemi Adams	Registered Nurse North Omaha Area Health Asian-American Council
Jack Gutierrez	Columbus, Nebraska Latino American Commission

The eleven people I have selected (without their permission) are people who dwarf existing Tourism Board members in terms of reputation, scope of influence and as a result of both, ability to generate publicity and funds for the state of Nebraska. These people reach out to new audiences and will "de-hickify" the state of Nebraska, adding color, resources and urbanity to a state that still acts as if it is still living in the days of the Gold Rush.

I expect responses to this proposal from all of those who receive it. Since you cannot do any better, then send back your concerns and criticisms. Until then, let me leave you with this Nebraska joke:

A country bumpkin family from Nebraska decides to go to the Big Apple for the first Time in their lives; Maw, Paw and their son.

They go into the Empire State Building. As they're walking around they notice the elevator.

Never seeing one before they stand in front of it bewildered.

While staring at it, an old lady in a wheelchair rolls up to it, pushes the button, the door opens, she rolls herself inside and the door closes.

The Nebraska redneck family watches as the lights for each floor light as it goes up. They continue to watch as the numbers go down again.

The door opens and out walks this tall gorgeous blonde. Legs to her neck. Great figure. Beautiful!

Paw looks at his son and says, "Quick boy, shove yer Maw in there!"

The nation's demographics are changing. When white people hear the shout, "Yee-hah!" they envision one thing; but when black people hear it, we get an entirely different vibe. Both images are rooted in history and perspective, but one is positive and the other is dangerously negative. You can decide which is which.

Give this paper and proposal the respect it deserves.

ENTREPRENEURSHIP: LIMITED AND LACKING

Overview and Explanation

Before getting into the article that I am about to dissect, let's offer a few preliminary notes.

Any discussion of entrepreneurship has to begin with and be wrapped around knowledge of the economy.

Warren Buffett's Berkshire Hathaway famously has its headquarters in Omaha, but so do Union Pacific and the food giant ConAgra. Accordingly, animal production, food manufacturing, and truck transportation all have higher shares of employment in Nebraska than elsewhere in the US. Nebraska had the second-lowest December 2014 unemployment rate at just **2.9%**. However, the state had the seventh-lowest rate of job growth, with a **0.82%** increase in nonfarm payrolls between December 2013 and December 2014. The state also came in seventh to last on wages, with the average Nebraska worker earning just **$US756** per week (Kiersz, 2015).

That low unemployment rate figure is misleading: there are a large number of African-Americans and Latinos who are unemployment and, in fact, that black unemployment rate is the highest in the state. Secondly the reference to that "food giant" Con-Agra has to be qualified; so dissatisfied with the Omaha workforce was

Con-Agra that it transferred its key officials to an office in Chicago and only left behind the blue-collar "grunts." This leads us to the third variable, that of "rate of job growth" and even these paltry figures of 0.82% are inflated; the fact of the matter is that the jobs that are opening up are at the low end of the service sector and soft-money jobs related to grants provided in the area of "social services."

A fourth factor that should be weighed is the fact that, "The state also came in seventh to last on wages, with the average Nebraska worker earning just **$US756** per week." Does this sound impressive to you? Because of these facts, there should be any doubt about the fifth important economic indicator: according to the article from *Business Insider*, Nebraska's economy ranked 25th out of the fifty states – in other words, middle of the pack (ahead of its neighbors South Dakota, Iowa and Kansas).

These are the contextual factors that provide form and function to any concept of "entrepreneurship momentum" that may exist in the minds of those whose job it is to promote such a fantasy. With the previous facts in mind, we can now get into the analysis of the presentation on and suggestions regarding "improving" Nebraska's so-called "entrepreneurship momentum."

"Improving Nebraska's Entrepreneurship Momentum:" Analysis of an Article by a "Senior Community Development Advisor

There are "professional niggers" everywhere you look around America. Former Omaha mayor Mike Boyle's public announcement (after a meeting) of the existence of such people paved the way for his eventual impeachment. But if he knew about it, it is a cinch that the majority of Omaha's white leadership recognized the existence of such "negroes" because they have been exploiting these individuals for decades. There is no other way to describe or define them. This term fits because they know what the reality is and they know that their job is to camouflage that reality with their very presence and the lies they concoct aimed at making the whites who control them appear to be beneficent, sincere and thoughtful.

Rather than using what education and information they get and glean for the defense and development of African-American communities, they instead become "professional niggerologists" and sell air sandwiches and hope pudding to ignorant hicks and backward folk (read: uninformed minorities) who are gullible and rife for the plucking. They get long titles like "Senior Community Development Specialist," "Director of Equal Opportunity," "Affirmative Action Officer," "Equity and Diversity Coordinator," "Minority Advisor," and so on.

Following is an article by one such person who gives public presentations that supposedly address entrepreneurship for the low-income and minority. My critique and commentary will filter throughout in hopes of showing how sheer and shallow the "information" that is given out truly is.

This particular presentation was shared publicly and via the internet on March 31, 2016 by Dell Gines, a "community development specialist" for none other than the Federal Reserve Bank of Kansas City. His role as niggerologist should be clearly seen by the fact that no "federal reserve bank" gives a shit about minority communities or minority development. They are about the bottom line and the management of various forms of profit and revenue. Since black people are poor in a country where power is valued above all else, any attempts at "outreach" are nothing more than attempts to comply with some type of "minority mandate" or prelude to some anticipated black takeover of a nearby minority or rural community. Following are his views – and mine. He begins, thusly:

> Entrepreneurship is a key driver of job creation and has the potential to give a further boost to Nebraska's growing economy. Nebraska, however, tends to lag [behind] … its state peers on measures of entrepreneurship. Although Nebraska's economy generally is strong, many communities, particularly small, rural towns and inner-city communities may still have economic struggles … (Gines, 2016).

These vague terms are being made because the speaker realizes that he is speaking in general terms and only makes references to Nebraska in terms of its "potential. "Potential" is defined as, "having or showing the capacity to become or develop into something in the future." The reason for the use of the term is that the speaker cannot offer guarantees based on the here and now because for the most part, the state of Nebraska is an entrepreneurial failure. Outside of the farm, the state has little else to offer other than what it can sponge off of the Federal government in terms of programs and grants.

This brings us to the next point that, "Although Nebraska's economy generally is strong, many communities, particularly small, rural towns and inner-city communities may still have economic struggles …" The speaker owes it to the audience to offer up proof that Nebraska's economy is strong. Is it strong because it manages to keep its head above water? Does "strong" mean "flourishing"? Of course not. To be "generally strong" is a nebulous term and can be found in the description of any entity that doesn't want to tell the truth. Even those entities that are about to shut down will use this term because they know that "generally strong" is a term that can buy them time to figure out what their next move will be.

Moving on:

> By increasing the focus on entrepreneurship, Nebraska can help
> these struggling communities also achieve economic growth while
> supporting the development of a more diverse and competitive
> economy statewide. The Federal Reserve Bank of Kansas City and
> other organizations are working to help accelerate growth in
> entrepreneurship across the state to ensure Nebraska continues to
> have a strong and diversified economy in the future. (Gines, 2016).

How can you "increase the focus on entrepreneurship" when you just recognized that small towns and areas are having economic problems and when I've just established that the state, as a whole, is barely staying afloat? To talk of entrepreneurship without financial backing to support any such efforts is nothing more than one more attempt for these "snake oil salesmen" to peddle their bullshit to unsuspecting populations – the way ministers do.

The question to ask is why this representative doing the speaking is making the claim that "The Federal Reserve bank of Kansas City and other organizations are working to help accelerate growth n the state to ensure Nebraska continues to have a strong and diverse economy in the future." First of all, you cannot continue that which has not been established or that which has not been proven to even exist. Secondly, why is this entity, based in Kansas City, concerned about a hick state like Nebraska? The answer is clear: because somewhere down the road they stand to make money from it.

The third question is why is this speaker promoting entrepreneurship. The answer is that the funding for any small businesses that may come about as a result of this "lecture" are going to *require loans* from credit unions and banks. Now what is the name of the entity that this speaker represents: The Federal Reserve BANK of Kansas City. Self-interest pawned off as community concern and commitment, pure and simple.

Quoting generic statistics (because Nebraska's are so deplorable he cannot draw from those), check out the following:

> Entrepreneurship, defined as the creation and growth of small
> businesses with less than 500 employees, is vital to a strong
> economy. Small businesses represent 99.7 percent of all businesses
> in the United States (Chart 1). Almost 50 percent of all U.S.
> employees work for small businesses. Moreover, small businesses
> also play a significant role in the growth of new jobs. Firms with
> less than 500 employees have created 74 percent of all new jobs
> since 2008 (Chart 2). (Gines, 2016).

What the speaker does is offer up a business definition of "entrepreneurship." It is, of course, a biased and somewhat narrow definition. The denotative definition describes the process, not just the end result. The definition that I use is, "Entrepreneurship is *the process of starting a business or other organization.* The entrepreneur develops a business model, acquires the human and other required resources, and is fully responsible for its success or failure."

So then, what is being offered in terms of working with the audience members who are interested in moving, step-by-step, to *becoming* entrepreneurs? Because only AFTER you become entrepreneurs can you *practice true entrepreneurship.* The fact that most employees work for small businesses is a fact that is only realized once those small businesses get the backing and resource support needed to actually turn enough profit to be able to begin hiring from the community. What is the Federal Reserve BANK offering in that regard?

Because the concept is generic and rooted in "what might be," the speaker then begins stating some obvious facts in an attempt to pawn them off as some kind of coherent strategy for growth:

> Entrepreneurship also can help address some challenges faced by specific communities in a region. For example, rural or inner-city communities often struggle to recruit outside firms. Other issues they may face are poverty, lack of a viable workforce, distance from key transportation hubs, or a population density insufficient to maintain certain types of industry. These disadvantages may lead to an out-migration of young adults, economic stagnation, or both. Research shows entrepreneurship helps alleviate poverty by increasing local employment and income … (Gines, 2016).

The speaker says that "entrepreneurship can help address some challenges." Sure it can; but to what degree? The fact is, entrepreneurship is moot unless there are certain economic foundations in place to serve as resources and supports. This speaker knows that. Entrepreneurship is no cure-all.

Moreover, he singles out rural and inner city communities and how they "often struggle to recruit outside firms." That's bullshit. These two areas know that they don't have the funding or contacts to be about "outside recruitment." Both contexts – rural and urban - rely on what they can afford, which are immediate contacts and partnerships. The speaker is ignorant of the workings of the small business in the inner city although he purports to be committed to them.

Third, he talks about the issues that these two areas "may" face, which he lists as, "poverty, lack of a viable workforce, distance from key transportation hubs, or a population density insufficient to maintain certain types of industry." These are universal obstacles! What is wrong with this guy? To begin with poverty is the issue that small businesses may face, but that they use as motivation. The lack of a viable workforce smacks of that "unqualified minorities" bullshit that these kinds of "consultants" talk about in hopes of getting grant money for "training programs."

Distance from transportation hubs is not a major issue because in the inner city and the rural community transportation is usually concentric: you have a site and then the transportation surrounds that site akin to a bull's-eye on a target. In other words, the smaller the venue, the more accessible the job is via transportation. Population density is a boom, not a bane! The more people per square acre the more accessible the transportation routes and the more easily such routes can be justified by the entities providing it. What this speaker is doing is capitalizing on the ignorance of his audience and tossing "Entrepreneurship 101" rhetoric to people who don't know any better.

The lecture continues:

> Developing and growing small businesses does not require extensive existing infrastructure, and it can reduce a community's dependence on attracting outside firms. Entrepreneurship also promotes economic diversity, which can offset some of the risk of economic downturns … Moreover, communities with solid entrepreneurial activity *may* realize faster and more sustainable economic growth … (Gines, 2016 – emphasis added).

None of these issues he has raised are issues that aspiring small business persons would raise! This is a "straw man argument," where bullshit explanations or assumptions are raised that make it appear as if they are viable ideas or solutions, while in reality, the counter-argument or solution refutes or offers nothing because no such argument existed in the first place.

The claim is made that, "Entrepreneurship promotes economic diversity, which can offset some of the risk of economic downturns." How can entrepreneurship promote economic diversity in and of itself? If economic diversity is going to exist you have to first of all have an appreciation for social and cultural diversity. No one wants to do business with an individual or group that they don't understand or refuse to acknowledge. "Economic diversity" is as shallow as the concept of "equity" and "engagement" unless both sides are willing to engage. And in most cases, especially in a biased and racist atmosphere like that in Nebraska, both sides are NOT.

Notice that the speaker makes no guarantees and offers no definitive statements. The speaker says that "communities with solid entrepreneurial activity may realize faster and more sustainable economic growth." So then, entrepreneurial activity is no guarantee of growth of any kind. Therefore, what good is it? Wasn't the title of his presentation, "Improving Nebraska's Entrepreneurship Momentum"? If there are no guarantees, then where is the evidence that any attempts at entrepreneurship are going to take place, let alone "improve"?

These speakers have to offer up some semblance of "hope" or else their entire mission has failed. If they cannot dupe people into thinking that they have a chance, no matter how slight, then they cannot justify the existence of their jobs or their vaunted job titles. Under the sub-heading, "Nebraska Improving, But Still Lags in Entrepreneurship," we find an example of bullshit under glass.

The speaker posits,

> **Nebraska Improving, but Still Lags in Entrepreneurship**
> Nebraska has gained momentum in supporting and fostering entrepreneurship but there still is room to improve. The University of Nebraska-Lincoln, the Kauffman Foundation and the Small Business & Entrepreneurship Council each produces a slightly different measure of state entrepreneurship. Each source, however, shows Nebraska has shown incremental improvement in recent state rankings of entrepreneurship, but still is only near the middle of the pack (Table 1). (Gines, 2016).

If Nebraska has gained momentum in supporting and fostering entrepreneurship, then why does he need to appear as a speaker and talk about it to audience members? And how can you gain momentum if you already had it? And why do you need to foster more if what you're doing is a sign that you've already gained it?

The institutional arrangements named all have a vested interest in trying to talk people into starting small businesses and taking out loans in order to do so. The University of Nebraska-Lincoln has a host of "institutes" that do nothing but attempt to foster economic development for the state, including the Buffett Institute which concentrates on kids and childhood development. As for the Kauffman Foundation, their goal is akin to that of the Buffett Institute. But, in concert with the subject of the lecture, the mission of the Foundation is to advance entrepreneurship and to "improve the education of children and youth."

So the funding source is in place, and the institutional arrangements that can provide meeting space, classrooms and other resources is also on board. The only people who seem to be benefiting from all this talk are the three organizations mentioned and, of course, the speaker. In total, they put together programs that can be placed on some kind of "community application" or grant that they can in turn submit to other funding sources, acquire more money, loan it out an a high interest and work in conjunction with the Reserve Bank to financially control whatever businesses are created as a result of all this "networking."

Speaking of networking, another word for it is "collaboration." According to the speaker, "One barrier to entrepreneurship in Nebraska may be a lack of collaboration among key players such as economic developers, educational institutions, support organizations, financers and policymakers." And there you have it: major groups including (paid) economic developers and institutions work together to foster a collective dependency on the part of the population in the name of "small business development." And remember: those employees who are hired and the people starting the businesses will all be paying taxes into Nebraska's coffers. They will be purchasing goods and services from other Nebraska businesses. It's about making money, with those who already have it receiving the lion's share.

Moreover,

> A key finding of the Battelle Study, a report prepared in 2010 for the Nebraska Department of Economic Development and the Nebraska Department of Labor, was that there are gaps in technology programs that focus on translating innovations in technology into market-based entrepreneurial opportunities. Such opportunities for the state identified in the report include improving the link between research and development and new companies and products, and focusing on growth-oriented startups. (Gines, 2016).

When these speakers make presentations any nuggets of fact that point to the backwardness of Nebraska are either omitted or sugar-coated. But since he is the one who mentioned the vaunted "Battelle Study" let's take some time to look at the findings and see if all it found were that there were "gaps in technology programs that focus on translating innovations in technology into market-based entrepreneurial opportunities."

The 2015 study was titled, Battelle Study: *Growing Jobs, Industries, and Talent: A Competitive Advantage Assessment and Strategy for the State of Nebraska*. The findings were almost all negative when it came to the "assessment" of Nebraska. The general conclusion was summed up, thusly:

> This review and update of the 2010 Battelle report's assessment of Nebraska's preparedness for an innovation-driven economy came to many of the same conclusions as the original report. Where the Research Division was able to reproduce Battelle's original work, the update from 2008 through the most recent available year, showed that *in many areas Nebraska remained below the nation*

and most of the benchmark states. However, in a number of areas, Nebraska's measure has shown *some improvement over the original 2001 through 2007 timeframe* (Battelle, 2015).

Really? Is this a conclusion that is worthy of boasting about? The fact that you made some minor improvements over a six year span is supposed to be cause for joy? And if that is the case, then why isn't this speaker talking about the problems, obstacles, pitfalls and shortcomings? In other words, why isn't he *warning the people* in the audience, instead of working to motivate and inspire them to walk directly into what I would define as a "business bear trap"?

More specifically, the 2015 Battelle Study found:

- In measures of educational achievement, *Nebraska remained below the national averages for science and engineering degrees* as a percentage of all higher education degrees, science and engineering doctorate degrees as a percentage of science and engineering degrees, and science and engineering doctorate degrees per 100,000 of population, *and the percentage of the population over age 25 with a bachelor's degree or higher* … (emphasis added)

- In measures involving entrepreneurial activity, average annual growth in new business establishments, job creation rate from new business establishments, and the number of high revenue growth businesses, *Nebraska again lagged behind the nation as a whole*. Bu (emphasis added).

- The availability of risk capital, measured in terms of venture capital dollars and deals, *showed Nebraska to be behind the nation and behind most of the benchmark states in terms of venture capital investment and venture capital deals*, and also in terms of per capita venture capital investments and per capita venture capital deals … *Nebraska was well below the national average in the time periods reviewed*, and below most all of the benchmark states in each time period. (emphasis added)

- In the measures of R&D capability, *Nebraska's academic R&D spending levels were below most of the benchmark states in terms of expenditures* … In measures of Industry R&D spending, *Nebraska's expenditure levels were below most of the benchmark states*. In terms of the intensity of industry R&D spending, *Nebraska was well below the national average and most of the benchmark states*. Nebraska did improve in these areas between 2006 and 2012.(emphasis added)

- *In Battelle's final measure of an innovation-ready economy, intellectual property generation and technology transfer, Nebraska again showed poor performance compared to national averages and against the benchmark states.* Measuring intellectual property generation by the number of patents granted on a per capita basis, *Nebraska had less than half of the patent awards per capita than the national rate in all time periods reviewed. Nebraska had the lowest rate of patents awarded per capita of the benchmark states in 2001 through 2007 period.* (emphasis added).

So now you see the real record. And now you see why it is so important for bright young men like Dell Gines to be ushered in to speak in front of a room full of people, and carry water for the state. He is burdened with the task for providing "hope" and "faith" and "dreams" – the same kind of bullshit that white people have fed black people for so long when it came to freedom, justice and equality.

The speaker was doing the best he could considering what his "assignment" most likely was. He continues to speak, telling the audience the same thing I had been telling Omaha's black community for decades. Take note:

> Additionally, a report commissioned by the Nebraska Legislature's Innovation and Entrepreneurial Task Force, also released in 2010, *described Nebraska's recent history of supporting entrepreneurship as "piecemeal."* The report also said Nebraska has focused on short-term actions, like developing micro lending, and a few key types of entrepreneurship such as agriculture. In comparison, the report identified that other states take a broader focus on developing the entire entrepreneurship ecosystem, which consists of a wide variety of stakeholders, activities and organizations that support the creation and growth of small business. While key organizations and activities are in place, *Nebraska as a whole lagged its state peers in both entrepreneurship policy and programs.* (Gines, 2016 – emphasis added).

The only reason that the previous information was provided is because it is the purpose of the speaker to promote the Federal Reserve Bank and its "approach" to small business development and entrepreneurship. By showing where Nebraska has failed even with its piecemeal approach, the implication is that the Federal Reserve can do better. And it's "community services" wing is there "to help."

Nebraska lags behind its peers for the same reason that an educable mentally handicapped child lags behind his/her peers: it's not intellectually prepared for the competition. Look at the population and where it is educated. Its largest school district is an antiquated joke and seems to reject the kind of energetic, culturally competent approaches that similarly sized district around the country are using. So bad is that system that it cut a deal with Metropolitan Community College to take in its graduates (since most them couldn't pass the University of Nebraska's entrance exams and qualifications), work with them and in two years once they get their Associate Degrees, they can then transfer into the four-year institution.

This is Nebraska's version of "education." And yet it continues to beg and leech for federal money. The largest school system, the Omaha Public Schools, spent over $130,000 ordering 8,000 "Diversity Manuals" for its entire workforce. That was more than three years ago. And in terms of degree of cultural proficiency, not a damn thing has changed.

These are the reasons for the findings in the reports that Dell Gines is attempting to smooth over. When he says that, "While key organizations and activities are in place, Nebraska as a whole lagged its state peers in both entrepreneurship policy and programs," he is proving my point: in order to develop or even write policy, you have to be able to spell, write, think and promote. Again, Nebraska is lagging behind economically because it is lagging behind educationally, and it is lagging behind educationally because it is lagging behind intellectually. The facts cannot be made any plainer than that.

Once you realize that the people you are working to exploit are worse off than you thought, the next step is to make excuses for them. An often used tactic is to take a reality that the group views as positive and then show how it can be negative if not used correctly. In that way the fault for the problem is placed on "incorrect application" and not what it is: the lack of a functioning brain stem! And here comes the excuse-making:

> Other factors that generally benefit Nebraska overall also may play
> a role in restraining the growth of entrepreneurship in the state.
> Nebraska's historically strong economy, for example, might
> diminish entrepreneurial activity, as the incentive to start a
> business can be greater in an environment of high unemployment.
> Entrepreneurship also involves risk, which does not always
> complement Nebraska's conservative culture. (Gines, 2016).

Bullshit! Any idea that can be developed that has a market has a chance for longevity and stability. You can be in a community inundated with Wal-Mart stores, but if you want to open up a landscaping business, a janitorial business or an accounting business, not only can you succeed, but you can flip it and pimp Wal-Mart for contracts and short-term projects. Innovation is what these Nebraskans lack, and the speaker is simply patting them on the head with the kind of things they want to hear, giving a "feel good lecture" because he knows the truth.

He then makes the claim that, "Entrepreneurship also involves risk, which does not always complement Nebraska's conservative culture." So what he's saying is that Nebraskans are cowards! These are people who came to a strange place, murdered off Native Americans, created a state made up of farms and corn, isolated black people who came into the state by action and law, and continue to make public mistakes at the state level, from the Department of Corrections and the Department of Tourism to the Department of Health and Social Services and the Department of Roads. They are not afraid of risk when they publicly steal money and comingle funds; they are not afraid of risk when they engage in perennial nepotism and discrimination. So again, the speaker gives them a "safe is best" alibi when in reality, nothing could be further from the truth.

The speaker then adds that, "Additionally, the state traditionally has focused on attraction-based economic development, which prioritizes attracting outside companies rather than focusing resources on growing existing businesses." This proves several of my earlier points. They go outside because there is nothing internal worthy of consideration; they realize they are too stupid to attract quality and are too racist to bring in businesses that might have a sizable minority labor force; and their "ideological incest" makes them feel more comfortable with fellow hicks and hillbillies than with "those urban types." These are the facts; what the speaker is talking about is nothing but fluff and sugar-coated rationalizations.

The next sub-head and section of the presentation is "Entrepreneurship Efforts Under Way in Nebraska." It begins as follows:

> **Entrepreneurship Efforts Under Way in Nebraska**
> Since the release of the reports in 2010, Nebraska has worked to improve the environment for entrepreneurship in a variety of ways. At the state level, Nebraska launched an "economic gardening" program through the Nebraska Department of Economic Development. Economic gardening focuses on companies with 10 to 99 employees, firms that traditionally create the most net new jobs, by providing in-depth marketing research and strategic management consulting. (Gines, 2016).

Economic gardening? Yeah – trying to grow something out of dirt and when necessary, use "hos" to do it (get it?). The approach is remedial as far as I'm concerned. Why didn't they call it "building blocks for business," "kindergarten capitalism" or "recess for revenue"? Those names would have been just as insulting and probably have about as much content and focus.

But the point is to treat those you are reaching out to as "know-nothings" and promote yourself as the expert. That is why they want small companies with only a few employees. Sure, they may create the most jobs, but they are also going to have the least amount of resources and capital to sue you when they realize they've been bilked. They are more likely to be vulnerable and have a lesser likelihood of lobbyists or supporters with real clout. The smaller the business the easier it is to control and this brings me to the next point.

The speaker adds, "In addition, the Nebraska Progress Loan Fund supports development of small businesses by providing loans of $50,000 to $2 million to existing and startup businesses." Loans. What did I tell you? Why else would the Federal Reserve BANK be interested in? Why else would an urban empire like Kansas City give a shit about a hick state like Nebraska, which has a city of about the same size (Omaha) as KC (which has 466,600), but far less going on in terms of night life, culture, business development, tourism, urbanism and so on? Like a dope dealer getting young kids hooked on crack, you give these farmers LOANS and get them "hooked" on having a business. All the while you are hoping that they default on that loan.

Fancy titles, big names and quadra-syllabic labels can also be used to mystify and mummify the unwitting:

> Nebraska Extension, under its Community Vitality Initiative, launched the Entrepreneurial Community Activation Process (ECAP) in 2013. To date, seven communities across the state have participated. ECAP helps communities identify entrepreneurial strengths and weaknesses and provides tools to help communities organize people, resources and policy to build strong local entrepreneurship ecosystems. Plans are under way to expand the program in multiple rural communities over the next year. (Gines, 2016).

The people creating, launching and sponsoring these "programs" are the ones who make the serious money. As for the identification of "entrepreneurial strengths and weaknesses," that should have been done before the person decided to go into business! So since it wasn't done, those running the programs know beforehand that they have a ready-made pool of idiots to exploit. And with such little progress having been made over the last century, it is clear that the program heads hit the nail on the proverbial head.

From talking about "inner-cities" in his opening, you can plainly see that the emphasis has shifted to the rural milieu. These people don't have the guts to talk about "inner city business development." Oh, they will talk about it (re-hashing the same bullshit that they fed to white farmers, only changing the word "rural" and using "inner-city"), but that would be about as far as it would go if it ever took place.

The speaker explains the following:

> The Nebraska Entrepreneurship Task Force, or NETForce, is a statewide collaboration that brings together organizations that

> support entrepreneurship and small businesses to educate and
> develop current and potential entrepreneurs. One example of this
> collaboration was a first of its kind conference in Nebraska in 2015
> that brought together educators, economic developers and
> policymakers with the specific goal of breaking down silos and
> building stronger networks to help enhance entrepreneurship in the
> state. (Gines, 2016).

This is why Nebraska keeps sliding downward – the same old tactics that end up reaping the same old results. Now, I call this the "Farm-Aid Syndrome." When the farms were going under, instead of Willie Nelson and the rest of those country-and-western hicks putting money together and helping out farmers, they decide to have a big-ass concert. In other words, promoting themselves and raising taxable monies and the farmer's did really get shit.

How about the so-called "AID concert"? You had the likes of Michael Jackson, Lionel Richie, Diana Ross and other mega-stars getting together to fight AIDS and HIV. Did they pool their money and make a massive donation? No. They made a damn record called "We Are The World' (when nothing could have been further from the truth) and used record sales. Promoting themselves while people died around them every day.

Now to apply these paradigms to the issue of entrepreneurship in Nebraska. They start off with a conference. Of course they charged and entry fee and since many of those interested were probably from out-state, that also meant paying for a hotel room. Then they had to pay for dinner and breakfast. And what in the hell was resolved as it relates to small business development and/or entrepreneurship? Not a damn thing. And yet the speaker boasts about a "first of its kind conference." It was not the first of its kind: it was the first of its kind in name only. This stuff has been going on for decades, all over Omaha, sponsored by groups ranging from the University of Nebraska Omaha and Metropolitan Community College to the Workforce Development and the City of Omaha. First of its kind? Don't make me laugh.

Now comes the reason for this lecture: plugs, promos and props for none other than the Federal Reserve Bank of Kansas City:

> Over the past five years, the Federal Reserve Bank of Kansas City
> has introduced a model of entrepreneurship-based economic
> development called *Grow Your Own*, which focuses on using
> entrepreneurship as the driver of local economic development. It is
> a community-based approach that concentrates resources on
> existing strengths, small businesses and supporting the
> development of job-creating entrepreneurs. (Gines, 2016).

If what the Bank has "created" is such a "model of entrepreneurship," then why hasn't it worked in Kansas City? Why hasn't it been applied and why doesn't it work in black communities? But that's not the real concern that I have about the program and its name.

The concept of "Grow Your Own" is exactly what black people had always done before white people interfered and, out of jealousy, started systematically destroying black communities by taking land, closing down black businesses, and stigmatizing the area so that others would not want to relocate there. Such tactics have a long history: read the story of Black Wall Street, the Greenwood community in Tulsa, Oklahoma, a community that was self-reliant and prospering before envious white people went in, with the help of the military, and leveled it, killing over 300 people. Never heard of it? Why would you? The school system is white and protectionist and white folks are (rightfully) ashamed of the kind of things they've done to undergird black financial initiative.

"Grow Your Own"? What was described in regard to the Greenwood (Tulsa) community in 1921 also took place in other cities but were called "riots." When white people attacked, they went after black individuals and businesses. This took place in East St. Louis (1917), Knoxville TN (1919), Elaine, AR (1919), Rosewood (1923), Rondo (outside of St. Paul, Minnesota in 1960s to build I-94) and North Omaha, Nebraska where a freeway divided the area and destroyed black business potential. And in New York, the white mob even burned a black orphanage, the home of more than 200 children.

Grow Your Own? Black people mastered it and envious whites now have the gall to take credit for the act of self-determination. And they use a black man to promote their lies. Look at how the speaker describes what black people engineered, mastered and actually practiced back in the day:

> The entrepreneurship ecosystem, which includes all the organizations, resources and policies that interact to instill and encourage a thriving entrepreneur community, is central to a *Grow Your Own* strategy. *Grow Your Own* models use a holistic approach to connect providers, resources and communities together so they can focus on sustainable economic growth. Resources from the Kansas City Fed can help guide the development of such synergy by providing an overview of the important components of a thriving entrepreneurship ecosystem and sharing examples of communities that have developed them. (Gines, 2016).

Either the speaker is abysmally ignorant of black history and black urban life or he is intentionally crediting his white "bosses" with paradigms and strategies that black people have long mastered (prior to white intervention). The "holistic approach" is simple enough when you ensure that white people control all the resources and avenues for growth and development. But black people had that going on as well when the communities were truly black. Dr. Martin Luther King, Jr., and his craving for "integration" killed most of the black businesses – hotels, movie theaters, cab stands, supermarkets, doctor's offices – that one time flourished, even here in Omaha.

Furthermore, the speaker says, "Resources from the Kansas City Fed can help guide the development of such synergy by providing an overview of the important components of a thriving entrepreneurship ecosystem and sharing examples of communities that have developed them." And there you have it: *the dependency connection.* First, induce people to start businesses and that you have what they need; secondly, push the concept of LOANS; and third, talk about "resources" that only the Kansas City Fed can provide.

The key is that the Fed provides the oversight, which is why the speaker used the term "synergy." When those in charge want to make it appear as if a process is quid pro quo, they use that term. Synergy is, "the interaction or cooperation of two or more organizations, substances, or other agents to produce a combined effect greater than the sum of their separate effects." The key is to convince the dependent entity that the entity with the resources and money needs the dependent entity as badly as the dependent entity needs the entity with the money. But the fact remains, "He who has the ability to satisfy human needs controls the humans with those needs."

But those humans are going to be white for the most part. And the following "example" proves it:

> One example of the implementation of a successful *Grow Your Own* model is Phillips County, Kan. After struggling to recruit firms to the small community of 5,500, its priority became supporting startups and existing small businesses. Using this model, Phillips County's sales tax revenue grew 120 percent between 2003 and 2012 and a once-declining population stabilized. By utilizing similar *Grow Your Own* models, many Nebraska communities may be able to foster a diversified economic development system that empowers local populations to drive economic growth through entrepreneurship. (Gines, 2016).

What an example to use. But it supports and reinforces the lily-whiteness of the priorities of the Federal Reserve Bank as well as the "Grow our Own" model. Phillips County, Kansas is described, thusly:

> *As of the census of 2000, there were 6,001 people,* 2,496 households, and 1,722 families residing in the county. The

> population density was 7 people per square mile ... There were
> 3,088 housing units at an average density of 4 per square mile ...
> *The racial makeup of the county was 98.25% White, 0.25% Black*
> *or African American, 0.30% Native American, 0.45% Asian,*
> *0.03% from other races, and 0.72% from two or more races.*
> *0.67% of the population were Hispanic or Latino of any race ...*
> *About 7.20% of families and 10.00% of the population were below*
> *the poverty line ...* (Wikipedia, 2016 – emphasis added).

And there you have it – towns don't get much whiter than that. The claim that the population stabilized should be qualified by the fact that there are only 6,000 people in the town. So "Grow Your Own" is a model for a small town, a village or a parish – not for a major city. And it appears to work best in areas that are homogeneous (read: lily white).

The speaker (mercifully) arrives at the conclusion of his presentation:

Conclusion
Nebraska has the potential for strong growth in entrepreneurship.
Many resources are available to support entrepreneurship in the
state, but they often are fragmented and disconnected. Fostering
greater collaboration among various economic development,
education and policymaking entities is important to building a
strong entrepreneurship ecosytem. In particular, looking at ways
entrepreneurship can help facilitate economic growth in small rural
communities with large population declines as well as inner-city
communities with high unemployment rates could help improve
the overall health of Nebraska's economy. (Gines, 2016).

The reason why Nebraska has such "strong growth in entrepreneurship" as I have shown you, is because it is so far behind in it! Its own studies show that in most of the areas of concern, the state is an abysmal failure. Of course there is nothing left to do but grow when you're been reduced to the lowest common denominator! The claim that, "Many resources are available to support entrepreneurship in the state, but they often are fragmented and disconnected" is contradictory: if there are so many resources that are available but they are fragmented and disconnected, then they are not really "available" nor can they be "availed of," now can they?

The entire presentation was nothing short of a regurgitation of general truisms. Even before the lecture even someone with but a scintilla of knowledge in business development knew that, "Fostering greater collaboration among various economic development, education and policymaking entities is important to building a strong entrepreneurship ecosytem." Feeding into the university system and the areas that were recommended by the speaker only increases dependency on those entities. And since "the hand that feeds, controls," it becomes clear what the real issue is: small businesses hire people and in turn, the ones hired can be controlled by the entities that control the small business. This is a form of what used to be called "neo-colonialism."

At the end, just as in the beginning, the speaker sneakily includes "inner city communities" in with the rural communities that his organization appear to prefer. So again, "blue skies promises" being made with an out-of-town banking interest using a young black man to outline what is being "offered and recommended." And as if my allegation about this entire fiasco being nothing more than a promotion for the Federal Reserve, the speech ends with the following information-laden conclusion:

> To learn more about the Federal Reserve Bank of Kansas City's work in small business and economic development, as well as entrepreneurship ecosystems, visit *www.kansascityfed.org/community/smallbusiness*. There you will also find information about the national Growing Entrepreneurial Communities Summit, May 4-5 at the Kansas City Fed. (Gines, 2016).

And there you have it: another example of how the "booty snatchers" continue to get paid even while making the claim of providing some form of businesses assistant and/or entrepreneurial training. But the "game" that is being run to keep an otherwise "countrified" state approach is far from over. Even while neglecting its African-American residents (except when using their collective situation and negative demographics to apply for and receive Federal grant money) the state continues to address its tax situation.

ON-GOING USE OF "TAX RELIEF" TO PACIFY RESIDENTS AND PREVENT THEM FROM LEAVING THE STATE

A hick state has to generate revenue somehow. So they have to keep what little population they've got. In order to do that they can't allow the property taxes to get too high or more people will leave. But even as they try to do that, the state of Nebraska still has the 7th highest property taxes in the nation. The only thing keeping people from moving to next door Iowa is that Iowa is ranked number 14 in property taxes and Kansas, Nebraska's neighbor to the south, ranks number 15 in that category. So the hick state is saved only because it works diligently to keep its already sky high property taxes under control.

The clown prince of journalism Tom Becka of Channel 42 said on December 9, 2016 that between 2011 and 2015 some 11,000 people with college degrees left the state. He said it was because there were jobs in other states. Of course he would say that because he is an apologist for Omaha, admitting during this same telecast that Omaha has a "small town feel" and that he considered that an attractive feature. For someone of his job-hopping ilk, it only figures that he would feel at home in Hooterville. But today's people, black and white, want that urban, sophisticated city feel, not the backwoods hillbilly veneer of a place that boasts about being a cow town.

They have to keep taxes under control to keep people from leaving the state. At the same time is the on-going leeching for every grant they can get. One of their major sources of revenue is the agricultural subsidy. One site explains that, "An agricultural subsidy is a governmental subsidy paid to farmers and agribusinesses to supplement their income, manage the supply of agricultural commodities, and influence the cost and supply of such commodities." That includes farm subsidies from the state legislature. According to Sen. McCollister on March 29, 2016, "In 2014 Nebraska farmers received more than $800 million in farm subsidies." Not only that, but according to one website, between 1995 and 2014, Nebraska got $18.2 billion in subsidies, ranking it 6th in the nation. These include commodity programs, crop insurance subsidies, conservation programs and disaster programs. Snatching all the "booty" they can get.

And the Nebraska Legislature is filled with farmer types, which explains the conservative (read: neanderthal) types of legislation that is favored and passed.

So the farmer's get paid to either grow their genetically engineered food or to not plant at all. In either case, you can see why the state of Nebraska has more millionaires per capita than any other state – and remains on the precipice of bankruptcy.

<u>The Tax Increment Financing Scam</u>

The City of Omaha continues to over-use what they call "Tax Increment Financing" for their bullshit projects. It usually begins with lies that are concocted by the City of Omaha Planning Department which labels a given "target" area (in a white area) as being "blighted," whether it is or not. McGraw (2006) provides an excellent example that also applies to Omaha:

> Until the 1990s, most states reserved TIFs for areas that could be described as "blighted," based on criteria set forth by statute. But as with eminent domain, the definition of blight for TIF purposes has been dramatically expanded. In 1999, for example, Baraboo, Wisconsin, created a TIF for an industrial park and a Wal-Mart supercenter that were built on farmland; the blight label was based on a single house in the district that was uninhabited. In recent

years 16 states have relaxed their TIF criteria to cover affluent areas, "conservation areas" where blight might occur someday, or "economic development areas," loosely defined as commercial or industrial properties. (McGraw, 2006).

In the case of Omaha, TIFs were not reserved for North Omaha. It was an economic and racial imperative that the black community remain poor. Without that "pocket of poverty" to use for their applications for free grant money, Omaha would be stuck using its own wits and skill sets to manage its finances. And if this book hasn't shown you anything else, this has never been a successful act or endeavor.

TIFs were instead used to expand businesses and generate tax revenue for the city and county, not for the masses of people. The example used above from Baraboo, Wisconsin also fits what these "booty snatchers" did in Omaha, Nebraska in and around an area that was an area that featured the international headquarters of none of other than Mutual of Omaha.

After Mutual bought up surrounding housing, tore it down and built mega-sized parking lots, all of a sudden the area was dubbed "blighted" by the city. I was there in front of the City Planning Board, a group of appointed incompetents who voted unanimously to use TIF to finance a "restructuring of the area," which they immediately dubbed "Midtown." It was an area that would have been developed eventually because it is less than a mile from downtown Omaha where there are 25,000 jobs. But as was stated above, this middle class area somehow became labeled as "blighted" and in came the developers and you should see it now.

Not only is there an ultra-e expensive hotel in the mix, but also s long three block line of small businesses and even a multi-screen Marcus Theatre. Parking meters adorn Farnam Street which mysteriously went from a one-way street headed west to a two way street to better accommodate the night life and the spate of businesses described earlier. Midtown Park is now a spectacle replete with night concerts and various other activities, and the area is marked as a tourist attraction. Meanwhile the real blighted area – North Omaha – looks worse now than it did in 1977 when I arrived in Omaha.

The use of TIF by these "body snatchers" is akin to their abuse of Community Development Block Grants, Urban Development Block Grants, Community Service Block Grants, Weed and Seed grants, Project Trigger lock grants, Project Safe Neighborhood grants and so on. The money goes to create jobs with high-status sounding names for white people while using a few of the pre-existing "negro" lackey groups to sign on in the name of "partnerships." With no power, these negroes basically attend meetings, say nothing, and serve as a buffer zone between the exploiting city administration and the low-income masses that are being pimped.

In other words,

> The result is that a TIF can be put almost anywhere these days.
> Based on current criteria, says Jake Haulk, director of the
> Pittsburgh-based Allegheny Institute for Public Policy, you could
> "declare the entire Western world blighted." (McGraw, 2006).

And as we know, "The man with the gold makes the rules." These white people know that the majority of the population in any given city, is so busy working to eke out an existence that they don't have time to monitor the abuse of taxpayers' dollars that is taking place right under their noses. When the city said that the Mutual of Omaha area was "blighted," not a single individual, white or black, who lived in the area rose in opposition to that insult. I was *standing alone* at the City Planning Board meeting opposing their use of the word "blighted" and it was reported on the local television stations as a "lone voice."

And following is how this scam continues to take place all over Omaha. Right now they are trying to do something with Crossroads Mall, a one time successful shopping mall that has since gone the way of the dinosaur. So what do the "booty snatchers" do? They label that area – the central core of the entire city of Omaha located at 72nd and Dodge – as being qualified for TIF funds! And these hillbilly business people in that area are saying nothing, although such a decision is going to hurt them in the end. Check it out:

> Largely because it promises something for nothing—an economic
> stimulus in exchange for tax revenue that otherwise would not
> materialize—this tool is becoming increasingly popular across the
> country. Originally used to help revive blighted or depressed areas,
> TIFs now appear in affluent neighborhoods, subsidizing high-end
> housing developments, big-box retailers, and shopping malls. And
> since most cities are using TIFs, … play them off against each
> other to boost the handouts they receive simply to operate profit-
> making enterprises. (McGraw, 2006).

Corporate handouts time and time again. The same thing that Mutual of Omaha received for standing pat while the city lied about the area they are in over on 33rd and Farnam Street – surrounded by their high rise buildings (by Omaha standards), condominiums to the west and a sloping view of downtown. They benefited from the use of TIF and the city ranked in the tax revenues that came from all of that new construction. The developers made a mint from erecting those specialty businesses and that movie theater, not to mention that Element Mid Town

Hotel. The mystique around a "Midtown neighborhood" was immediately used for tourism purposes.

These foolish Nebraskans and Omahans don't care about the residents and they look the other way. Again, McGraw writes,

> … TIFs only add to the problem: Although politicians portray TIFs as a great way to boost the local economy, there are hidden costs they don't want taxpayers to know about. Cities generally assume they are not really giving anything up because the forgone tax revenue would not have been available in the absence of the development generated by the TIF. That assumption is often wrong. (2006).

And it is going to be wrong in Omaha, a city that is annexing nearby areas to increase its population but in doing so, is also increasing its tax burden. They have to stretch their already buffoonish police force, their fire department and so on. As they seek to expand and make Omaha appear to be more populous than it really is, they are also assuming more responsibility, including garbage, sewers, lighting and roadways. Omaha is already a pothole-ridden "town" that is in need of serious infrastructure attention. And TIF is used to construct huge buildings and change the skyline of a town that is sorely in need of marketing and promotion.

Omaha will begin using TIFs as they assume increasing control over what was at one time the black community. In the name of "development" and "progress," greedy people like Warren and Susie Buffett, along with the Omaha Chamber of Commerce, the City of Omaha Planning Department and all their negro appointed lackeys will use TIF to invade the community, take over housing and construct new housing for the yuppies who can no longer stand the long commutes from suburbia to jobs downtown, to the airport and the newly developed riverfront. Black people will be relocated to the northwest:

> TIFs have been around for more than 50 years, but only recently have they assumed such importance. At a time when local governments' efforts to foster development, from direct subsidies to the use of eminent domain to seize property for private development, are already out of control … (McGraw, 2006).

It's all about "American greed." The people don't count as anything much more than taxpaying thralls. That is why these huge skyscrapers are being constructed and downtowns are being developed. The more revenue that can be generated from restaurants, casinos, shopping malls and the like, the more taxes paid into the city's coffers and the more money the financial managers can finagle, manipulate, steal and co-mingle, the way the city of Omaha, Douglas County and the State of Nebraska have been getting away with for decades.

Wasting taxpayers' money and double-dipping. Or, as one scholar explained it:

> Local officials usually do not consider how much growth might occur without a TIF. In 2002 the Neighborhood Capital Budget Group (NCBG), a coalition of 200 Chicago organizations that studies local public investment, looked at 36 of the city's TIF districts and found that property values were rising in all of them during the five years before they were designated as TIFs. The NCBG projected that the city of Chicago would capture $1.6 billion in second-stream property tax revenue—used to pay off the bonds that subsidized private businesses—over the 23-year life spans of these TIF districts. But it also found that $1.3 billion of that revenue would have been raised anyway, assuming the areas continued growing at their pre-TIF rates. (McGraw, 2006).

So in the home of the "booty snatchers" they end up exploiting their own residents. Like fiendish vampires, the leaders tax their own people so that they can construct buildings and upgrade properties that, in turn, will generate tax revenue so that they can pay their bills. As Omaha goes, so goes the state of Nebraska, a state with a predicted $900 million budget shortfall in 2017.

THE FEWER BLACKS THE INCREASED NEED FOR POVERTY GRANTS

Nebraska is a lily-white state and when funders look at the general picture they don't see much poverty in general. They see rich farmers, a low unemployment, a constant median income and quality housing. That is, until they come to a section of the state known as "North Omaha." The area has been so stigmatized that even rednecks in the western panhandle recognize it as "the ghetto." And it is that ghetto whose status and negative demographics generate on-going Federal funding for the state's largest city. And it is for that reason that Omaha makes sure that North Omaha remains poor and for the most part, moribund.

Nebraska is a large state, ranking 16th in square mile total and 15th in land area. And yet for the most part the African-American community covers less than ten square miles of it. That is segregation by any measure. In 2000, a ranking of the states by percent of population selecting the race of Black/African-Americans alone, Nebraska came in 32nd, even lower that lily white enclaves like Rhode Island, Kansas and Indiana.

As long as black people remain poor, Omaha can lie on its grant applications and claim to be working on the problem. They've done it since 1975 with the Community Development Block Grants and since that time have received more than $216 million in free money. And North Omaha has not changed positively since that time and in fact, looks worse than it did in 1975 when the city received its first grant.

And what about the Social Service Block Grants? You can only receive those if you have low-income areas. That translates to mean Blacks and secondly, the Latinos. But it is the black population whose demographics are a combination of factors that lead to endemic poverty: drug use, crime, gangs, homicide, teen pregnancy and so on. And Omaha goes after every single one of these in hopes of landing a grant that they can use to employ white people who couldn't land a job sweeping floors were the position a matter of real qualifications. They know it and so do the businesses that "pass" on Nebraska and Omaha once they glean the type of people and the low-level skill sets these people possess and display.

Turning Death Into Dollars: Guns, Grants and Gooniness

I wrote the following essay in early June, 2014 in response to a 2010 article that appeared in Nebraska's major newspaper. The article, titled, "Turning Death Into Dollars in Omaha, NE.: How the City and Cops Get Rich From Black Homicide," appears below in its entirety.

In a 2010 article (specific date unavailable), Henry J. Cordes of the *Omaha World Herald* wrote an article about violence in Nebraska with a special emphasis on violence in the Omaha black community. The article was titled, "Epidemic of poverty, violence," and is filled with the kinds of conjecture and distortions that paves the way for begging for Federal grant money, undermining black people, neglecting the source of both black poverty and violence and essentially represents the type of bullshit "reporting" that the *Omaha World-Herald* is notorious for.

> Over a recent span of five days, gunfire rocked northeast Omaha. A teen gunned down outside a bowling alley. A 15-year-old shot in the face while walking to a bus stop. A man shot dead inside a home. A young woman shot in broad daylight, followed by a rolling gunbattle through north Omaha streets. The surge of violence left three dead and another gravely wounded and heightened the tensions in several Omaha high schools. But more than that, it underscored how Omaha's streets in recent years have become among the deadliest places in America for blacks.

This is the way that white reporters bring the news to their lily-white readers: as if they don't know why these murders are taking place. Their conclusion? Blacks must hate each other. They don't ask the obvious questions: where is the police work? What are the cops doing other than coming in and sweeping up the mess? What is going on with all that cop-related grant money that pays for more police overtime? Nothing is being done. How did the kids get the guns? What is the "gang task force" doing? Moving on:

> Fueled by gun violence in northeast Omaha, Nebraska has the third-highest black homicide rate in the nation, according to the latest compilation of detailed national homicide statistics. The figures are based on homicide data from 2007, but they aren't a one-year fluke. Nebraska's black homicide rate for 2008 was even worse, and should again Police Chief Alex Hayes. "All these efforts are still ongoing. It takes a collaborative effort." rank with the nation's highest when national figures become available.

That which is referred to as "fuel" means that it is the instigator, the power that makes something go. If the end result is "gun violence," then how does it begin? What is the source? If a community is powerful enough to foster and fan "gun violence," then shouldn't it be able to "fuel" some jobs, some economic development, some improved housing stock, a fair and equitable education for their children, better health care and so on? No.

The white man is in charge of all of these things, and takes his time with their implementation – that is, when he chooses to do anything about them at all (usually after a spate of violence – check Omaha history). No, black people don't "fuel" gun violence. The city allows it to justify social service programs, more police overtime and more Federal grant money such as "Project Triggerlock," "Weed and Seed," "Project Safe Neighborhoods."

> Nebraska's black homicide rate did drop considerably in 2009, a welcome change that police and north Omaha community leaders attribute to initiatives aimed at tamping down gun violence.

See how foolish these "decision makers" are. They are talking about the impact that "initiatives" had on decreasing the black homicide rate in a state where there are only 80,000 blacks out of a total population of 1.7 million. And what is a "north Omaha community leader"? Shouldn't that just be "leader" no matter what section of Omaha you're in? Shouldn't the cops assigned to patrol the area be "north Omaha leaders"? Of course not. What is meant is "Black leaders" and that doesn't mean that they actually lead; it means they are black and have been dubbed by whites as being "influence peddlers."

> As the recent outburst of gunfire showed, there is still work to do.
> "When we do have a flare-up like that, we absolutely pay attention,"
> said Omaha. Both nationally and here, gangs, guns and black-on-
> black youth violence are at the center of the black homicide epidemic.

Recent outburst of gunfire as opposed to not-so-recent? Why make such a distinction? Because Omaha got caught "accidentally on purpose" forgetting to put black homicide stats with the rest of the stats. So there was no "formal" recognition of how concentrated the violence was, but informally the cops knew (they help to fan the violence with snitches, selective gang manipulation, arrests and so on) about it all along. The police chief, sounding like an idiot, claims that when there are "flare ups," they pay attention. Why do they wait? A flare-up is a response to the laxity of attention that is already not being paid! The Christians say that, "an idle mind is a devil's workshop." The cops wait and play around, manipulate the youth with snitches and Uncle Tom cops coming in from New York to create a snitch system, and then stand back and watch what happens. A flare-up, under such conditions, is inevitable and well they know it.

> Though Nebraska's 82,000 black residents make up about 4.5
> percent of the state's 1.8 million population, blacks have accounted
> for nearly 40 percent of the state's homicide victims over the past
> three years. In Omaha, 55.5 percent of the homicide victims in that
> time were black.

I think that the 82,000 figure is exaggerated, but that's fodder for another day's discussion. My point is that if blacks have accounted for "nearly 40 percent of the state's homicide victims," then there had to be some help along the way. How could such a high percentage of anything be generated by such a small population unless, somehow, somewhere, the white man was involved? Providing guns? Providing bullets? Using zoning to only allow taverns and bars, alcohol selling establishments, to be built or opened up? Instigating rivalries between black gang members? Using social services to instigate conflict between black youth and parents, and black men and women? Somewhere down the line, the white man is wringing his hands and allowing – and enabling – this homicide to take place.

> A black Nebraska resident during that span was 18 times more likely
> to be a victim of homicide than a white resident. That black-white
> disparity is much wider in Nebraska than the nation, where blacks are
> about seven times more likely to be a homicide victim.

The reason for that statistic regarding a black being 18 times more likely to be a victim of homicide than a white is because of the segregation status of the black community. On top of that there is high population density, blacks living on top of one another and a high person-per-square acre density level. If whites lived in the same situation, there would be white homicide that would be sky high as well; it's all about spacing and reliable studies show that the higher the population density, the higher the potential for conflict. White planners know that, but they do and say nothing because black on black conflict generates grant money

> That two of the recent victims were teenagers was hardly surprising. More than half of last year's black homicide victims were between 16 and 24, ages where many north Omaha youth are at high risk of falling into street gangs. Omaha police have identified 3,038 suspected gang members, up almost 300 from a year ago.

North Omaha youth? White boys and girls are "falling into gangs" as well, but they live in the same communities as many of the cops, more than a few of the news reporters and therefore it doesn't get the publicity. More importantly, black kids and guns generates more grant money from the government than a white kids who is "on the wrong track' might generate. It's all designed and pre-designated, but no one wants to believe it because of the myths of All-American city, Christian populations and high moral values. None of these is even close to being the truth.

> Guns were the weapon used in nearly nine of 10 slayings of black residents in Nebraska over the past three years — including all 15 in 2009. And in the vast majority of cases where the shooter was identified, the shooter also was black. "It tends to be intra-racial, focused in urban centers, and guns are the weapon of choice," said Josh Sugarmann of the Washington-based Violence Policy Center.

The fact that the homicides were committed with guns is only part of the issue. If these white people were being honest, the question they would be posing is this: "How can a section of town that is the poorest, the most denied, the most policed, the most monitored, the least educated and the most hated by people in power, have access to all these guns? How are the guns being obtained and from whom? Again, Josh Sugarman is one of those white people who enjoys documenting problems (violence), but offers nothing to alleviate them. Might I suggest the formation of a Violence Policy FOUNDATION that gives grants to black groups like the Urban League and NAACP (for what they're worth) to deal with the issue?

> The toll goes beyond the victims and the people who loved them. There were children in north Omaha during the recent eruption of violence who saw people they knew gunned down in front of them. Willie Barney of the African-American Empowerment Network, a

community action group in north Omaha, said the Nebraska statistics and recent violence are sobering. But he said he's been encouraged by the community reaction in the days following the latest shootings. Not only in north Omaha but in neighborhoods far beyond, people are saying loud and clear: It's time to stop the killing.

If Willie Barney was dealing with the situation in a realistic manner, he would not be talking about being "encouraged" about people who can only RESPOND and REACT to crises (such as himself). He would know, for instance, that the Nebraska statistics were there all along and he would have taken it upon himself to avail them. He would have called a press conference, announced his findings, and instead of sheepishly talking about how "sobering" the statistics found, he would have been expressing ANGER. Saying "enough is enough" and "let's stop the killing" are the signs of impotence unless the people you are saying it to have the commitment and "juice" to do something about it. All those statements do is further piss off the people who hear the words and know that these so-called leaders "ain't gonna do shit

The article continues: "But to make a difference, he said, such words need to be turned into action by expanding street intervention programs that reach out to gang members, providing more mentors and viable activities as alternatives to gangs, and implementing new training and employment programs. All will require money, manpower and focus."

"When you say 'Enough is enough,' the next step is, what are you going to do about it?" Barney said. "This is a critical juncture for Omaha." Though concern about gun violence in Omaha's black community is not new, what wasn't known until now was how the violence has made Nebraska among the deadliest places for blacks. *That's largely because Omaha homicide statistics haven't been reported into a detailed FBI national homicide database for almost two decades.* (Cordes, 2010: emphasis added)

Who is this Johnny-come-lately to talk about a "critical juncture for Omaha?" Where has he been all these years? What he is known for is serving as a water carrier for Susie Buffett and those other white-controlled members of a so-called "Empowerment Network." Empowerment? A term introduced to North Omaha by me in 2002, starting with a Nebraska Humanities Funded-grant conference that I held at Mount Moriah Missionary Baptist Church titled, "Self-Empowerment and the North Omaha Community." The Johnny-come-latelys came along after I held three more conferences in 2003, 2004, and 2006 and then left

Omaha for Dallas. They made their move and allowed white folks to define what THEY saw as "empowerment." Someone should have filed a lawsuit against the Omaha Police Department for failure to file those homicide stats. But apparently nobody had the time, the knowhow – or the guts.

> A Violence Policy Center study based on that FBI database and released last month found that Nebraska ranked 42nd in black homicide rate. But the study included only the five black homicides in 2007 that occurred outside of Omaha.

The fact that these people are keeping homicide rates by race should tell you something about how black people are viewed. If a small group has access to guns at a high rate and then kills as a result of that, and the people they are killing are their own, why should the white man care? This is what he wanted all along and has always wanted since the days of slavery! That is why in-house prison deaths that are black on black are not taken seriously; this is why black on black youth homicides are dismissed; this is why the ghetto, the barrio and the reservation have higher rates of homicide than those communities that are spread out. Compartmentalization by race is a successful white historical habit. Were it not, there would be no ghettos, barrios and reservations to speak of, now would there?

> When the 22 black homicide victims from Omaha are added to the study, Nebraska shoots up to third in per-capita black homicide rate, behind Pennsylvania and Missouri. Nebraska's rate of 34 homicides per 100,000 black population in 2007 was 65 percent above the national rate. If the Omaha numbers are added to the group's two previous studies, Nebraska ranked 14th in 2006 and eighth in 2005, its per-capita rate in both years well above the national average.

Now that the information has been reported by the World-Herald, the cops and others clip the article and send it in to the Federal government, leeching for grant money to "help the Negroes." The proposals for aid will come from the area hospitals, social service nonprofits, the cops themselves and a host of others, all feigning a concern for and a commitment to "doing what we can to decrease these horrific numbers." Again, they lie so they can get PAID.

> But violence surged even higher in 2007 and 2008, pushing Nebraska's rate among the very highest. Even with the significant drop in homicides in 2009 — from 28 down to 15 — Nebraska's rate fell to only slightly below the typical national average. Police Chief Hayes and north Omaha leaders said that the high rankings may be startling at first but shouldn't surprise anyone in light of the similarly high poverty rates and dropout rates seen among Omaha blacks in recent years.

Recent years? Where have these "north Omaha leaders", whomever they are, been? They are not "leaders" because if they were, the high poverty and dropout rates mentioned above would not be a surprise because there would have been an on-going battle to fight and address these issues. These problems exist because these "leaders" are in cahoots with the racists who are in power; these "leaders" are being paid under the table and are assigned to carry water (translation: kiss ass) of white decision makers who are in charge of the fate and future of North Omaha. "Recent years" my ass! Black kids have been getting mis-educated, suspended, expelled and pushed out of school, and high poverty rates have existed, for more than 80 years. Where were these "north Omaha leaders" at THEN?

> The latest U.S. Census survey indicates Omaha has the 11th-highest black poverty rate among the nation's 100 largest metro areas."I'm extremely disturbed by those numbers, but I'm not surprised by those numbers," said Ben Gray, the Omaha city councilman who represents north Omaha. "It goes hand in hand with the poverty we see and the racial separation which is obvious to anyone who comes to this town."

Ben Gray is part of the problem. The "leadership" that he and his City Council predecessors have provided was self-centered, wholly inadequate and sophistic, to say the least. Since State Senator Chambers got district elections passed for city council which meant a mandatory black district, North Omaha has been presented by two attorneys, a former KETV reporter and now a former KETV camera man. And since time of the first stint by Councilman Fred Conley, North Omaha has gotten progressively worse aesthetically, socially and economically. Under their watch the community has been divided and decimated with a freeway, the destruction of housing projects, the co-optation of North 24th Street and the on-going abuse of Community Development Block Grant dollars. But in all truth, you cannot blame selfish and silly people who come into office and act in such a jejune manner: it's the people who vote for them – the same ones who allow their ministers to sit back and do NOTHING from the pulpit other than make promises, promote "hope" and collect the hard-earned money of their congregation members. Gray, like his predecessors does a lot of talking, but the outside forces controlled every single one of them. He is the reactionary rule, not the exception.

> When the director of the State Office of Violence Prevention sees the numbers, he sees the reason his office was created in 2009. It's likely no coincidence, Mike Friend said, that lawmakers were moved to act in the wake of violence we now know was among the nation's most severe.

Nebraska's white leadership, several of them named Friend, were cops and legislators and had no foresight when it came to community issues. They were like most whites in Nebraska: a world of "mefirst" and not really giving a damn about poverty unless they can wrangle a job out of it – and most of them have done just that. Therefore, the creation of this State Office of Violence Prevention is a sham: how can you prevent violence if you lack the will and the resources? How can you prevent the very thing that white people seem to thrive on, whether you're talking about economic violence, political violence, cultural violence, religious violence or, of course legislative and/or legal violence?

> Indeed, the escalating gun violence in 2007 and 2008 — including a month in the summer of 2007 when there were 31 shootings citywide in 31 days — got a lot of people's attention. Police responded by cracking down on illegal gun possession and collaborating more in the community, seeking to break a culture that discouraged "snitching" in the shootings' wake.

How can you "collaborate more in the community"? Don't you mean "collaborate more WITH the community?" Maybe you do – but maybe you don't. Maybe all these racist and ignorant cops want to do is collaborate in the community while they park their cruisers next to one another in store parking lots during evening hours passing a joint. Or maybe they want to collaborate while cruising through the community trying to pick up on black women (as several got busted doing). In either case it's not a "culture that discourages snitching," although I wish it was. It's the fact that black kids know that white men hate them and unless they are forced to (or tricked into doing it), black kids despise the police because they have seen and heard from friends and relatives, how chickenshit the Omaha Police Department has been and continues to be. And these kids are also getting an increasingly more profound understanding of how worthless the so-called "North Omaha leadership" has been:

> Gray, Barney and other north Omaha leaders launched the Impact One intervention program to open lines of communication with gangs and stop retaliatory killings. Some of the program's counselors are former gang members, giving them credibility in efforts to lure youths to more productive lives. A summer jobs program for at-risk youths started modestly in 2008 and then, through federal stimulus funds, expanded to 500 kids in 2009, giving them work experience, some income and keeping them off the streets.

The time that these so-called leaders are spending launching programs could be spent actually engaging in some ACTION. They're failures on a personal level and then they take that next step of seeking out some white folks to "adopt them" and they are then given a platform to spew forth specious and spurious claims of "creating a program." Token ideas and ass backwards concepts create ass backwards results. What was described above about summer jobs and counseling has been tried since the 1960s. What made them work before was that the people in charge were black and really cared about more than just getting paid. Today, with these "black leaders" under the thumb of Susie Buffett (Warren's daughter) the priorities are just the opposite: get paid first and worry about the kids later.

> The entire anti-violence campaign has grown into Omaha 360, a
> coalition of business, philanthropic, community and faith groups
> inside and outside north Omaha. A key test for the effort, said Urban
> League of Nebraska Chief Executive Thomas Warren, will be finding
> funds for an expanded youth job and training program this summer.

Coalitions? Coalitions are formed for immediate reasons and ad hoc in their substance. They usually deal with a problem and then disband. Don't these idiots know that? Jobs for kids that last a summer. Training for people for jobs that don't exist and pay hardly nothing. And that's the best that people like Barney, Warren and Gray can come up with. And that is why the kids are pissed off: they see these Uncle Toms on television making problems aimed at jacking off viewers and have little long-lasting substance. The same thing goes for the ministers in Omaha. Put it all together and you've got an entire community of cowards controlled by an outside crew of racists with a long-range plan of relocation black people to the northwestern sector of the city so that they (the whites) can re-take the ghetto and be close to the airport, to downtown jobs and parks, and right near the riverfront.

> There were noticeable drops in violence during months the program
> was in place, the former Omaha police chief said. Mayor Jim Suttle
> has been lobbying for more federal dollars, and other sources are
> being explored. "Even as chief, I always felt violent crime was a
> symptom of poverty," Warren said. "If we're going to prevent violent
> crime, we have to start dealing with the causes, including under-
> education and lack of employment."

Warren was one of the worst chiefs the city ever had, if you judge it by the way he treated black people. He acted white, talked white and he treated black kids like dogs. He got the job because he scored highest on the chief's exam, meaning that he answered the questions the way the white man would. And he's still got that white way of viewing things as you can see by the preceding commentary. The Urban League of Nebraska, like the national chapter, is largely invisible and certainly irrelevant. The article concludes, thusly:

> Barney said everyone in the community has a role to play. "Not
> everyone is a gang intervention specialist," he said, "but you can be a

mentor."

It's the same old shit, year in and year out. Lies told by politicians, promises made by rich white folks, scams run by the City's Planning Department, and poor North Omaha stays poor. This is the formula for how you turn the negative demographics generated by the ghetto's deprivation into dollars for white folks (and their negro lackeys). Now that it's in writing, no one can say that the truth hasn't been shared.

THE "RACIAL GAP": CONCEPTS AND CHARACTERISTICS

Far too many people want to write about the "racial gaps" that exist between blacks and whites as if they just appeared out of nowhere. The obvious and simple fact is, racial gaps are the result of racist thinking. Before getting into the gaps in education, health and other areas that exist everywhere, including Omaha, I will offer up some case studies of examples of recurring incidents of racism that demonstrate that the racist atmosphere and ethos of Omaha is what paves the way for maltreatment of blacks and other people of color; in a word, the gap is designed and intentional. Following are some random case studies and examples of it before moving into the "gap in living standards" that have permeated Omaha for a century.

<u>Basis of the Racial Gap: Recurring Racist Activity as Normative Behavior</u>

The maxim teaches that, "Once is chance, twice is coincidence and three times is a pattern." Another version says that "three times is enemy action." This may be more fitting because it is clear that when it comes to the actions of white folks in Nebraska, there is no problem establishing that the racist activity that permeates Nebraska in general and Omaha in particular is the part of an on-going, recurring pattern ("enemy action"?) aimed at showing the disregard that the state and city have for African-American people.

The similarity between all of the examples I am about to show you is that white provocateurs take their chickenshit actions always claiming to be defending their race and always claiming that they want to make the racial situation better.

<u>Exhibit 1</u>: Back on February 6, 1972, a white man wrote a response to an article that appeared in the World Herald, penned by a black man who was then chairman of the Black Studies Department. The white man, a student, who wrote the World-Herald article, Buck Jones, was responding to an article by Dr. Milton White that had appeared in the January 30th edition of the newspaper. Following is

Jones' response, representative of the majority of white students and white Omahans, no doubt, under the heading, "Further Divisiveness: 'Prof's One-Sided Article Widens Black-White Chasm'." The article appears in its entirety:

> Considering the great concern exhibited by the press in recent years over justice and freedom, I was nothing short of amazed that you let Milton White manipulate you into printing "his" one-sided, diversionary article Jan. 30 ("Black 'Sure' UNO Trying to Fire Him"). Surely you could see through his "position" to his ulterior motive of denying the UNO administration any semblance of freedom of deciding upon the renewal of his contract as director of the Black Studies Department.
>
> In trying to determine why you decided to assist him without clarifying the real issues, questions came to mind:
>
> 1. Regardless of White's view point on the new (or should we say elimination of) discipline "required" for the Black Studies Department, and his opinion that he should not be required to cooperate with the administrators hired to supervise him, the primary question is, what does he really stand for and preach to his students? Ethnocentrism? Pluralism? Black culture separatism? Liberation? Revolution? What?
> 2. Does he not classify "Negroes" as those who seek to improve their lot through integration as differentiated from "Blacks" who believe in revolution for the attainment of their goals?
> 3. Implicit in his definitions, does he not consider "Negroes" as nothing more than "Uncle Toms" who should be looked down upon by "Blacks?"
> 4. Is he indoctrinating the younger blacks with his beliefs and are those beliefs not being spread to the entire black community?
> 5. Concerning the above question, will more or fewer of Omaha's "Negroes" brave the ostracism of their "Black" brothers and sisters by moving out of the black ghetto areas to provide a better environment and better schools for their children?
> 6. Now, considering a few of our white citizens (some of whom never intend to have black neighbors nor want their children to have black friends or even black classmates), are their purposes not ultimately being served by Milton White?
> 7. Finally, who is the establishment press really helping? Milton White, whose current ego trip will eventually be paid for in full by his own people in terms of self-suppression, limited horizons, or worse? Or is it Omaha's white racists who are gambling that they as individuals will never have to pay the price for the long-term consequences of Milton White's policies. Or is it both?
>
> There is one thing we do not need at this time in our nation's history; further divisiveness.

> The normally moderate tone of your paper indicates that you
> recognize this. Yet by publishing one-sided "dictated" articles as
> you did in this case, you are not only denying the university's
> administrators the freedom to make a responsible decision on
> Milton White's record, you also are serving to further widen the
> chasm between the black and white "Americans" of Omaha.

See? The white man knows what the black man needs and is always acting in a capacity of unsolicited "advisor." Bear in mind that Jones was a mere student taking on a black man with a doctorate and a position on campus. But in Omaha, white people realize they are the beneficiaries of white privilege and therefore need no credentials, need no real merit and need no active brain cells to spew forth their specious and spurious attacks on black people.

Exhibit 2: December, 1980.

Toward the end of December in 1980, the *Omaha World Herald* once gain displayed a callous disregard for objectivity and for the black community when the newspaper leadership decided to play God at the expense of race relations. As Matthew Stelly wrote in 1982:

> On December 7, 1980, there appeared in the Omaha World Herald
> the picture of a young white boy receiving and eye examination
> from Creighton University medical student Johnnie Sanders. This
> picture was to be used in conjunction with promotion of the World
> Herald Good Fellows 1980 Christmas fund-raising drive. Truly
> humane, right? Wrong. The boy was not really a boy, nor was
> he/she really white. Sounds strange,doesn't it? The World Herald
> art department was ordered by the city desk to alter the photo of a
> young black girl to make her look like a young white boy ..."

The plot thickens and, again, it is Senator Chambers who catches the newspaper with its hands in the proverbial cookie jar. As Chambers wrote:

> The falsification extended to the story: "The wording in the story
> was also edited to delete the girl's name and make the child male.
> World-Herald employees confirmed." The incident was such a
> journalistic travesty that Steve Kline, an 8-year veteran with the
> newspaper, resigned in protest. G. Woodson Howe, the executive
> editor of the World Herald, refused to return phone calls from the
> Omaha Sun newspapers, who were the first to expose the incident.
> Not only did the World Herald skirt the issue, but 'ran a tiny item
> ... which declared simply that Kline resigned after 8 years with the
> W-H and that 'we are sorry to see him leave." Not a word about
> the hoax has appeared in the W-H."

Exhibit 3: The Police and the Mass Arrests of Central High Students. On November 10, 1993, the police handcuffed and arrested 26 Central High School students on suspicion of jaywalking and obstructing traffic in the downtown area. Earlier in the month, merchants had complained that the students were making a nuisance in the area when school was dismissed. The police planned the mass arrests and were ready for the students with video cameras, handcuffs and paddy wagons. The police arrested the students and forced them to face the wall as they were handcuffed. The arrests, which caused a great deal of controversy in and around the black community, prompted even Mayor Morgan to express a concern that the police action was "excessive." Because of the criticism and promise that the community was willing to work with the police, the charges against most of the students were dropped (Burbach and Brennan, 1993).

Exhibit 4: Joe Friend and the Parental Responsibility Crime Proposal. In March of 1994, yet another controversy in the name of "crimefighting" involved the young people of Omaha's black community. City Council member Joe Friend, a former Public Safety Director, proposed an ordinance that would make parents responsible for the criminal acts of their children. Friend said that there were three options to his proposal. First, if a child gets in trouble for the first time, parents would be fined $200. If a child gets in trouble for a second time, the parent would be fined $500, and for the third time, the parent would be fined $1,000. If the parent could not afford to pay the fines, the fine could be worked off through community service. Also, the parent could make arrangements to attend personal counseling.

If a child were to get into trouble three times, the parent would not have the choice of only paying the fines, but they would have to attend parent training. The Ordinance failed because the Black community stood up against it, but Friend said that the failure was due to a church coalition, Omaha Together One Community, or OTOC. He said that he had the votes of five council persons that he needed, but OTOC spoke before them and, according to Friend, "scared them." Friend felt that the other councilpersons did not vote for the ordinance because OTOC convinced them they could impact upon the voters which, in turn, would hurt Council persons politically.

In an interview with Carrie McVicker, a student at the University of Nebraska at Omaha, Councilman Lee Terry said on March 13th, that then council person Brenda Council (an African-American) refused to sign the proposed ordinance because she felt that it represented a lack of due process for both youth and the parents. He said that the fines were excessive for members of the Black community due to the depressed financial condition of the area (meaning, North Omaha).

Furthermore, Terry said that the parents and children would have to go through a mock tribunal process in the Mayor's office. He added that every youth who gets in trouble was not the responsibility of parents, and that if a student did get into trouble oftentimes it is used as a learning experience. Terry added that the enforcement of the ordinance, had it passed, would be discrimination because it might not be equally enforced in all parts of the city. Even if it were, the parents in wealthy suburbs could afford to pay the fines, whereas in the black community, most parents could not.

These arguments basically echoed the arguments offered by the Black community and its leadership, including the Urban League director George Dillard, then UNO Black Studies Department chairman George Garrison, long-time activist Frank T. Peak and a host of others who filed into the City Council chambers to protest what they viewed as one of the most racist proposals in recent Omaha history.

Exhibit 5: The Cotton Patch Doll Incident at OPPD. The year was 1980 or thereabouts, when the Cabbage Patch Doll was the craze. Some MUD employees thought it would be funny to place posters of black dolls parodying the then popular Cabbage Patch Dolls under the name "Cotton Patch Dolls." The black dolls with white lips would be sold and come with a welfare card and other stereotyped documents. Senator Ernie Chambers got involved and the "prank" was immediately quashed. The Metropolitan Utilities District is the leading gas and water supplier in the state.

Exhibit 6: An article titled, "CEO Rebukes Those Behind Flier Advocating for 'White Man' that appeared in the July 23, 2016 edition of the *Omaha World Herald* is typical for a number of reasons. First of all, the headline, aimed at absolving the leadership of Union Pacific from any involvement in or knowledge of the racial incident you are about to read about. Secondly, the article attempts to make the incident occur as an "isolated" phenomenon when, in reality, such racist actions in Omaha are recurrent. From the campuses of UNO and Creighton University to the corporations of OPPD, Mutual of Omaha and Peter Kiewit, such incidents take place and after a few people say "ooops," the actions are swept under the rug until later, when similar incidents can take place elsewhere. The point is clear: white men don't like their fellow black employees and refuse to acknowledge them as human beings. Examples are in abundance.

In this case, the incident is described in the article by Brad Davis, reporter for the state's largest newspaper:

> A group of purported Union Pacific employees saying they will
> advocate for "European American males" drew a sharp
> condemnation from the company's top executive (Davis, 2016).

This is a tendency that white men have once black people begin kicking them in the ass. Under the mask of some stupid shit called "reverse discrimination," they want to allege that they are being passed over by lesser qualified people of color. That would make it outright "discrimination," and not "reverse discrimination". These dummies therefore display their stupidity, tendency toward embellishment, and outright lies through their own actions, which is why they are being "passed over" more likely than not.

The information continues:

> A flier saying it was for the "European American male Employee
> Network at Union Pacific" made its way around social media this
> week. In the flier, the group said it was "dedicated to developing
> and advancing the careers of men of European ancestry – the white
> man –at Union Pacific" (Davis, 2016).

If the white man is so "superior" as he claims and seeks to be, why all the concern? His people are the ones at the top? They only hire black people when pressured to do so. Could it be "fear" by these white boys that make them sit around on their bar stools and come up with bullshit like this? Omaha political leadership, like these clowns, has a history of being led by drunks, including former mayors Al Veys, Bernie Simon and Mike Boyle. The article adds that,

> The group, which calls itself "Teamen UP," said it would fight
> against "diversity for diversity's sake as a virtue" and said U.P.
> departments were "cluttered" with "token minority employees."
> Omaha-based U.P. has sanctioned employee groups for several
> minority groups, veterans and women. The company says these
> groups help attract and maintain a diverse workforce" (Davis,
> 2016).

Racism will always exist and will always permeate Omaha. Despite their bullshit programs and mastery of buzz words like "inclusion," "diversity," "multiculturalism," "community engagement" and so on, these white cowardly cowboy corporate types have always been homoerotically envious of black people in general and black men, in particular. The only black men they can accept are those on the University of Nebraska football team, running up and down the field with numbers on their backs as they (the white males) shout, "Go Big Red."

But when it comes to the workforce, it's a different story. Observe:

<blockquote>
…The flier said less-qualified minorities had been hired in favor of more-qualified white men. "E have sat back and watched as blacks and other minorities run around us for promotions based on nothing more than race and gender," it said. "We believe it to be reverse racism and discrimination against white men" … Union Pacific employs 8,000 in Nebraska and around 44,000 people nationwide (Davis, 2016).
</blockquote>

This is nothing new in 2016. Exactly thirty-eight (38 years ago, in 1978, Alan Bakke made similar "less qualified minorities" arguments as he sued the University of California system. This is the case that ushered in the oxymoronic and jejune term, "reverse discrimination." Similar cases followed, but my point is simply that the white man has always been insecure when it comes to people with skin color walking around in the same building he is in. He sees black people as competition for his sluttish white female who in her own words prefers her men, "tall, DARK and handsome." Omaha white males are most comfortable when black people occupy obviously inferior positions.

In this particular case at Union Pacific,

<blockquote>
The flier said the group would be 'discreetly recruiting members. It said there were seven members working from Omaha to get other employees involved. "Of course, this is tricky because we will be fired if we are found out and losing our jobs would obviously be counterproductive to our cause" (Davis, 2016).
</blockquote>

The concept of being discreet is a key in the updated and modified white supremacist structure. But know this: where you find discretion with white men in charge, you will find racism and discrimination. From judges and cops on the street, to university instructors and medical doctors, these white boys selective pick and choose the people who they will support and oppose. And most of those decisions are based on race.

<u>The Racial Gap: "Two Societies, Separate and Unequal …"</u>

The Kerner Commission Report, also known as the National Advisory Commission on Civil Disorders, concluded in 1968 that America was two societies: "One black, one white, separate and unequal." In the Omaha of 2016 – some 48 years later, this dichotomy remains a reality. Therefore any "racial gaps" that exist cannot be considered a "quirk" or an "accident." These gaps are the result of programs, plans, projects, and paradigms that are intentional and are *designed*.

Omahans continue to fall for the okey-doke when it comes to discourse and discussions regarding the "racial gap," which as we know, is a reality any place you go in the United States. But in Omaha, the racial gap represents free money – grants from the Federal, state and local governments. We used to call it "poverty pimping" but today's it's just plain "doing business as usual." The following analyses will show how this perversely parasitic modus operandi is alive and well and operating at full throttle in the State of Nebraska in general and the city of Omaha, in particular.

The concept of a "racial gap" has existed in Omaha for decades. Typical of the "news" surrounding the gap can be found in a February 23, 1989 article in the Omaha World Herald by Sharon Rosse under the headline, "Efforts to Bridge Racial Gap Outlined: Board Backs School Equality Proposal." Now, Ms. Rosse didn't pen that headline – the World Herald "editors" did. As an all white male enclave of decision makers, you can see the silly errors inherent in the headline – they mention a "racial gap" and they claim that "efforts" are being made and then have the gall to claim that there is such a thing as an "equality proposal." That was twenty-seven (27) years ago.

And the gap still exists.

The fact of the matter is, this "racial gap" is often used by racists to make it appear as if the existence of it lies at the door of black people themselves. Such as the case in a published article in the Omaha World Herald on February 6, 1972. Written by someone named Buck Jones, the headline of the opinion piece was, "Further "Further Divisiveness: Prof's One-Sided Article Widens Black-White Chasm." The article was written by a black studies scholar who was accurately discussing the race problems in Omaha. Such a reaction by Jones is not the exception, but the rule when it comes to "white leadership" in the River City. And remember: the World Herald's editors decided to print it and they gave it the headline.

A February 23, 1980 article by Sibyl Myers, the lone black reporter for the Omaha World Herald at the time, carried the headline, "Report on Black Omaha: Gap in Living Standards Cited." That was 36 years ago. And yet Omaha continues to lie and claim that they are working "their garsh darndest", not to eliminate the "racial gap," but to "close the gap." How will they determine when and if the gap is sufficiently closed?

Racial gaps are the result of a long-term and perpetual design. They are not accidents or quirks. These gaps generate money so that those in power can dupe the public into believing that with more money, the gaps will close. The public, being the idiots that they are, fall for the lie every time. These gaps or "disparities" as they are often called, generate Federal money for the city and the state. As a result,

Omaha has the fifth-highest African-American poverty rate among the nation's 100 largest cities, with more than one in three black residents in Omaha living below the poverty line. The percentage of black children in Omaha who live in poverty rank ranks number one in the United States, with nearly six of 10 black kids living below the poverty line. Only one other metropolitan area in the U.S., Minneapolis, has a wider economic disparity between blacks and whites (MedLibrary, 2016).

An article by Paul E. Barton and Richard J. Coley titled, "Those Persistent Gaps" offers some elements of the various gaps that I talk about and I will draw from their article and analyze each component to show how "the invasion of the booty snatchers" is most successful when they can feign a commitment to "problem solving" or "closing" a particular "gap" that they helped to create in the first place.

> Although we've focused more and more attention on dealing with the seemingly intractable gaps in achievement between black and Hispanic students and white students in the last quarter century, we've made little progress in closing the gaps. All subgroups of students have, in general, improved as measured by the National Assessment of Educational Progress. But disparities related to race/ethnicity and socioeconomic status remain.

Who is this "we"? If you're talking about educators who are white, all that activity in addressing the racial gaps is nothing more than a façade. As stated throughout this book, the racial gap is just another revenue stream that white people capitalize on in order to apply for and receive grant money from the Federal government. The talk about "closing the gap" is a way to hire more white people as social workers, classroom teachers, truant officers, police officers and so on, and a way to promote their "attempts" so that the world and the nation can truly believe that they are putting in work.

Moving on:

> Although the gaps may seem intractable, they are not inevitable if we continue to enlarge both our understanding of why they exist and what it will take to close them. A 2003 report from the ETS Policy Information Center titled Parsing the Achievement Gap(FN1) answered two questions: What life and school conditions are correlated with cognitive development and school achievement? and, Do gaps in these conditions among racial/ethnic and income groups mirror the gaps we see in achievement? (Barton & Coley, 2010).

What the authors are attempting to do may be admirable. But if your strategy and vision is based on or rooted in a bullshit thesis, then the product will inevitably be fucked up as well. This is what the previous paragraph shows us. Much of it is alright as it defines their intentions; but the flaw lies in the claim that, "Although the gaps may seem intractable, they are not inevitable if we continue to enlarge both our understanding of why they exist and what it will take to close them." They've got it wrong: the "gaps" that they outline and document are by design. They are intended. And most importantly, these gaps generate money for people who lie and claim that they have a 'remedy," a "solution" or a "cure" that will close those gaps. It's a complex game of Three-card Monte.

Now the authors offer up 16 gaps and what I am going to do is show you how, in the case of each of the gaps that these authors (Barton & Coley) claim to be so committed to "eradicating," their vision will not be realized because one man's "gap" is another man's "revenue stream." And it takes place "from the womb to the tomb." For instance, one gap deals with birth weight:

> Birth Weight
> Research has long established that low birth weight can lead to
> severe problems, ranging from mortality to learning difficulties.
> Children having a birth weight of less than approximately 5.5
> pounds are more likely to end up in special education classes,
> repeat a grade, or fail in school. ? (Barton & Coley, 2010).

If low birth weight can lead to problems, then that means that the mother – the person carrying the baby – has to be placed in harm's way as well. Thanks again to the farmers and their genetically engineered food, doctors who prescribe anything that is experimental and use pregnant black women if the drug has anything to do with that which is prenatal or gestational and the general conditions that low-income mothers live in, low birth weight is more common than not it appears.

In a racist society, discrimination is the wheel on which that racism turns. Invariably, black women are the backbone of the black family and if you infect, affect and cause her harm, the children she produced will be affected. One study found that,

> Factors such as genetics, unequal prenatal care and poverty only
> partly explain why blacks are three times more likely to deliver
> very low birthweight babies (less than 3.3 pounds). For example, a
> substantial black-white gap persists even among mothers who have
> college degrees. (California Black Women's Health Project, 2004).

It's about race on two levels. First, the black woman carrying the black child and secondly, more likely than not, the doctor who is her pediatrician is going to be white. Not only that, but because of the fact that medicine is racialized, how he helps her and what he prescribes are issues that are also in the hands of white people. Pharmacies pay out huge sums for doctors to "recommend" their medications, and many vitamins and supplements that appear are not even approved by the Federal Drug Administration. Add to that the conditions of the black community that the pregnant woman most likely lives in and all of the associated social issues and the *product* may be low birth weight, but the *process* is definitely a racist one.

Information on the racial gap as a moneymaker continues;

> Duke University researcher Sarah Mustillo and colleagues analyzed births in Chicago, Oakland, Minneapolis and Birmingham, Ala. Among black women, 50 percent of those with preterm deliveries and 61 percent with low birth weight babies had experienced discrimination in at least three situations. Among white women, the corresponding rates of racial discrimination were 5 percent and zero percent. (California Black Women's Health Project, 2004).

When certain things continue to re-occur, it is clear that they are not quirks or anomalies. Once is a fluke, twice is a coincidence, three times is a trend, as the saying goes. Low birth weight, because of the factors I've mentioned throughout this report, is designed by the powers that be. And money is made by doctors, pharmacists, social workers and a host of other "professionals" at every level. The more the black man or woman suffers, the more likely it will be that some white person designs a "program," a "project" or a "model" that can generate funds and revenue for the system:

> In a second study, researchers asked 312 black women who delivered babies at Stroger and University of Chicago hospitals whether they had experienced discrimination looking for work, at work, at school, in public settings or while getting medical care. Those who had experienced discrimination in at least three settings were 2.6 times more likely to deliver very low birth weight babes (California Black Women's Health Project, 2004).

Black women face discrimination every day of their lives. And this also includes the ones who are well off or even celebrities. This society continues to have problems dealing with its paleness and discrimination against black people (read: keep them out of our sight) is more popular and cheaper than the multibillion dollar tanning industry.

The old saying teaches that, "When white folks have a cold, black folks have pneumonia." An example of what this means appears in the following excerpt:

> Between 2000 and 2005, there was an increase in low birth weight
> for blacks, whites, and Hispanics. However, the percentage of
> black infants born with low birth weight in 2005-14 percent--was
> approximately double that for white and Hispanic infants. ?
> (Barton & Coley, 2010).

See? So this reality is turned into a revenue stream by those in power. The media gets into it by airing fear-based commercials on the "importance" of pediatric care and services. The insurance of the poor is continually pimped by the system and those who don't have it have their status turned into a new and innovative grant program that in turn, will create jobs for everyone but black females.

Next is the issue of lead poisoning. As you may or may not know, high lead levels are associated with the paint that exists in older homes. And where are older home located? In poor areas of the city, long abandoned by white people who ran away ("white flight") when they realized that black people were moving in. As a result, black families were affected and infected by the lead based paint in those homes and many of the kids developed intellectual problems, problems that again were turned into a revenue stream by those in the housing, education, and health industries.

Barton and Coley (2010) write,

> Lead Poisoning
>   Research has established that lead poisoning can seriously affect
> children, causing reductions in IQ and attention span, reading and
> learning disabilities, and behavior problems. As a result of laws
> focused on cleaning up the environment, the levels of lead in
> children's blood have dramatically decreased over the decades.
> However, we have not eliminated lead in the environment. A
> synthesis of recent studies has established that there is no safe
> threshold for blood lead levels. (Barton & Coley, 2010).

So what we are talking about is another way for white people to get rich off of black adversity. Low IQ scores means more placements in special education courses which requires the hiring of more white teachers. But it also means that the school qualifies for more "remedial education aid" and that is free money. Learning disabilities and behavior problems are handled with special classrooms and equipment, which are placed in the annual budget request, submitted and then funded. Mo' money, mo' money, mo' money.

And as for the lead in the houses, organizations and agencies are quickly formed and bullshit "credentials" are handed out by white folks who "train" people to learn how to remove paint chips and other areas where lead is present: the soil, window landings, stair rails, etc. As Barton & Coley further explain,

> Children in minority and low-income families have a higher risk of exposure to lead as a result of living in old houses or around old industrial areas with contaminated buildings and soil. Black children have considerably higher blood lead levels than white or Hispanic children have. The levels are about four times higher for blacks than for whites, and they are more than twice as high for children below the poverty line than for those above it. ? (Barton & Coley, 2010).

So it's poor black people once again. And in Omaha that means North Omaha because the city is residentially and racially segregated. All the old houses are in an eight square mile area on the northeastern sector of the city. And that is why the area represents a treasure trove of different types of federal and state grants. Black poverty becomes another revenue stream for the City of Omaha, Douglas County, and the State of Nebraska.

And the beat goes on:

> The trend: Although the 1980s saw dramatic drops in blood lead levels, these have leveled off in recent years. The gaps between whites, blacks, and Hispanics and between poor and non-poor children have remained relatively constant. ? (Barton & Coley, 2010).

And that is how things are going to remain. Even after the lead has been cleared out of the housing and out of the soil, there will still remain the after effects as the kids who were affected and infected continue to need special education to get them up to par. By that time the program will have been bled dry and once again, black poverty and adversity has been a major revenue stream as a result of "the invasion of the booty snatchers."

Hunger and Nutrition

> Science supports the commonsense view that hunger impedes student learning. Adequate nutrition is necessary for the development of both mind and body. The differences show up early, as revealed by studies of inner-city kindergarten students.

> Children in these studies who were underweight tended to have
> lower test scores. ? (Barton & Coley, 2010).

These white people knew that. Just like they knew that lead-based paint was slowly poisoning young children. But they turned it into a revenue stream through the educational system. They took those kids who had the "lower test scores" and put them in those special education classes. At one point the Omaha Public Schools was getting double the money for every special education kid they had; so who were they going to use to pay their bills? Black kids, that's who. That's why when I filed a grievance against them in 1980 for the disproportionate numbers of black kids in what they called "Educable Mentally Handicapped" classes, I was able to get the Office of Civil Rights to come to Omaha, investigate my charges, and get that situation overturned.

The more illness, the more money the booty snatchers can make. This is both a long- and short-term strategy. For instance, take note of the following:

> Black and Hispanic children are more than twice as likely as
> their white peers to live in food-insecure households. In 2005, 29
> percent of black children and 24 percent of Hispanic children were
> food insecure, compared with 12 percent of white children. The
> situation was more pronounced among households below the
> poverty line--43 percent of these households were food insecure,
> compared with just 6 percent of households with incomes more
> than double the poverty line. ? (Barton & Coley, 2010).

These numbers may well be worse now, especially in Omaha where it was revealed several years ago that the city ranked number one in the nation in black child poverty. In my view that means family poverty, and is directly linked to high unemployment which, as we know, is in the hands of the booty snatchers. By keeping unemployment high, when added to high population density, you have the perfect recipe for conflict and crime. And that means more money for another set of booty snatchers: the police. Free money from the federal government through such programs as Project Triggerlock, Operation Safe Neighborhoods, Weed and Seed and so on ensure that the lion's share of that money goes for police overtime.

With the children hungry and impoverished, the parents unemployed and discriminated against, and housing stock under the control of white absentee landlords, what you have in Omaha is a scenario reminiscent of the South African "Bantustans" that once were the homes of segregated black people in that nation. After all, apartheid is apartheid no matter where it is located.

Continuing:

> The trend: From 1999 to 2005, the gap between black and white

children remained unchanged. The gap between whites and
Hispanics narrowed because food insecurity rose slightly for white
children (from 11 to 12.2 percent) but improved for Hispanic
children (from 29.2 to 23.7 percent). ? (Barton & Coley, 2010).

Under another heading I've written about "the economic benefits of the racial gap" and showed who the bigger the gap between black and white is, the more profits generated by whites because of black impoverishment. The more studies, research teams, programs, projects, social workers and "assistance" can be rendered to make it appear as if the "gap" is being addressed. But in reality, nothing could be further from the truth.

A "gap" that you hear people talking about is the education gap. This gap is as old as American education itself. One blame for that gap is too much TV viewing by kids:

Television Watching
Research shows that excessive television watching is
detrimental to school achievement. In fact, one study by the
American Academy of Pediatrics found that for children ages 1 to
3, each hour of television watched daily increased by 10 percent
their risk of having attention problems, such as attention
deficit/hyperactivity disorder, by the time they were 7. In 2006, 57
percent of black 8th graders watched four or more hours on an
average weekday, compared with 20 percent of white 8th graders.
? (Barton & Coley, 2010).

One point not mentioned in the previous excerpt are the negative images that bombard the minds of children of color even as they view these programs. If a kid thinks lowly of him or herself, how can they study in a classroom where the same stereotypes about their race persist? As an example, take the case of how the booty snatches stereotyped, programmed and yet made money poking fun at Latinos:

The Frito Bandito was the cartoon mascot for Fritos corn chips
from 1967 to 1971. The Bandito was created by the Foote, Cone &
Belding Agency, and animated by Tex Avery. The character was
voiced by Mel Blanc, who used an exaggerated Mexican accent
not unlike another character of his, Speedy Gonzales. The Frito
Bandito spoke broken English and robbed people of their Fritos
corn chips, a reference to the "Mexican bandit" stereotype in
western movies. He also complained that he was being pursued by
the "Frito Bureau of Investigation." (Wikipedia, 2016).

Who created this shit? White people. And they did it on purpose, just like Helen Bannerman, the author of "Little Black Sambo," did. Originally she was picking on Indian kids, but the child was still black, so what difference does ethnic background make? What about Agatha Christie and her works, including one called *And Then There Were None*? Wanna know what the original title of that book was? It was called *Ten Little Niggers*. You heard me! These white people picked on people of color and then put it in cartoon or fairy tale form with the *intention* of fucking up the minds of young black kids and giving white kids something/someone to laugh at.

And here's something else: as a kindergartner back in 1959-60, I remember one of the songs we would sing in class was that "One little, two little, three little Indians …" song. Remember that? Can you imagine how it must have felt to be a native American, have to hold that inside because of fear of reprisal, and then have to sing these song while sitting next to the descendants of the people who killed off and/or relocated your people?

The fact is, stereotypes maintain any gaps that exist and as long as the gap exists, there will be plenty of profits for the booty snatchers.

In order to dupe the public into thinking that "racial progress" is being made, you will occasionally read an excerpt like the following one:

> The trend: There was no change in the gaps from 2000 to 2006. However, we need to track the time students spend with newer devices--such as mp3 players, video games, and cell phones-- because use of such devices is growing. ? (Barton & Coley, 2010).

Again, a peripheral and superficial assessment. The advent and rise of technology doesn't neutralize or cut back on racism – it exacerbates it! The scholars that these teacher education departments are still relying on and testing future teachers on remain white and racist; the teacher attitudes in classrooms that are gradually becoming blacker and browner remain as staid and static as they have ever been; white teachers scamper for suburban homes after their jobs and spend more time trying to survive until pension time than anything else. Once tenured, white college professors sit on their fat asses and use the same "the white man is right as usual" type material that permeated higher education since the 1960s, and so on. The use of "devices" may be growing but more importantly, so is the use of "devilishness."

The racial gap, as I say, is by design. Barton and Coley (2010) have the following to say about the role of talking and reading to children:

Talking and Reading to Children
> By talking and reading to their children, parents play a crucial

> role in children's language development and early literacy.
> Research has found that by the time children are 36 months old,
> the vocabulary of children in professional families is more than
> double that of children in families receiving welfare. ? (Barton &
> Coley, 2010).

The white man has known this for centuries, which is why from the outset he forbad blacks from reading at all. After that he allowed them to read that bullshit Bible which was used to associate Jesus and the white man as being one and the same. And even after the Brown v. Board decision of 1954, the talking and reading consisted of white nationalist views of the world, of politics and of general protocols. To this day kids still believe that George Washington never told a lie, and teachers don't mention Thomas Jefferson and his rapes of slave women; the schools still offer mandatory courses in western civilization where the white man gets the credit for inventing the air, and so on. So the issue is not about "talking and reading;" it's about what is being said and what is being read to children that is important. And the racial gap persists because pro-white curricula, test mandates and competencies remain the order of the day.

The data are then used to make a point:

> In 2005, 68 percent of white children ages 3-5 were read to
> every day, compared with 50 percent of black children and 45
> percent of Hispanic children. Poor children were also less likely to
> be read to than their more affluent peers. ? (Barton & Coley,
> 2010).

Again, point missed. It's not how often you read, it's not even what you read. It's how well and fairly you explain what is being read. And when you have limited cultural competency, you can only tell kids what you were told by the racists who were your teachers and mentors. This is how racism can be maintained and perpetuated over centuries despite all these alleged technological advances.

The issue of "gaps" is a scam that is used to beg for money to "close the gaps." But the gaps just don't close because they are not supposed to. How can the myth of white supremacy be maintained if the gaps close? If the gaps close that means that everyone is on the same "level playing field" as the pundits say. And if that happens, the white race will inevitably lose (as long as decision makers are culturally competent). The fact is, white folks didn't get what they have based on merit: they tricked and stole much of it. The gaps remain as a way to maintain the lie by the white decision makers that they "earned" what they have based on intellectual superiority – hence the "gaps."

In the art of prestidigitation, you dupe people into looking at one hand while you play a magic trick with the other hand. So the belief that the "gaps" can be closed come from a wide number of places. And as a result, "findings" like the following continue to "meet the press":

> The trend: From 2001 to 2005, the gaps remained about the same. All groups slightly improved, with the largest improvement occurring in the "near-poor" group (100 to 199 percent of the poverty line), narrowing the gap between near-poor and non-poor families. ? (Barton & Coley, 2010).

How silly. The gap exists between the poor and non-poor because that is the foundation of how capitalism works! Anyone who has taken even the most rudimentary introduction to economics class knows that in such a system there are going to be "the haves and the have-nots." And in America, for the past four centuries, the "have-nots" have been based on race and class, in that order. Black people, Native Americans and Latinos and the lower class whites. But the white group, no matter how backwards, still has the benefit of white privilege and while there are admittedly poor whites, always remember: they ain't poor because they're white!

In 1968, Dr. Paul Ehrlich published a book called *The Population Bomb*. It was written at a time in American history when black people were burning the country down and was written by a white professor who was at Stanford University, right next door to where the Black Power movement in the Bay Area was kicking much ass. In other words, he was scared so he wrote a book, along with his wife Anne, that basically said that "the niggas are eating up all the food." Of course this is said in jest – but meant in earnest. The book may have been criticized, but it was Ehrlich's view that it was the populations of color that were growing and that was the major fear.

What does this have to do with the racial gap? It has everything to do with it since everyone has to eat! Who is going to decide who gets what? Who is going to be able to afford to purchase groceries? Who grows the food and more importantly, what is being put into that food? Who distributes the food? Haki Madhubuti once cogently said that black people depend on white people for everything that is life-giving and life supporting. And today in 2016 we take this fact for granted, as if we, as blacks are somehow "owed" by our oppressor to do right by us.

When something take place that negatively impacts on black people, we blame the white man for not treating us the same way he would treat his own race. How ridiculous is that? The gap exists because the white man is showing Blacks and other people of color just how he feels about us. He takes it out on our children because he knows that they represent the future generations. And if he can poison their bodies and minds, then he can control the race. As Mao taught, "He who has the ability to satisfy human needs controls the humans with those needs."

Speaking of "population bombs" and people of color, the racial gap exists because of the concerns by the decision makers about the procreation ability of black people. In other words, we're having too many children. So here come the "studies" that associate having children with the problems that black people have. In other words, we're bringing all these problems on ourselves. Here is what Barton and Coley (2010) had to say:

> **The Parent-Child Ratio**
> Both common sense and a large body of research establish that students who have two parents in the home have better chances of doing well in school than students who just have one. This is partly because one-parent families have lower incomes, on average, and partly because of the absence of one parent. The gaps are large: Just 35 percent of black children and 66 percent of Hispanic children live with both parents, compared with 74 percent of white children. ? (Barton & Coley, 2010).

This is so much bullshit. Two parents in the home who get along and work in a partnership to support and help the kids is one thing. But two people who argue about money constantly, one who works and the other who stays home and backstabs the other one – a conflictual relationship – that's but a few examples of two parents being worse than one parent. White people destroy black relationships and the former welfare system split people up and then had the nerve to publish articles and books (read: Daniel Patrick Moynihan) about the black family, *sans* males, being a "matriarchy."

Since white people control the job market and the employment sector, their decisions play major roles in black relationships, as sad as that may sound. In America, it takes money to raise a family and white people would rather force dependency on black people by locking them into social services than to see a functioning black family. This trend started during enslavement and continues on to this very day, and it is by design. That is why the following fact is in effect:

> The trend: The good news is that the steady decline of the two-parent family, for all subgroups, has recently stopped. However, the gaps have not changed from 2000 to 2006. ? (Barton & Coley, 2010).

And again, those "gaps" generate snaps (money). Those gaps are by design because they persist despite the social indicators. Those gaps, for the most part, are based on and rooted in issues of race. And even in places like Nebraska, which is a state not known for having a large black population, nevertheless takes its ire out on what few blacks they have: compartmentalized in the largest city (Omaha), occupying less than eight square miles of it on the North side, and ranked just last year as number one in the nation in black child poverty and black youth homicides.

What Barton & Coley refer to as "those persistent gaps" (as if they were gnats or mosquitoes that could be swatted away with the brush of a hand) are really example upon example of the degradation campaign that has been heaped upon the heads of the poor in this country for centuries. From the white ethnics on the east coast and the enslaved black people in the South, to the barrio-filled enclaves in California, this system has continually made money off of minority and low-income grief. From that grief comes the "booty" akin to that which the pirates stole from ships back in the day.

Summer school: another money making scam. It is summed up like so:

> **Summer Achievement Gains and Losses**
> Educators have long known about reading losses that occur over the summer. Accumulating research has established that depending on their summer experiences, some students gain over the summer and some lose. Clearly, changes in test scores cannot be attributed entirely to what happens during the school year. ? (Barton & Coley, 2010).

The fact is, the kids have to return to the conditions where they live. And those conditions play a major role in their socialization. So do the schools. So it matters not if school begins in the fall or the summer, the same aim of mis-education continues to take place. It can't be a coincidence if black children are failing in different parts of the nation and at all levels. The classroom environment is inherently not conducive for the black child to succeed. All summer school does is prolong the inevitable push-out or drop out.

But summer school also generates more money for the system. Far too many parents use summer school as a surrogate baby sitter, sending the kids off for a full or half day so that they (parents) can catch a breather. If child care is paid for by the state, then it usually is not paid for during the summer. The more extenuating circumstances there are, the more costs to parents, the more impoverishment takes place which, in the final analysis, benefits the state of Nebraska.

Furthermore,

> The quality of summer experiences varies by family income. Students isolated in high-poverty inner-city areas often experience little or no enrichment. Large gaps exist between white and minority students in the degree to which achievement grows during the summer. (Barton & Coley, 2010).

Again, we find the family income "difference" and it is this difference that maintains the pocket of poverty that the "booty snatchers" have created, continue to manipulate and perpetuate, and are truly reliant upon. The state of Nebraska needs minority poverty and Federal programs in order to help keep them from falling off the edge of the budgetary cliff. Summer school is not free in most cases, and even when it is, the economy still gets a boost from the poor who have to find child care, purchase materials and attend meetings where white administrators are telling them how their child needs "special programs." And that, in turn, generates even more Federal funding. Did you know that if a child is found educable mentally handicapped, the school gets DOUBLE the funding for that child?

Frequent School Changing
Changing schools is a challenge both to students and their teachers. A change in schools may mean that a student faces work he or she is unprepared for, a teacher who is unfamiliar with his or her previous school records, and a new environment in which he or she is an outsider. ? (Barton & Coley, 2010).

As I've said, the problem is with the teacher attitudes and the classroom settings. The reason for the "change in schools" – which is known as a "Mobility issue" by the way – is that students are moving because the parents are being evicted or facing some kind of financial problem that has to do with economics. But if the schools were consistent, the change in location would not be the major setback that it becomes. The fact is, suburban schools have the best teachers because that is where people choose to be. The inner city schools are more like babysitters and disciplinarians and therefore have an agenda that is totally different. The result is more turmoil, more suspensions and in some cases there are "fines" associated with truancy. Again, the booty snatchers at the school administration level, come out on top.

But,

Not all school changing is the result of residence changing. According to research, 30 to 40 percent of such changes are the result of school overcrowding, class-size reductions, suspension and expulsion policies, general school climate, and, possibly, the parental choice options in No Child Left Behind. ? (Barton & Coley, 2010).

When white boys talk about "according to the research," and then don't name the source, I question their conclusions. They claim that 30 to 40 percent of residence changes are responsible for school movement for the student and the family. That is bullshit, and it depends on the demographic you're talking about.

White landlords control black tenancy, and the white employer controls that tenant's ability to pay rent. That is why so many of those landlords are putting their houses under Section 8 so that they can get a federal check. But most of them are so cheap they don't want to make the changes and upgrades so that they can pass the Section 8 inspections and qualify. So they rent out slum housing until they bleed the tenants for all they can get, hence the on-going "movement."

Put another way,

> Minority students change schools more frequently than white students do. Although the mobility rates for all groups declined from 2000 to 2006; the largest decline was among Hispanic households. The trend: From 2000 to 2006, the gaps changed little. (Barton & Coley, 2010).

Why? Because Latinos have more cultural stability. It is not uncommon for two to three families to live together in a single house or next door to one another. In other words, they practice operational unity. This difference should be explained by Barton & Coley. Again, their generic and glossed over analyses omit the "booty snatcher" mentality of the culprits behind black student mobility, most of them white and most of them getting paid one way or another.

In the education thrust of the "booty snatchers," other than in higher education, the parents are the ones who shell out the money in the name of "working to close the gap." The school programs, projects and plans sure enough are not closing it! And why should they: the bigger the gap, the more money the schools and the district can receive!

That is where "parent participation" becomes the source of exploitation:

> **Parent Participation**
> Although teachers play the predominant role in student achievement, substantial research has confirmed that parents play an important supportive role. One key aspect is the degree of parent-school interaction. On some measures of parent involvement, such as whether parents attend a scheduled meeting with a teacher, little difference exists by race and ethnicity. However, on measures that require greater involvement, such as volunteering or serving on a committee, larger differences emerge. In 2003, 48 percent of white parents reported volunteering or serving on a committee, compared with 32 percent of black parents and 28 percent of Hispanic parents. ? (Barton & Coley, 2010).

Black parents don't have time for that committee bullshit. For one thing, white women dominate them, they elect each other to this chairmanship or that coordinator slot and they give all the juicy assignments to each other. They are the ones who are in the face of the TV cameras and the media and by the time the real work is put in, the white women get all the credit.

Furthermore, black women don't have time for that bullshit. Many of them are single parents and they know that all these meetings ultimately come down to submitting proposals, requests, and agenda minutes to higher ups, and these are the same people in those higher up positions that created the problem in the first place. All these committees do is make the system appear to be functioning when, in reality, it is not. Black parents and Hispanics work in most cases and don't have time for that "volunteer" bullshit; white women have that option. Why didn't Barton & Coley go into details like these?

Since what they did was a fluff piece for the most part, they are quick to add the following:

> The trend: The good news is that parent involvement showed an increase from 1999 to 2003 for all racial and ethnic groups. The gaps among groups narrowed for attending a school event but remained about the same on measures requiring greater involvement. ? (Barton & Coley, 2010).

Why no explanation or theory about why there would be an increase in black parental involvement? Because the explanation would not fit their "booty snatcher" rationalizations. Black parents may be attending these meetings more because white women attended, saw that black women might be coming, and decided to bow out. White women and black women do not have similar interests. It could also be that the sistahs formed their own committees and decided to focus on issues of concern to them (a so-called African American Achievement Team was formed by some "negroes" in support of the Omaha Public Schools but, like the people who made up the group, achieved very little.

Rigor of the Curriculum

The next issue, as thousands of parents have been telling these white curriculum specialists for decades, is the curriculum. These white people want to impose their one-sided "teachings" onto kids who, in this day and age of the internet and social media, are beginning to learn from other parts of the country about the heinous history, the brutality and rampant racism that permeated this country's foundations. White kids and black kids alike are insulted by the fact that this information is not being provided in the classroom setting.

According to Barton and Coley:

> Research supports the unsurprising fact that students' academic achievement is closely related to the rigor of the curriculum. There

> has been progress across all groups in taking a "midlevel"
> curriculum in high school. A midlevel curriculum is defined as at
> least four credits in English and three each in social studies,
> mathematics, and science; completion of geometry and Algebra II;
> at least two courses in biology, chemistry, and physics; and at least
> one credit in a foreign language .. (2010).

The subject matter has to have honest content. English and math are understandably boring and rote, but what about social studies, government, civics and the like? Even in biology you learn things that make it appear as if the white gene is somehow "normal" instead of being the albinism variant that it is. You learn nothing about the power and dominance of the brown gene, which the overwhelming majority of the world's peoples possess.

And it gets worse by the time the students arrive in high school:

> The trend: The gap in taking a midlevel curriculum in high
> school has closed between black and white students, with 51
> percent of blacks and 52 percent of whites completing a midlevel
> curriculum. There has been no narrowing of the gap between
> whites and Hispanics, however, with only 44 percent of Hispanics
> completing a midlevel curriculum in 2005. The gaps have changed
> little since 2002. ? (Barton & Coley, 2010).

In a district that is over 25% African-American, the Omaha Public Schools have only a handful of black history classes. What kind of message does that send, especially when it is clear that white people know little or nothing about the black role in forming this country – other than their favorite subject, which is "slavery." When it comes to that, they have lectures, films and all kinds of handouts to show "how far the negroes have come." Again, this is directly related to the kind of curricular "rigor" that Barton and Coley continue to ignore. *It's not just about the outcomes (giving out grades based on how well you regurgitate the bullshit that has been imparted in the classroom setting) : it's also about the content – cultural content.*

Teacher Preparation

If Barton and Coley have ever been classroom teachers (which I doubt), then they were of the same mediocre variety that the Omaha Public Schools is inundated with. On November 14, 2016, there was a "special meeting" held to discuss kids who were "unruly and getting out of control." The claim was that they were fighting and attacking teachers. White people and black people were whining about it, and they were whining to white people who had already shown that they didn't give a sit.

This is all related to teacher preparation in my view. An article by World-Herald Reporter Erin Duffy titled, "Nathan Hale Seeks Ways to Deal With Unruly Students" is a perfect example of a system that is out of control and principals, black and white, who are lacking in teacher preparation. According to the article,

> Nathan Hale Magnet Middle School parents and staff called for higher expectations, more parental involvement and greater diversity among teachers Monday night at a meeting organized to address unruly student behavior. **Teachers also have called on the district to have their back when they take disciplinary actions.** This year, teachers have complained of widespread discipline problems at the school, including assaults on staff and other students. Even the consultant brought in by the district had strong words for what he has seen at Nathan Hale.(Duffy, 2016 – emphasis added).

The photo that accompanied the article was a black principle speaking to these white women. As a "magnet school," Nathan Hale is host to the best and the brightest. If the kids are out of control or "unruly," do you know what that is a reflection of? It's a reflection of the children's awareness that the teachers are weak and don't have their shit together. When these kids sense weakness – as they do in the case when there's a substitute teacher – they take full advantage. These white women cannot even handle their own spoiled kids in their suburban homes, but they get to have jobs where they drive to the urban center (where Nathan Hale is located) and "tolerate" black kids. Again, the lack of cultural competency and poor teacher preparation are the reasons, in my view.

The teachers in the Nathan Hale situation are talking about leaving. If they are afraid of black kids, why take the job in the first place? The district's spineless superintendent had the gall to attempt to "summon" the black principals to a meeting several months ago, and none of them responded. This was just before he made the announcement that he was going to step down in June of 2017. So he got his money and decided to cut and run; the white teachers appear to be wanting to do the same thing. After all, there are plenty of lily white school districts in the area that would be glad to hire the "combat trained" white women who come crying about how difficult the situation as in the Omaha Public Schools.

It was because it was their premature assumption that black people were under control and that they (the teachers) could use the social service approach, talk down to them and act as if they (the teachers) were somehow "missionaries" that were the key to the salvation of these black kids. Evidently some of these kids had other ideas.

The article notes that,

> Teacher quality is strongly related to student achievement. Yet sizeable gaps exist among racial/ethnic groups in the percentage of students whose teachers are fully certified. In 2007, 88 percent of white 8th graders had certified teachers compared with 80 percent of black 8th graders and 81 percent of Hispanic 8th graders. There are also gaps among students whose teachers have a major or minor in the subjects they teach. ? (Barton & Coley, 2010).

Vague generalities is what Barton and Coley have to offer.

To begin with, the statement that "Teacher quality is strongly related to student achievement." So is a student getting his ass kicked in the hallway, but the question is, is it a positive or negative correlation? Malcolm said that a long time ago when he postulated, "If you live in poor neighborhoods, you go to poor schools; if you go to poor schools you have poor teachers; if you have poor teachers you get a poor education …"

If there is a gap between the percentage of students whose teachers are fully certified, and that gap is a racial one, then is shows an intentional plan, a design and a strategy! And if there are teachers in the classroom who are lacking in the major or minor they teach, and those teaching assignments are based on race, then of what use is all this bullshit about "racial gaps"? They exist because the system wants them to and those gaps generate money that the school system can use in any way they want to.

Therefore:

> The trend: There has been little change in the gaps in teacher certification among groups. However, for teachers prepared in a given subject matter, the gap between Hispanic and white students increased from 2003, whereas the gap between black and white students remained about the same. (Barton & Coley, 2010).

The "booty snatchers" are the ones raking in the money from these "gaps," and that is why these gaps persist. And they persist by race which means that there is a formula or design. If you need more evidence, look at the next area: that of "teacher experience."

Teacher Experience

Research has shown that the amount of teaching experience has an effect on student achievement. Specifically, having five or more years of teaching experience makes a difference. The gaps by race

and ethnicity are large; black and Hispanic students tend to have
less experienced teachers. In 2007, 20 percent of white 8th graders
had teachers with four or fewer years of experience; this was the
case for 28 percent of black 8th graders and 30 percent of Hispanic
8th graders. The trend: The gaps have remained unchanged from
2003 to 2007.

The older a white person gets, the more they get locked into the old ways of teaching and viewing reality. That is the basic problem in the Omaha Public Schools: old fuddy duddies looking at black kids with that kind of "pickaninny" mentality that their ancestors had. And then, when they try to communicate with that condescending racist approach and end up getting cussed out or getting their asses kicked, it is the student who is deemed "unruly."

Older black teachers can be just as bad. Having programmed to be "coons" and to answer "yes sir, boss," to the white man, far too many of these bruthas and sistahs judge these young students by these same standards. When they meet a student who has been schooled in race relations, they (the "negro" teachers) view that child as an opponent. It is as the late Dr. W.E.B. DuBois once said,

> Dr. DuBois proceeded then to explain in careful detail that he was
> making no special plea for segregated schools, or mixed schools,
> but for *education*. To use his language: "*... a separate Negro
> school where children are treated like human beings, trained by
> teachers of their own race, who know what it means to be black in
> the year of salvation 1935, is infinitely better than making our boys
> and girls doormats to be spit and trampled upon and lied to by
> ignorant social climbers, whose sole claim to superiority is ability
> to kick "niggers" when they are down.*"(quoted in Wesley and
> Perry, 1969 – emphasis added).

None of the "consultants" that the Omaha Public Schools has contracted, black or white, have the guts to say what was just said in the previous paragraph. For the most part they are grant-chasing apologists who don't want to bite the hand that feeds them. Like their white masters, they too blame the children for the problems and do not even research where these white classroom teachers drive to when they leave school at the end of the day. Since Omaha is racially segregated, the obvious conclusion should be that the context and the teacher are the problems, not those who are victims of both.

Related to this point is the following one: "teacher absence and turnover."

Teacher Absence and Turnover
More minority students than white students attend classes in
which teachers are frequently absent. In 2007, 8 percent of white

> 8th graders experienced high teacher absence rates compared with
> 11 percent of black 8th graders and 13 percent of Hispanic 8th
> graders. Many more have teachers who leave before the end of the
> school year. Such disruptions have a negative effect on student
> achievement. (Barton & Coley, 2010).

That first sentence speaks volumes: "More minority students than white students attend classes in which teachers are frequently absent." Even the most naïve and nonproductive education expert has to see that this cannot be a quirk. When the white female or male teacher feels that they cannot get their way, they get burnout. When they cannot impose their will on students without bothering to explain process, procedure or protocol, like spoiled children they take their marbles and go home. They call in sick or lie and claim that there is a family emergency.

As a substitute teacher in the Lancaster Independent School District (ISD), the Cedar Hill ISD and the Duncanville ISD (Dallas, Texas), I was always working. Those teachers, ill prepared based on what I was left with during their absence, were more than happy to take time off. Maybe some of it was legitimate, I don't know. But I do know how white people "cut and run" when they feel that they are being dominated by a non-white group. Remember the "white flight" from the inner cities? That is but one example of it.

What do Barton and Coley conclude? They write that, "Many more have teachers who leave before the end of the school year. Such disruptions have a negative effect on student achievement." This has been going on for decades, and the teacher administrators know it. So the question is, why hasn't something been done about it? The answer is clear: these absences by the teachers are a part of the design. They want to get paid and they want the benefits but that is where the "social promotion" phenomenon came from and its been going on for decades.

In "The State of Black Omaha 2000" report, put together by the UNO Center for Applied Urban Research and the Urban League of Nebraska (the worst of the five reports ever written and distributed), even that group had to admit the following as it relates to social promotion and its effects:

> These problems include: schools that do not teach but graduate
> functional illiterates; high unemployment rates; hundreds of people
> who have never held a job and probably never will; the staggering
> increase in families headed by single women; and violent crime
> where blacks are both principal victims and perpetrators (p. i).

The key words? "And probably never will" when it came to holding a job. Remember: these are the conclusions of white social scientists from UNO and a black organization in Omaha that is supposed to be "serving" the African-

American community. And such a blanket stereotype fits perfectly in future grant applications submitted by those who are the leaders in "the invasion of the booty snatchers."

White folks justify social promotion with definitions like the following one: "Social promotion is the practice of promoting a student (usually a general education student, rather than a special education student) to the next grade after the current school year, regardless of when or whether they didn't learn the necessary materials or they are often absent, in order to keep them with their peers by age, that being the intended social grouping."

That is such bullshit. These scary white teachers pass the black kids on because they simply shake and shiver at the prospect of having that same child back in their classroom the following year. In their view they allow them to pass because (1) they fear getting their asses kicked by the parents for flunking the kid; (2) they fear getting their asses kicked by the kid after his peers make fun of him or her for being "held back"; and/or (3) the flunking of that child may be viewed as a "failure by the teacher" on some of the records and might jeopardize future job opportunities.

The "negative effects" that were alluded to earlier by Barton and Coley are the ones that the teachers fears for financial reasons. Flunking a black child who can't cut it would show a level of compassion, care and concern that far too many of these white teachers simply do not possess.

At any rate, Barton and Coley conclude that the trend is that, "For teacher absence, the gap grew between white and Hispanic students from 2000 to 2007 and narrowed between black and white students. For teacher turnover, the black/white gap remained unchanged, and the white/Hispanic gap narrowed slightly" (2010). All of this is bullshit because "teacher absence" is more than just not showing up physically. In my view as an educator, you can be standing in front of the classroom and be miles away. You can show bullshit films to take up time or give assignments and break the kids into groups and turn them on each other. There are a number of "teaching strategies" that can be used so that far too many of these teachers can "relax" at these kids expense. I've seen it up close.

Class Size

Although many studies have found that class size makes a difference in student achievement, the issue is controversial. But few would disagree with the proposition that minority students should not be subject to larger classes than majority students. Also, some research shows that black students, particularly males, benefit from smaller classes. Minority students are, on average, in larger classes than majority students are. (Barton & Coley, 2010).

This is more peripheral analysis. Class size makes a difference but those differences are, in themselves, cultural. When these white people were invading what is now called "the Old West" and they opened up schools, those classes were always packed, sometimes standing room only. And they weren't divided up by age either. If you were in fourth grade, it wasn't unusual to find kids in there who were teenagers. Adjustments were made and everybody got along, and do you know why? Because they were all white.

When the schools began to have some color in them, class size became an issue because for the most part, the black kids were packed into black schools in black areas of town. The white kids followed their cowardly parents to areas of town where new larger schools with shiny new classrooms were built. The classes became smaller. When segregation was forced to end and black and white attended school together because of busing, class sizes were larger – and split: black kids sitting with their pals and white kids sitting with theirs. These are just a few of the cultural differences that should have been delved into by Barton and Coley.

They nevertheless claim that the trend is that, "From 2000 to 2004, the class size gap between schools with high and low proportions of minority students increased." (Barton & Coley, 2010). And the Federal funding kept coming in to construct more buildings, to expand existing buildings, to expand the number of bathrooms per building and so on.

The next area of the "gap" is in the area of technology:

Technology in the Classroom
In general, research supports technology use in classrooms, particularly for drill and practice. The availability of computers in the classroom, along with Internet access, continues to increase. By 2005, 92 percent of schools with 50 percent or more minority enrollment had Internet access in the classroom, compared with 96 percent of schools with less than 6 percent minority enrollment.The trend: The gaps among groups narrowed between 2000 and 2005. ? (Barton & Coley, 2010).

Again, the analysis is superficial. In this day and age of classroom technology, the fact remains that what goes in is what comes out. Just as the racist teacher stood in front of the classroom and imparted information using the chalkboard, which has morphed into the white board, or just because the white teacher is now using power point instead of an overhead projector does not in one bit offset the racist curriculum that is at the basis of what is being offered in the classroom. Technology may help to disguise the ethnocentric outcomes to an extent, but today's black students are more culturally confused than any generation before them. Even with the i-pod and other technology, today's minority youth are not learning, are not graduating and even when they do both, come out as what Nathan Hare would call "Afro-Saxons" than anything else. Education then, is more about assimilation (forgetting what you used to be) than it is about integrating kids of color into the system.

Continuing with the next "gap":

Fear and Safety at School
Research has established that a positive disciplinary climate directly links to higher achievement. In many schools, maintaining discipline may be the largest problem that teachers face. Minority students more often avoid certain places in school because of fear of an attack, experience the presence of street gangs, and are involved in fights. (Barton & Coley, 2010).

They are not writing what they really mean. When these white people talk about fear they are talking about their own fear. When they write about safety, they are talking about the need to protect white kids. They view black kids as being able to adapt and fend for themselves. When it comes to consider black kids being afraid or safe, it is because they believe that the fear may have a residual effect and turn those scared black kids into "attack mode." Where was all this concern when these peckerwood kids were greeting buses of black kids, carrying signs and shouting "niggers go home"? Where was all this concern when grown-ass white adults were rocking school buses with black kids on them and making death threats to schools that were forced to integrate? Nowhere to be found.

Further,

The trend: Between 2001 and 2005, there was an increase in black and Hispanic students reporting gangs in the school--36.6 percent of black students and 38.4 percent of Hispanic students reported such an increase compared with 16.6 percent of white students. For physical fights, the gap between white and Hispanic students widened, with 18.3 percent of Hispanic students typically involved in this behavior compared with 11.6 of white students. There was no change in the gap among students experiencing fear of attack or harm in school. ? (Barton & Coley, 2010).

But just as they document all this information about fights and deviant behavior, they take that information and turn it into a grant application so that they can get money for hall monitors, added security, paid police overtime, extra counselors, in-house suspension rooms and so on. The booty snatchers turn all adverse situations into money making programs that enable them to hire their own people or to publish some kind of document about a "model program" that they have created. Remember: it is very rarely about the well-being of the children.

Having skimmed over the realities of the "gaps" that exist in education, the authors have another section that they call "the truth of the matter." As if these white people know the truth or have the guts to share it. They know that if they share the truth – as I have done – their grant money will dry up right away. At any rate, note what they have to say:

The Truth of the Matter

People frequently ask which of these factors are the most important or whether out-of-school factors have larger or smaller effects on student achievement than school factors. Given the research currently available, we are unable to answer these questions. However, we can be sure that both school experiences and home and early life experiences are important. And the two are related: Low-income neighborhoods where there are few resources in the home also tend to have low tax bases available to support high-quality schools. ? (Barton & Coley, 2010).

If people are asking which gap has the most adverse effect, and you have the gall to write an article outlining some of those gaps, then you have an *obligation* to answer the damn question! If I say that your mother is a whore, and then I name the men she's screwed, and you ask me which one was the worse to her and I say, I can't answer that question – what does that say? It says that your mother never really mattered in the first place because she was a whore! In the same way, you show how the system is racist, you show how black kids suffer, and yet you offer not a single solutions. Conclusion: black kids don't matter.

What Barton and Coley did offer was the same old 'blame the niggers for their problems" formula that has been used ever since formal education started. These peckerwoods know full well about these "gaps" because, as I've shown and explained, they create and maintain those gaps so that they can acquire funding and create jobs for their own race, hence "the booty snatchers." Therefore, blaming the victim is the only way to absolve the perpetrators of their responsibility.

The authors further conclude,

Those who argue that what happens outside of school and before school begins should not play a role in the ability of the "good" schools to raise all students to the same high standard seem to assume that students are empty vessels that schools can fill up with knowledge. But students are not empty vessels. (Barton & Coley, 2010).

More bullshit based on straw man arguments so that they (the authors) can sound "profound." Nobody in their right mind is assuming that a student is not shaped by what happens before or after school. The fact is, these white people know what it takes and they provide it for white kids while denying it to kids of color. It's as simple as that. They use kids as experiments, for survey purposes and as social guinea pigs. Then they apply for a grant to "help" them – hence, the "booty snatchers" approach once again.

Moving on with more general truisms:

> For those who argue that these early and out-of-school experiences are the sole reasons for achievement gaps found in schools--and that schools are powerless to remedy them--we know for a fact that schools can make a difference. As Daniel Patrick Moynihan once said, "Students do not learn their algebra at home." How well teachers are prepared, how much experience they have, how often they show up in school, and how well they maintain order and discipline in their classrooms all make a difference--and minority students are getting short-changed on all those fronts. (Barton & Coley, 2010).

They don't have a clue when it comes to changing anything because it is not their job to change anything. These white scholars merely document the problems so that their "findings" can be used in future grant applications and as "evidence" that more money needs to be pumped into the education system. That is their goal. They also get a publication out of the deal and that solidifies their tenure on campus as instructors and they can then become experts on the subject and get on the lecture circuit and make more money. What people like Barton and Coley do has nothing to do with solutions or salvation for black and other students of color.

And in the rare instance that they do attempt to offer a solution, it is of the bullshit fairytale variety akin to the one that appears in their concluding paragraph:

> To address the achievement gap, we need to focus on equalizing access to high-quality schools. We also have to focus on conditions beyond school to compensate for challenges that many students experience in life outside the classroom. (Barton & Coley, 2010).

So as far as students of color are concerned, it's a white ladder with white steps leading to nowhere. The idea of "equalizing access to high quality schools" isn't changing the curriculum any. The more "quality" the school, the more racist it will more than likely be, the more lily-white it will be (that is what quality means to white people), and the more stringent its administration will be. It will be lacking in cultural competency and the suspension and expulsion rates for students of color will skyrocket. It will be like the education version of the police "weed and seed" program: weed out the kids of color and seed the school with resources for white students.

As for that idea to "focus on conditions beyond school," it has been tried by the people in the neighborhood but not supported by the schools. And that is where the conditions are going to have to be changed from: the community and neighborhood efforts. The school ranks are made up of people who live far out in the suburbs and therefore feel that they have no vested interest in helping "those people."

Education is a mandate in America and white people control it. But it is but one institution that upholds the white supremacist system. Without it, there is no way to perpetuate the myth that white people deserve to be where they are. Even the media would not be as successful were it not for the pre-school through high school bullshit that is force fed to young people about the American Dream and all of the lies that buttress that particular myth.

As an institutional arrangement in such a system, it is funded by that system and its on-going funding means that "the hand that feeds, controls." Whatever the power structure dictates, that is what the educational arena is going to do. Even the so called "black colleges" basically teach reactionary "be on time" and "be a good nigga" tips as a part of their curriculum. The United Negro College Fund is an annual check that gives the leaders of the small black colleges a chance to catch upon their Lexus and Cadillac payments and little else.

The "invasion of the booty snatchers" is alive and well and is quite visible throughout the educational spectrum. I have touched upon only a few of the many ways that black inequity is pimped by a system that continues to boast of "equal education."

COMMUNITY DEVELOPMENT

After years of living in Omaha, it has become clear to me that when the majority population talks about "community," they are referring to the white majority community that resides in the suburbs and downtown high-rise apartment buildings. Even though the city is prone to pimp black poverty so free money can continue to come in to address "urban development" and "social services," the fact of the matter is in Omaha, community development is aimed at perpetuating the residential and racial segregation that has been a part of Omaha history for as long as the city has existed.

TABLE 1: Distribution of Community Development Block Grants in Milwaukee and Omaha, 1975 to 1997

City/CDBG Recipient	Year of Allocation	CDBG Amount (per $1,000)

Milwaukee	1975-1976	$13,383
Omaha	1975-1976	1,390
Milwaukee	1980-1981	22,794
Omaha	1980-1981	5,912
Milwaukee	1985-1986*	17,684
Omaha	1985-1986	4,833
Milwaukee	1988	25,090
Omaha	1988	3,715
Milwaukee	1989	15,362
Omaha	1989	3,868
Milwaukee	1990	15,328
Omaha	1990	3,654
Milwaukee	1991	14,342
Omaha	1991	3,470
Milwaukee	1992	16,233
Omaha	1992	5,587
Milwaukee	1993	16,101
Omaha	1993	6,409
Milwaukee	1994	20,500
Omaha	1994	7,024
Milwaukee	1995	22,000

Omaha	1995	7,335
Milwaukee	1996	24,274
Omaha	1996	7,056
Milwaukee	1997	24,705
Omaha	1997	6,950
	TOTAL: Milw.	*$247,796*
	Omaha	*116,748*

***Switched from fiscal year to calendar year**

<u>Example: The Urban Development Action Grant</u>

The Urban Development Block Grant was applied for and abused in the same way as the CDBG outlined earlier. Omaha simply applied for the grant claiming that they were going to help to upgrade the North Omaha "pocket of poverty" (read: copies word for word the lies told on the CDBG application) submitted it to the carelessly inattentive Federal government and received one large check after the other. Remember that this is in addition to the CDBG that the city had been getting since 1975. UDAG came along in the early 1980s, and lasted about five years before the funds petered out. But by that time Omaha had amasses millions that were used for its own pet projects, placing white people on the payroll and as usual, ignoring the poverty and the area whose predicament qualified the city for the money in the first place.

The purpose of the UDAG, according to the rules, was to assist distressed cities and urban counties in promoting economic development." And what qualified those cities as being distressed? Black and Brown poverty. The problem was that without sufficient government oversight, the grant was abused on a regular basis. For one thing, the money was being spent on projects that would have been done with taxpayers dollars in most cases. But in Omaha the philosophy when it comes to the black community is if they can't get free Federal dollars to do something, it's not going to get done. In other words, spending taxpayers' dollars on North Omaha has historically been viewed as a waste of money. The "booty snatchers" strike again.

Secondly, the city kept on submitting jacked up budgets to the government, requests for funding that were grossly overstated. With UDAG now long gone, the same booty snatching "game" is still being played with the remaining CDBG funding. And North Omaha looks worse today in 2016 than it did when Omaha received its first CDBG check in 1975.

The Empowerment "Movement"

When I first brought the term "Empowerment" to the fore back in 1996, the word was preceded with the word "self." "Self-empowerment," in my view, is a survival tactics, providing skills and or training to people who have a particular savvy for doing a particular thing. As I viewed it, there are jobs that, wherever you go, you can always make money (generate income). Those jobs include: auto mechanic, barber, child care provider, grant writer, plumber and/or various types of contractors.

Empowerment means "to make stronger" in some capacity, and it was a great idea—or so I thought it regularly on the air, in writing and at three consecutive "self empowerment conferences, one of them featuring the great Senator Ernie Chambers. I gave out scores of awards, fed the masses and at no time did I see a single person who now claims to be a part of the "empowerment movement" present.

I suppose it was logical to bring in some novices and out-of-towners to become the voice of the people regarding "empowerment."

But that is understandable: mine was a grass-roots movement, a bottoms-up kind of approach. Stripped of the word "self" and employing more of what we urban planners call an "elitist model," today's empowerment movement has been true to form: it is truly "empowering" a number of people. But the question is whom—and for what??

Can there be any doubt that with all this construction going on—new sewers, 75 North, North Star, expansion of Girls, Inc.,, riverfront development, a so-called Fair Deal Plan and a North Omaha Village — that there is someone making money and planning to make even more? Here's my point: what does any of this have to do with the residents of 68111, 68110 or for that matter, 68104?

Times, they are a'changing. When I was attending the University of St. Thomas for a year, I learned a lot about the St. Paul-Minnesota area. One thing I learned was about the disappearance of a small town, mostly black, called Rondo. While in Milwaukee I studied and learned about a small black town called Lake Ivanhoe, made up of folks who moved from Chicago to settle that area. And that popular movie "Rosewood," which came out some years back, had more realistic counterparts than many people would care to admit. When people became jealous of Black Wall Street in Tulsa, Oklahoma, they attacked it and even went so far as to drop bombs on it. I'm one of the officers of the Black Wall Street movement, so I know what I'm talking about.

Councilman Ben Gray told the Omaha World Herald back on or about October 9th his views of North Omaha, the area he represents. He said that the area was "a neighborhood inhabited by people of various income levels, with businesses and offices mixed with the residences … That's the way North Omaha used to be," he said.

Then he cogently and correctly added that, "This is a prime confident that the rest of the development will happen because of "the caliber and commitment of people willing to invest and of the people doing the groundwork."

What does this have to do with "empowerment" of black people? Nothing. It has to do with empowerment of the people that Councilman Gray described, and that sho' don't mean the residents of the area that Triple One represents. You had your chance, and sat back and waited for lions and lambs to fall in love and pose for pictures. The "Empowerment Movement" is not about empowering those who don't already have power; it's about providing more power and opportunities to partake in it for those who can appreciate it.

I'm telling you after almost 40 years of organizing in black communities around this country: *our halcyon days are over*.

Most of you came here from the South acting as if you were free when you landed jobs at the packing houses. Jobs were so plentiful that you can get fired from one packing house and walk across the street and find work at another one. You moved your families up here and then, for someone reason, you forgot where you came from. You started thinking that you had it made because you didn't see any lynch ropes or "for whites only" signs. And it went to your head.

From there, you used the resources you scrounged up and started spoiling your kids. Now look at 'em: pants and draws sagging, talking back atcha, skirts as short as blouses and no idea of their history: too weak to do anything but wander. You can't "empower" people when the key to their lack of power is one of the fundamental sources of city, county, state and federal revenue! That would be counter-productive, would it not?

The low-income folks from North Omaha—black, white, Latino and Asian— they are the ones supporting this city. They do it with the social service jobs that other people get, they do it by riding the Metro bus line, they do it with their on-going ordering of premium cable channels while suburbanites stick with basic cable because they're never home, they do it with higher interest rates on that rent-to-own crap and so on.

You can't "empower" people who wouldn't know what to do with power if they had it. The only people of color you see directing and leading the neighborhoods are not people who

 have power — they are influence peddlers! And that's how and why the neighborhoods have deteriorated and outsiders have bought up the housing and the vacant lots—empowerment means investing and then building so that your kids can have something to live on.

Admittedly, I've left town a couple of towns and made some major inroads in some areas. But that's MY legacy, and it sure hasn't improved the lives of the majority of black people and other people of color in the neighborhoods that seem to be getting relocated to other sectors of their respective cities. It's not just Omaha: most of them have these buzzwords they use to solicit grant funding and dupe the growing minority that they are going to "make things better"

Scott Knudsen, a former Republican city official during the Daub Administration who was an Election Commissioner who screwed over more than a few election rights for black people, recently informed me by email that he was about to get his real estate license. His wife, who already works for Berkshire Hathaway, already has hers. In other words they will both be working for Susie Buffett. It is clear that the plan is to buy up property all over Omaha and then use those purchases to manipulate the population so that black people are relocated from the inner city area to outlying areas. The "booty snatchers" are alive and well and have a long history of real estate manipulation along with the banking and developer associates.

EDUCATION

The segregationist history of the Omaha Public Schools will first be provided before delving into the areas of the American student exodus, higher education in Nebraska, and a so-called "cultural proficiency journal" that was distributed to the employees of the Omaha Public Schools. All of these, though negative in outcome, are positive in one thing: they all add to the coffers of the "booty snatchers."

Let us begin with the so-called "poverty allowance" in Nebraska.

During a March 30, 2016 session of the Nebraska Legislature, a member of the Education Committee provided the following information and insights. In his words:

> Nebraska is 49th in the nation in state support of their schools and
> 18th in the nation on expenditures per student. Cost of living in
> bottom 20s … We spent this year $125 million for poverty

> allowance, this year over $450 million spent by schools for poverty allowance. OPS last year went from $46 million to $56 million in poverty funding in one year. Grand Island went from $4.4 million to $9.5 million. We need to get rid of the common levy, get on an even playing field, the one hot button issue that divides rural and urban in Nebraska. (Sen. Negroni, 3/30/16)

Poverty allowance. That's what these white boys have been leeching for and living on in one form or another for a century, hence the name "booty snatchers." Omaha's history in denial of equal opportunity while raking in the poverty money because of the "ghettoization" of black people has been taking place ever since the inception of the Omaha Public School system.

In 1975, the Eighth District Court of Appeals ruled that, indeed, the Omaha Public Schools were segregated and that the system should get to work to desegregate. In response to the decision, James Evans, director of the Urban League said, "This is the fastest way to bring about equal opportunities in our schools." But right or not, the OPS spent in excess of $300,000 fighting against the desegregation order. Segregation in Omaha had always existed; but the formal maintenance of it can be traced back to the 1930s.

In fact, an editorial appeared in the August 27, 1938 edition of the Omaha Star under the headline, "Why Not Negro Teachers in Our Public School System." Following is that page 4 editorial, in its entirety:

> Why not Negro teachers in the school system of Omaha, that is the paramount question in the minds of every forward thinking Negro in Omaha.

> It is pure nonsense that two races who are mixed and mingled, as are the blacks and whites in Omaha, can share the same streets, dwell under the same roofs, act civilly with each other 99 times out of 100, graduate from the same schools, having studied under the same instructors, and passed the same examinations, cannot qualify as teachers in our school system.

> In the face of such environmental condition, can anyone say that out of the many Negro boys and girls who have received from a bachelor's degree to a doctor of philosophy degree from reputable institutions, be not qualified to reach in our school system? The answer is that there are those who are qualified and we as a group must fight to see that these individuals so prepared, as in the case of one of our born and reared Omaha boys who was forced to take his Ph.D from the University of California and transverse the country into Washington, D.C. on quest of a job, receive what is rightfully due them here in Omaha.

> This young man, who at the age of 23 was the recipient of a Ph.D degree, would be a credit to our school system.

> The Negroes in Omaha pay for the support of government,
> from the city tax to the federal tax. The truth is that they pay more
> pre capita in proportion to earnings than the others. Yet they are
> not granted the privilege to share that for which they are taxed.
>
> The spirit of the law, handed down from that far off day
> when the patriots dumped British tea into Boston harbor to
> emphasize their unwillingness to be taxed when not represented, is
> against taxing when not sharing. Black America, we have no tea,
> but thank God we do have a right to the ballot box. When the time
> comes, let's as a unit answer the question: Why not Negro teachers
> in our public school system?

Therefore, the Eighth Circuit Court of Appeals, in its decision to desegregate the Omaha Public Schools, provided background and insights into the segregated state of Omaha and the role that segregation played in making the schools inequitable. All of this was a part of the report that the Eighth Circuit released as part of its decision:

> The evidence established that segregated housing patterns were the
> result of discriminatory state and private actions. Between 1938
> and 1953, the Omaha Housing Authority opened five large family-
> occupied public housing projects. Four were constructed in, or
> adjacent to, the Near North Side, and each was over 95 percent
> black in 1973. One was located in South Omaha and became a
> "white project." The Housing Authority encouraged racially
> discriminatory housing assignment by allowing white applicants
> for public housing to turn down openings in "black" projects while
> remaining at the top of the priority list (Omaha World Herald,
> 1975).

Furthermore,

> An early school report published in 1951 recognized that … there
> is a tendency toward the restriction of the residence of Negroes,
> which has caused a certain amount of geographical segregation.
> The report also stated: "Segregation, even though it is the result of
> residence rather than administration, is almost undesirable
> educationally (Omaha World Herald, 1975).

In Omaha white folks dominated the school board for a century. Since all of them resided in segregated communities, it only stood to reason that maintaining segregation would be one of their priority goals. And the Report on desegregating the OPS pointed to the results of such segregated policymaking:

> We conclude that sufficient evidence was presented to establish
> that segregation in the Omaha Public School District was
> intentionally created and maintained by the defendants … The
> Omaha public schools are segregated. The District Court so found,
> and the defendants do not contest that finding. In 1973-74, the
> School district of Omaha had a student population of 60,502, of
> whom 10 percent were black. It operated eight high schools,
> twelve junior highs, one middle school (grades 5-7) and seventy-
> eight elementary schools. Over 50 percent of the black students in
> the district attended schools which had an 80 to 100 percent black
> enrollment, while 73 percent of the white students attended schools
> with black enrollments of less than five percent (Omaha World
> Herald, 1975).

But even those few black teachers who were already in the system were isolated for the most part. The Eighth Circuit Court established the fact that,

> The faculties also were segregated. In 1972-73, the district employed 193
> black teachers. Of that number 121 were assigned to majority black
> schools, and 159 were assigned to the twenty-three schools which had a
> black enrollment exceeding 25 per cent. Thus, only 18 percent of the
> black teachers were assigned to the seventy-five schools with
> enrollments less than 25 per cent black (Omaha World Herald, 1975).

Furthermore, another key to maintaining such segregationist thinking was at-large elections, where school board members were voted for by the city as a whole. With blacks in the minority, this ensured that no black person would ever sit on the boards. But interestingly enough, "prior to 1915, the school board was elected by ward. In that year, the legislature "imposed" at-large school board elections upon the citizens of Omaha (Sink, 1975) , a system which remained in effect" until Senator Chambers got it passed in May of 1975. District elections officially went into motion in 1976 because of a bill sponsored by and pushed through by State Senator Ernie Chambers.

But before that, school board members, superintendents and various white interests groups made all the decisions and that explains why residential segregation remained intact; school board members and the other players, so firmly raised and rooted in segregationist living themselves, made decisions and acted in the name of segregation. *It was, to them, the natural order of things.*

Prior to district elections, the disdain held for black education could be exemplified best by the condition of Tech High School. Tech was predominantly black (98%) in terms of students, but only 5% of the teachers were black!

Furthermore, it is the building that the schools said could not be repaired but today, at that same site, is a multimillion-dollar renovation of that school. Now, of course, it is the home of the Teacher Administration Center, where administrative offices, the school board meeting room and other spacious offices can be located.

The problem of mis-educating and segregation of the school system was inextricably bound to the problems and poverty that plagued the North Side.

In February of 1971, if you were to visit Tech High School, you would have found a school where most restrooms had sinks with inoperable hot water faucets and of the 169 shower stalls in the girls' shower room, 60 would be working. (Omaha World Herald, 1971). When State Senator Ernie Chambers brought this to the attention of Rudy Dufek, Tech High's chief engineer, Dufek claimed that he had submitted a work order and "didn't know why" it took so long. But Paul Thompson, director of the division of supplies for the district said he "was not familiar with the request" from Dufek. But this same system was more than willing to expend monies for "extra private police guards at Tech." (UNO Gateway, 1972: 1)

But it was more than just manipulation of the physical plant of Tech High which showed how much the school board hated black students. The board fired two well-liked teachers, Eddie Chambers and Otis Westbrook, deciding not to renew their contracts. Chambers was a counselor and Westbrook a music teacher. (Omaha World Herald, 1971: 10; Omaha World Herald, 1971)

When the students organized a black student group and requested that Chambers come to speak, the board begrudgingly accepted because of student pressure.

At the same time, the school board showed its racism by its violation of the rights of Chambers, who appeared before the school board and was treated so badly that he transcribed the work and issued to the community under the title, "The Right to Know: The Closed Hearings of Eddie Chambers". Three hundred copies of the work were printed at a cost of $900, defrayed by a community-based advisory board and other concerned persons. *The school board, in the meantime, closed Chambers' hearing to the public which is what prompted the release of the document.*

Poverty reigns supreme and tends to generate all forms of resources, money, assistance and yes, social workers. An article titled, "OPS Has Eye on Sherwood Foundation Grant to Boost Number of District's Social Workers," more evidence of leeching and "booty snatching" is evident.

Remember: the white man's school system was a bastion of inequity even before it started becoming increasingly black and brown. The teachers today are old and set in their ways, and the Black ones they recruit are those "yes sir boss" types from the Deep South. The kids run over them and many of them are whining about how "rough" things are without realizing that this is the way it is all over. I know from first-hand experience, having substitute taught in three school districts in much tougher Texas: Lancaster ISD, Duncanville ISD and Cedar Hill ISD.

With that having been said, OPS wimpishly seeks to place their lack of adult control on the kids by looking for "social workers" which is basically another "booty snatcher" trick to hire more white people based on black peoples' adversity. As the article makes clear,

> The Omaha school district is exploring a $7.4 million grant from Susie Buffett's Sherwood Foundation that would increase the corps of school social workers who deal with behavior problems, truancy and connecting families with outside help (Duffy, 2016)..

Susie Buffett, the self-appointed "white mammy" of Nebraska education, is constantly involved in "booty snatching." She opened up Edu-Care in the heart of the black community and helped to move Operation Headstart from Parker Street in North Omaha to the Omaha Public Schools before the latter group decided to drop it as well. Now the same system that couldn't handle Operation Headstart begs for money to bring in social workers to "deal with behavior problems." Translation: "mo' money, mo' money, mo' money!"

Now, check out the following:

> If approved, the grant would allow Omaha Public Schools to hire 40 more social workers over the next several years. OPS currently has nine social workers, mostly spread out across seven high schools, but could use more to reach elementary and middle school students, officials said. (Duffy, 2016).

They want to "reach" younger kids – younger minority kids. The white people in Omaha are those kind who find black kids "so cute" and are constantly posing for pictures with them, but that is because they know that at the end of that photo shoot they (white people) are going to skidaddle back to their suburban homes while those black kids that they pretend to care so much for go back to a community that, as of 2015, ranked number one in the nation in black child poverty.

Moreover,

> "In a district of 52,000 students ... obviously more than nine social workers would be good for us," Assistant Superintendent ReNae Kehrberg said at a Feb. 17 board meeting where the proposal was discussed. (Duffy, 2016).

These white people are as out of touch in Omaha as they are anywhere else in the nation, and the previous quote by ReNae Kehrberg proves it. It's not just with high school kids or those going through puberty; even at the pre-school and elementary school levels these cultural competence-lacking white folks don't have a clue. Remember those 8,000 diversity manuals that the district purchased? Do you think any of these peckerwoods turned the pages and read what was inside? Of course not because many of them are know-it-alls, having studied under other clueless white teachers in Teacher Education programs that rely on the theories and models of old-school racists.

All while they were "discussing" this, school superintendent Mark Evans was busy planning his exit. He had collected his largesse and was ready to blame his aging parents as the reason. The burnout that he felt is what is being described here with the hiring of these social workers. Here is what the proposed grant would have financed:

> The school board could vote on the grant proposal sometime this year. But at least one board member is questioning the financial implications of hiring more social workers whose salaries and benefits would eventually fall to OPS. (Duffy, 2016). The Sherwood grant would initially cover the salaries of 40 social workers, a supervisor and an external evaluator. About eight social workers would be hired each year for five years, and OPS would start contributing a portion of salaries in the fourth year. (Duffy, 2016).

Remember elsewhere in this book I charge that the Omaha strategy is to get free money wherever they can if the issue has to do with people of color. They lie in their applications, get the money and then use part of it to implement some type of "program" and the rest to hire their own race members. This is one more example of that. They want money from Buffett but are worried about actually having to PAY for social workers' salaries once the grant runs out. Even though its five years away, these white people don't want to pay for anything that has to do with kids of color. Their history proves this is the case: remember that in 1976 the district had spent in excess of $300,000 fighting the Federal order to desegregate!

After the five year grant period ran out here is what would happen:

> By the sixth and seventh years, OPS could opt to hire 22 additional social workers with district funds and would have to take over all social worker costs from Sherwood. Over the span of four years, those salaries and benefits could cost OPS an estimated $17.8 million. (Duffy, 2016)..

Knowing the track record of OPS, the fact that the system would "opt" to hire an additional 22 social workers means that they would renege on the deal. They will come up with some kind of excuse or financial reason why they "simply can't do it. Susie Buffett won't care: she's wasted money before and made all kinds of silly investments that she couldn't account for in the past. And in each of those cases, the "donation" or "contribution" somehow involved low-income or minority people.

My accusation bears fruit as the following passage makes clear:

> At the board meeting, member Matt Scanlan called the grant "very generous," but questioned whether OPS should commit to paying millions of dollars' worth of future salaries."What happens if we start this program and it's going along great, but ... we can't support that financially because of cuts in the budget?" he said. "I'd hate to see that go away." (Duffy, 2016)..

As long as the money is free, these people are standing line with their hands out – the same thing they used to blame black people for doing during the days of welfare. But when there is a financial obligation involved, even if it doesn't kick in for five years, they start shakin' and shiverin'. If you track the history of the OPS board you will see that for the most part it has been comprised of buffoons and individuals who know little about education other than the information they receive in their "packets" just prior to the beginning of each meeting.

It gets worse:

> Superintendent Mark Evans said it would be difficult to predict OPS's budget and funding picture several years down the line. The state funding formula for schools is frequently tweaked, and Nebraska legislators are currently debating outright eliminating or replacing the Learning Community common levy with other funding sources. With the common levy, OPS came out ahead $2.1 million this year. (Duffy, 2016)..

The coward Mark Evans, school superintendent, was concerned about the future of the budget at a time when he knew he was going to be putting in his resignation. Having already collected more than $700,000 in salary over three and a half years, he didn't give a shit: he was so gutless that instead of being a man and stating that he just didn't want the job, couldn't cut it, or got burned out, he blamed his "elderly parents" and the need for him to spend more time with them. The fact is, those parents were "elderly" when he took the job! So he's doing the same thing the school board does: go through the motions, feed the World Herald some bullshit excuse (knowing that they won't fact check) and live to rip off the citizenry for another day.

Continuing:

> "It may be that we can't support it to that level, I'll just be quite frank," Evans said. "Depending on what happens in Lincoln, we don't know all those dynamics." (Duffy, 2016)..

I think Evans had an idea that things didn't look good, which gave him all the more reason to cut and run. If he didn't "know all those dynamics," it was incumbent upon him to share what he did know and to seek to learn more. That is what education leaders do. If they don't do that, then they are throwing the students to the lions.

This is not to say that they're not doing that by accepting the social worker grant:

> Evans and several other board members acknowledged the large price tag of expanding the current social worker program. But they said the district should seize the opportunity to beef up its mental health and support offerings, especially with philanthropic dollars on the table. The Sherwood Foundation did not return a call seeking comment. (Duffy, 2016).

See? Instead of working to ameliorate, lessen or neutralize their problems, ass-backwards Omaha leadership, using the "booty snatcher paradigm" merely seek to expand upon money making ways to "address" the problem. Not "solve" it – "address" it. And that is why the problem continues to persist. You can "address" a rattlesnake that is staring right at you through either fight or flight. But if you don't address the problem and work to get rid of it, it's going to stay around and either bite you or someone else. It's fight or flight. And cowardly Omaha leaders usually "choose the path of least resistance."

So just "beef up" the mental health and support offerings because after all, the system they are running can guarantee you more bodies to put into those programs – either legitimately or otherwise. I proved that back in 1980 when I filed a major grievance with the Office of Civil Rights in Kansas City and brought those "negroes" to Omaha to look into why so many black kids were being "placed" in Educable Mentally Handicapped programs and so few in Gifted and Talented. My findings, courtesy of the Urban League of Nebraska, won out. But today, some 36 years later, they're back in the "goon building business" again under new names, new definitions and new (fake-ass) outcomes.

Again, it is the idiocy and laziness of the school board that should never receive short shrift:

> "I look at this and think, yes, it's expensive, but when you get
> down the road, maybe we won't need as many social workers if we
> can get some issues addressed," board President Lou Ann Goding
> said. "But in the first three years you have the opportunity to touch
> the lives of children who are in very difficult situations." (Duffy,
> 2016).

This woman is supposed to be a leader. But because she has no concrete plan or commitment, what do you read? Words like "maybe," "if" and "some issues." These are the kinds of tell-tale signs that the people in charge are asleep at the wheel. The adds that in the first three years of the social work hirings "you have the opportunity" to touch the lives of children. Let me tell you something: these white people have had more than a century to touch those lives. And what did black kids and parents of those kids get in return? Intensified segregation of the schools, bullshit busing programs that put all the pressure on black kids standing on street corners, tenuous "projects" and programs (like "Project EMPATHY, for example) and so on. They kick the can down the road but the public is so busy with their bullshit, they don't have time to see what is being done. That is why when they keep seeing history repeat itself, to most people, it's a "new problem" when, in reality, the "old problems" never stopped.

Now come the comparisons that are not even logical:

> Other school districts, including Millard, Bellevue, Papillion-La
> Vista, Westside and Lincoln, have social workers on staff whose
> job it is to bridge the gap between what's happening at school and
> at home. Millard, which has more than 23,000 students, employs
> 11 social workers spread out across the district's elementary,
> middle and high schools. Lincoln, with an enrollment of nearly
> 40,000 students, has 29 social workers who visit each school in the
> district at least a half-day every week. (Duffy, 2016)..

The districts that were named above are damn near lily white. Those white kids don't come close to having the kinds of issues that black and Latino kids have. They are small districts with small teacher-student ratios and top level technology. Those social workers don't do a damn thing but baby sit and pacify. Black and Latinos kids have to deal with crime, drugs, cop harassment and parents who don't have the time to interact with them in many cases because they (the parents) are facing similar harassment!

Now you have to find a token Negro to use as an example of what you want the public to think that social workers "may be doing." Following is an example of what could be called "the Ritz-cracker-with-cheese syndrome." This is what I call a situation that could handle itself over time (Ritz crackers taste good enough on their own) but someone comes along with a "booty snatching "paradigm or proposal to add some cheese to it, thereby making it more of a health threat and impairing the taste of the original cracker.

With that theme in mind, now note the following:

> LaKeisha Bonam is a social worker at Blackburn Alternative School in OPS. On a typical day she might help a student secure a bus pass, mediate a disagreement between a student and a teacher, or meet with a group of teen parents and bring in a speaker to talk about budgeting or car seat safety. Social workers also make home visits and work with special education students or those with attendance issues. (Duffy, 2016).

Secure a bus pass? Don't OPS kids ride the bus for free? Of course they do. But by pretending that you're "helping," you justify the job of that social worker. But the white reader of the Omaha World Herald wouldn't know that because they live out in the suburban hinterlands. Mediate a disagreement between a student and a teacher? Are you kidding? Those are usually issues involving the lack of cultural competency, the lack of teacher preparation and outright gooniness on the part of the teacher.

After on-going, almost daily examples of mind numbing inability to deal with kids of color in the Omaha Public Schools, the time has come to blame the kids – a key component of the "booty snatcher" paradigm:

> "That's one of the biggest things we deal with — getting our kids to come to school," she said. Blackburn has one guidance counselor, who focuses more on academics — checking grades and reminding students of college scholarship deadlines. The two work together to cover the academic and social needs of teens, Bonam said. (Duffy, 2016).

Ass backwards thinking yields ass backwards results. Getting kids to come to school would be no problem if the system weren't functioning inside of a context that promotes the abuse of black people. You live in a segregated situation then it's easy to "tee off" on black kids who, in turn, take their frustrations out at school once they walk in the classroom and have to listen to a teacher talking about how "wonderful" Omaha is and how "great" diversity can be. Guidance counselor? What is this – the blind leading the blind? Guide them where – to Metropolitan Community College because once they get socially promoted they find that upon graduating they don't have what it takes to pass the entry tests at nearby University of Nebraska at Omaha?

Finally, how are you going to "cover the academic and social needs of teens" when you didn't cover those needs during their pre-teen years? How are you going to cover anything when you treat their parents like shit so that you can qualify for more "poverty pimp" grants from the government? And how are you going to "cover" anything other than your own ass when the problems and predicaments of those black kids are the key to you securing that federal grant money and handout programs like those inherent in the social work proposal?

It gets worse:

> She might pull a student out of class for a "cool-down" if he or she is mouthing off to the teacher or fighting with another student. A parent might call wondering how her child will get to school now that the family is homeless, or to ask if Bonam can serve as a liaison between the family and a student's probation officer. (Duffy, 2016).

She's not a social worker – she's a truant officer! This is the kind of work that "officers," "hall monitors" and "juvenile workers" perform. She's got a job where her daily routine is seeing the worst of what low-income people have to offer after a wealthy system does its job to destroy their lives. She is there to sweep up the residue in the same way that the cops are called to "sweep up" the bodies only after a homicide has been committed (although in many cases proactive policing could have prevented the homicide in the first place).

Bonam adds, "We let them know we are here, we're a community here to help and serve students," Bonam said. "If they can't focus on all those issues they're dealing with prior to coming to our building, they can't be any good in our classroom." (Duffy, 2016). This is old news and the Omaha Public Schools should have known it. The Black Panther Party, back in the 1960s, Malcolm X, Stokely Carmichael and so many others tried to tell these peckerwoods that black kids were being subjected to negative conditions and that once in school, they were being punished for reacting to those conditions. White people found a way to "market the pain" and here come the booty snatchers, seeking out free money to hire more nurse maids like Bonam, to deal with their (the system's) dirty work.

Evidence of my allegation of the "dirty work" approach by these so-called "social workers" appears in the following excerpt:

> That's been the driving philosophy of other programs that have cropped up in the metro region to help students dealing with mental illness or hardships associated with poverty or unstable homes. "If the family's not successful, we're never going to educate that child, because their mind is going to be in 20 other places," board member Yolanda Williams said. "They're thinking

'Where am I going to eat tonight? Where am I going to sleep
tonight? Am I ever going to see my mom again?' When we're
talking about this, let's think of the child and not the dollars."
(Duffy, 2016).

Williams is one of the reasons why the school board has been constantly
ineffective and culturally bankrupt. She's African-American but thinks and acts
white, just like the other two black board members, Justin Wayne and Marque
Snow. They are not committed to education or to the kids; they don't return letters
and they certainly haven't responded to the reports and studies submitted to them
by the Triple One Neighborhood Association. This lax response is indicative of
people who are on the outside looking in – just like the traditional Nebraska-
sanctioned white social worker used to do. *Just because they change the color of
the social worker doesn't mean that they change the consciousness or the
competence of that individual.*
And yet they continue to "sic" these unqualified social workers on black
children, the younger the better. That is because if they are young, they are more
impressionable and also they are less likely to be able to kick the asses of those
workers when and if insulted. Continuing:

If OPS gets the grant, social workers would be added primarily to
elementary and middle schools. Schools struggling with discipline
or academic achievement would be prioritized. "When I look at
our persistently low-performing schools, one of the things that
always shows up is the need for not only mental health services but
also family services ... because these young people are in need,"
Evans said. (Duffy, 2016).

Get to them while they're young: train them to be the willing thralls of the
people who oppress them and teach them to associate all that is powerful with
white folks. Those social workers are borrowing from and imparting the same age-
old paradigms that they used back in the 1950s. They give credit to these white
women who maternalistically set up shop in the "slums" and catered mainly to
white ethnics who were wallowing in squalor, due to the maltreatment they faced
at the hands of their own people. And when it came to black people it was the same
old method: sacks of flour, some rice and a Bible so that they could learn that Jesus
was white and had blue eyes. That image hangs in many black churches around the
country to this very day.
Mental health services? I've written extensively on the fact that medicine
and health care are "racialized." Contrary to the bullshit myth, we are not "all the
same under the skin." We don't even think the same way. So what constitutes good
mental health to the white social worker and school psychologist may not be in the

best interests of a black kid who sees white people for what they are due to having parents who were raised in the 1960s or who were otherwise "conscious" when it came to race relations. Any act of militancy or any sign of knowledge of black history sends a red flag to the mind of the white social worker.

Writers like Richard Wright document the short shrift that their teachers gave them, as did Malcolm X in the following recollection regarding one of his teachers:

> He told me, "Malcolm, you ought to be thinking about a career. Have you been giving it thought?" The truth is, I hadn't. I never have figured out why I told him, "Well, yes, sir, I've been thinking I'd like to be a lawyer" … Mr. Ostrowski looked surprised, I remember, and leaned back in his chair and clasped his hands behind his head. He kind of half-smiled and said, "Don't misunderstand me, now. We all here like you, you know that. But you've got to be realistic about being a nigger. A lawyer – that's no realistic goal for a nigger. You need to think about something you can be (Malcolm X, 1965: 38).

The fact is that when it comes to young black students, the white teacher tries to often play social worker and the white social worker tries all too often to be a "teacher" of sorts. What you just read happened all the time in the Omaha Public Schools and State Senator Ernie Chambers has the records to prove it, as does the local NAACP and Urban League. White social workers learn white approaches, theories and models, and those were created by white people who studied other white people. In far too many instances, the white social worker is clueless when it comes to people of color because they were never taught about the value of cultural competency; only about paternalistic control, how to mete out sanctions and otherwise work to control black family systems (which are deemed "deviant").

Continuing:

> "I know some community members who say 'They ought to take care of it themselves,' " he continued. "Well, that's a nice thought, but it doesn't always happen. The young person deserves the resources regardless." (Duffy, 2016).

Those "community members" that are being referred to are white suburbanites who fled the inner city to get away from black people. And from there the segregated patterns of Omaha persisted and that served to support the "us versus them" atmosphere that these white people feel. Their false sense of superiority can only exist when there are no black people around to show them how "average" they really are. This is the case in sports, in popular culture and anything having to do with creativity, and well they know it. That is why the "resources" that are always lagging are kept away intentionally because when all is said and one, powerlessness creates a race of beggars.

Continuing:

> Goding asked why more social workers weren't being directed to the high schools, where students might experience more issues such as teen pregnancy, drugs and homelessness. "Ideally, we'd love to add 150 positions and put four of them at the high school," special education director Kara Saldierna said. "We tried to look at where we can have the most effectiveness, where can we do some early interventions? What are the schools that have some of the least amount of support? (Duffy, 2016).

See? The concept of "early interventions" raises a red flag in my mind. To begin with, interventions for what? When you intervene in something, it means that you are taking an action to improve a situation, especially a medical disorder" (Merriam-Webster, 2016). That was their choice of words. They see black kids as being some kind of diseased individuals who are in need of "improvement." And the white man views assimilation as the ultimate form of uplift. And that is what is meant by "early" intervention: a group of people are much easier to control if you can get to them before they have had a chance to mature.

Saldierna, the "special education" director (read: retards) continues:

> "High schools have a lot of students, but they also have a lot of counselors and administrators, where some elementary schools maybe only have a principal and a counselor," she said. Scanlan wondered whether OPS could maximize its partnerships with community and government agencies that focus on social work and counseling, instead of schools taking over those responsibilities. (Duffy, 2016).

It's all about white people providing the direction, vision and strategy and black people coming in to do the grunt work with the students. This kind of setup hails back to the days of enslavement and has carried over into the American workplace for the past two centuries. The white man makes a mess and the black man is brought in to clean it up, though the positions may be token, the titles very long, and the keys that are given to the black person usually don't fit anything. And they readily admit it, as is the case in the following quote from Scanlan:

> "The job of OPS is education," he said. "When you get into family issues and social issues, you do need some boundaries to keep you from bleeding over." (Duffy, 2016).

Bleeding over? See what I mean. If education was what is used to be when it was all white, then it would be relying heavily on those "family issues" as part and parcel of not only the direction, but also of the curriculum. The coming of Black Studies to college campuses, for instance, wasn't done in isolation on those lily-white campuses who were resisting: the families in the community came forward and forced those educational settings to change their ways. The same can be said for women's studies, ethnic studies and so on. So for Scanlon to act as if education functions in a vacuum is for him to display and abysmal ignorance of the very basics of what education is supposed to be.

The article concludes, thusly:

> Goding said she's asked for another presentation next month to
> answer additional questions, including a breakdown of the
> different roles and responsibilities of guidance counselors, social
> workers, school psychologists and community counselors.
> "I think we need a little clarification as board on that," she said.
> (Duffy, 2016).

Why don't they ask Senator Chambers, a pioneer in the education reform efforts in and around Omaha? Why don't they ask me – I have more degrees than any of them and exponentially more writings and research. The answer is clear: it is because the "booty snatchers" want confirmation of the mistakes they have already made with only a "tweak" to make it appear as if progress is being made. If they overhaul their mistakes, they might threaten their grant potential to rake in more free money at the expense of black students.

And while they work to proselytize and bamboozle the elementary and middle school kids and socially promote the high schoolers (therefore ensuring that they won't be able to pass any college entrance tests), they also have a fuzzy focus on higher education as well.

A February 22, 2016 article titled, "Omaha Sees Spike in Black College Grad Rate, as Outreach Programs Aim to Close Education's Race Gap" by the *Omaha World Herald's* Henry Cordes provides the falsified fluff piece that the major newspaper so often provides in order to neutralize criticisms of how little UNO is actually doing in terms of its overall educational "vision." Stripped of the bullshit personal accounts, the key points will be addressed and my analyses will filter in and out in the name of serving as a "social corrective."

Now, the article:

> … According to U.S. Census Bureau data, the number of black residents in
> the metro area with at least a bachelor's degree has spiked nearly 80
> percent since 2000. Today nearly one in five black adults in the metro area

has at least a four-year college degree. In 2000, it was less than one in seven.

That doesn't mean that they got the degrees from UNO! People come to Omaha for a number of reasons, as I did, and end up staying. Not only that, but the question is how did they get those undergraduate degrees? Most black kids are being forced into Metropolitan Community College under some kind of sick matriculation agreement with the Omaha Public Schools, go to that junior college for two years, graduate with an Associate's degree, and then transfer to UNO for the rest of their undergraduate work. On the transcripts this process is documented and employers don't see it as going from high school straight into a four-year degree; they see it as not being able to cut it and having to take a kind of "remedial route" via the community college.

But even more profoundly than any of those points is the fact that, according to Tom Becka of Channel 42, between 2011 and 2015 some 11,000 people with college degrees left the state. He made these comments on December 9th. Why didn't Cordes mention this fact even as he was propping up the numbers of black college graduates? Wouldn't it make sense to do so? He didn't do it because people reading his article might take the lead of those who already left because after all, there are jobs in bigger and better climes. This is the kind of selective bias that the World Herald has perennially been guilty of.

Next come what I believe is an outright fabrication:

> Among America's metro areas with the largest black populations, only two have recently seen bigger growth in the rate of black college grads than Omaha. "What's nice to see is the trend, which has been consistently going up," said David Drozd, a demographer in UNO's Center for Public Affairs Research. "It's important because we know education is a pathway out of poverty and to higher-paying jobs."

Look at all those qualifiers: two metro areas with the largest black populations have seen bigger growth of black college grads than Omaha. This is bullshit. Define a metro area, of which in the larger scheme of things, Omaha is not one. Omaha ranks something like 41st in the nation in size. What are the other two areas? Are they talking about Chicago or Detroit? Philly or Los Angeles? Of course not. So the way you write an article speaks volumes about the reality of the situation that you are trying to describe. Omaha is a hick town and some of the black people have undergraduate degrees. So what? The unemployment rate in the black community is four times higher than it is in the city as a whole. So what good are those degrees in a racist and segregated city. Where is the pathway out of poverty when Omaha ranks number one in black child poverty?

The manipulated manifestations of reality continue on in the Cordes article, a regular apologist for the educational screw-ups of UNO:

> The growth trend is largely mirrored on the state's college campuses, with UNO, Bellevue University and the University of Nebraska-Lincoln in particular seeing sizable increases in black graduates. UNO, which enrolls more black undergraduates than any other four-year school in the state, now awards bachelor's degrees to more than 100 black students a year, up from just over 60 during the early 2000s.

These figures are fudged. Do they consider continental Africans as "black students." How are students from the middle east defined? Some of them call themselves "Indo-Europeans" even though they may be darker than you or I. UNO has a history of lumping African bruthas and sistahs in with the American crop to send in to the Federal government. You cannot rely on their figures because in a recent news report it was documented that overall, high school graduation rates have leveled off. So if that is the case, from where will UNO draw its future crop of "negroes"? There should be a federal audit of UNOs admissions records because the school, as I have shown in the past, has a tendency to lie in order to cover up its discriminatory treatment of students of color.

Here is another question for the apologists and administrators. If there are 100 black students a year graduating with undergraduate degrees, where are they going to go in a discrimination-laden environment like Omaha? Will they be janitors pushing brooms, or will they try to do them like they tried to do to me, provide them with an opportunity to travel around the public school system and put light bulbs inside overhead projectors? Graduating with a degree means leaving Omaha and venturing forth across the country to seek out a job. Nowhere does UNO motivate students of color to open up their own businesses, and the graduate school is an option where you have to flip a coin.

Now comes a scintilla of truth:

> However, the picture for black student success is not completely rosy. Black students in Nebraska are still less likely than whites to attend four-year colleges. At UNO, the black graduation rate is up only marginally since 2000, and the gap between white and black graduation rates has grown.

After that rosy picture filled with questionable information, Cordes comes clean and admits that there remains that famous "education gap." You know, the one that they have lied and claim to be working on in other sections of this paper, the one that generates millions in Federal dollars for this mediocre campus. If the gap is growing then the rise in black graduation numbers leaves the black graduate in the same place relative to his white counterpart: competing with white kids for jobs in a white system where the hiring decisions are made by white people. How do you feel about those odds?

Always willing to make the Lincoln campus somehow seem better (I taught there for three years – there is no major difference except that the Lincoln campus students can get drunk quicker within walking distance of the campus and they have a major football team). Check out the next passage:

> Conversely, UNL has seen a sharper increase in its black graduation rate and is narrowing its black-white gap. In fact, a recent national study found UNL over the past decade has reduced its graduation gap between whites and historically underrepresented minorities more than any other school in the country.

This is bullshit. Those black graduates from UNL are disproportionately athletes who have their term papers done for them and their tests taken for them. They take Mickey Mouse courses and are babied by professors because they are members of "the Big Red" football or basketball team. They are socially promoted so they can remain eligible for athletics. They are on scholarship. Other than athletes there are few undergraduates who are black that attend that campus on a full time basis. When I taught there in the 1980s I had four and five sessions of Introduction to Sociology and the classes were lily white.

And look at the following statement: "a recent national study found UNL over the past decade has reduced its graduation gap between whites and historically underrepresented minorities more than any other school in the country." Bullshit! The graduation gap may have been reduced, but take notice that the writer doesn't tell us by how much! One additional black person graduating over the previous year would be a reduction in the gap if all other factors remained equal! Think, people, think! If what Cordes just wrote was true, then these white people wouldn't be hemorrhaging money and the NU system wouldn't be putting a freeze on conferences and travel for its faculty! Impressive racial rates generate funding, and UNL apparently isn't getting any funding from outside sources that would benefit black students – just more buildings and more coaches for the football team.

If what Cordes wrote was true there would have been a chart or a graph showing the schools that UNL had beaten out. Just because it appears in the World Herald doesn't make it so. You have to challenge their lies and realize that it is a newspaper that has a history of being steeped in unethical behavior, including the fact that several of its top administrators were involved in pedophile-type behavior. And remember: this is a newspaper that owns all of the other newspapers across the state. So lies spread quickly. But facts speak volumes and Cordes is peddling lies about this racial graduation stuff. History, not the easily assembled lies of the oppressor, is best qualified to reward our research, as Malcolm X taught.

The flaws at UNO were well documented in my 100 page analysis of lies told by UNO Chancellor John Christensen, seconded by another administrator Dan Shipp, and then recorded by an earlier article by Henry Cordes of the World Herald. Now with that in mind, kindly read the following excerpt:

> At UNO, recent concerns over lagging black graduation rates have prompted the launch of new programs aimed at early identification of struggling students and better connection of often-isolated black students to the campus and each other.

So the word is out about the lagging rates and then voila! It's time for the admissions office and the World Herald to get together and lie about overnight progress. Don't forget that the person in charge of public relations for UNO, Chris Reed, is related to the former graduate dean who still works in the administration along with her husband, BJ Reed. Nepotism that never goes reported because UNO and the World Herald control the news streams. (The city of Omaha is rife with nepotism. An article by Henry Cordes regarding Goodwill's ripping off of people and their high salaries revealed, "He called Goodwill's executive pay fair and deserved, arguing that the Omaha charity is unique and so complex that it can't be compared to any other nonprofit organization here or elsewhere. He also defended the employment of close relatives within Goodwill's upper ranks — including his own daughter — saying the charity is lucky that it gets referrals "from friends and family that already bleed Goodwill blue." (Cordes, 2016).

At any rate in the UNO case, that's how this miraculous "increase" in "black graduation rates," sans future prospects for those graduates, can make it into print. And as we know, the major television stations – KMTV (Channel 3, CBS), WOWT (Channel 6 (NBC), KETV (Channel 7, ABC) and KPTM (Channel 42, Fox) all get their news tips from the World Herald. And so the vicious lie-filled cycle is complete.

Next come statements from the liars who want to make it appear as if they care as much about black students as they do white ones:

> "We are taking it very seriously," said Dan Shipp, UNO's vice chancellor for student affairs. "I think we can do a lot better, and we have leadership on campus committed to doing it." Leaders in higher education say all Nebraskans have a stake in continuing to close the state's racial education gap. With the baby boom generation aging into retirement and the state's population growing increasingly diverse, Nebraska needs kids from all races and backgrounds to succeed in school if it's going to have the workforce needed to fuel future economic growth.

Let's look at the previous falsehoods before moving on with the rest of the Henry Cordes propaganda piece.

What do you expect Shipp to say? He was hired away from California to come to UNO and be a water-carrier for a failing system. He's one of those white boys who thinks he knows about black people and having met with him and made him look like an ass, I have first-hand knowledge that the only difference between him and the lily-white ol' boys network that permeates the UNO administration is that he's younger. That's about it. He says he "thinks" they can do a lot better, which isn't the most rock strong testimony in the world but once again, he had better say that in public because his job description demands it and his job requires it.

Secondly, the lie about closing that gap. Notice how they always mention that. The University of Nebraska Medical Center has a Center for the Reduction of Health Disparities and talks about closing the "health gap." In this document you have seen other references by these white people about closing racial gaps in education and other areas. But what must be remembered is that they were the ones who created the gap in the first place! They are the ones who chose racial segregation – American apartheid – as their choice of living arrangements and that is the arrangement that maintains the gaps! Talking about closing gaps while living in lily-white gated communities and redlining and steering Blacks and Latinos is like claiming that by robbing a bank you are helping the economy!

Two facts in need of juxtaposing. First, the previous claim that, "With the baby boom generation aging into retirement and the state's population growing increasingly diverse, Nebraska needs kids from all races and backgrounds to succeed in school if it's going to have the workforce needed to fuel future economic growth." Now, recall an earlier point made that between 2011 and 2015, Nebraska lost 11,000 people with college degrees. Can you see what these hicks are doing? Again, they want to build up their economy on the backs of blacks. You can believe that when these kids go into the workforce they will be replacing white retirees and will be paid a fraction of what those old white boys earned. In other words, a savings for the workforce and on-going disparate pay for people of color just as is the case with women.

Despite my logic and facts, the article claims, "We are seeing things trend in the right direction, but there's still a long way to go," said Mike Baumgartner of Nebraska's Coordinating Commission for Postsecondary Education. "It has to be a top priority for the state." These people don't know what the hell they're doing. As has been said before, "You can't teach what you don't' know and you can't lead where you won't go."

Black people will get the blame. Note the following:

> When it comes to raising achievement rates, there are few places it's more
> critical than in north Omaha, which in recent years has been home to one
> of the most impoverished black communities in the nation.

This is the "hero syndrome." These white people want to make it look like they are out to save the negroes, to close the poverty gap and all that, but they don't want to admit that they created both. It was because of white racism and greed that black poverty exists in the first place. The article further asserts that, "The metro area's black poverty rate ranked as the 14th-worst among the nation's 100 largest metro areas in census surveys between 2006 and 2010. More starkly, Omaha ranked fifth among those metro areas in the disparity between its black and white poverty rates."

Those figures are false. Omaha ranks number one in the nation in black CHILD poverty, which is the most severe kind because it is a family indicator. The black community has an unemployment rate four times higher than the city average, the median housing value in the black community is half that of the rest of the city, and the average income for blacks is a fraction of what it is for white folks. These are all indicators of the results of a designed social program based on racism! Even the passive and submissive long-time black residents of Omaha have to admit that they have been the victims of discrimination on all levels. So this stuff about poverty "in recent years" ranking Omaha in the national rankings is a fabrication: Omaha's black community has ALWAYS been impoverished, and the white folks in the city administration made sure that it stayed that way.

But who do they blame? The victims:

> Historically low rates of college success for blacks contributed to such
> numbers. In 2000, 13.5 percent of Omaha-area blacks age 25 and over had
> at least a bachelor's degree. That was less than half the 28.5 percent white
> rate in Omaha and nearly a percentage point below the U.S. black average.

If the low rates of college success for blacks contributed to black poverty, then who controls the colleges? Who controls the teaching taking place? Who controls the high school graduation rates and the social promotions? Who allowed these things to exist for a protracted period of time? White people did. So if you want to raise the issue of race as a "bragging point" as you talk about "progress" being made, always remember the race that stifled black progress from the get-go. And it is the same race that controls black progress, defines it and makes sure that it is limited only to those who agree to two the "company line."

What better way to ensure that the lie about "progress" is spread than to interview one of the culprits. First, check out the following truth claims:

> But more recent data compiled and analyzed by UNO's Drozd shows
> considerable progress on that front. Census surveys from 2010 to 2014

show the rate of black four-year grads shot up to 19.8 percent, and it's
trending still higher. It's also now slightly above the U.S. black average.
Among the 100 metro areas with the largest black populations, Omaha's
percentage of black college graduates now ranks 33rd, improved from 55th
five years ago. More impressively, among those metro areas, only
Savannah, Georgia, and Tallahassee, Florida, in that time have seen a
bigger percentage-point rise in black grads than Omaha.

The most racist department on the UNO campus is the department of Public
Administration. It is lily white except for a black woman who is powerless to bring
about changes, and so corrupt that it allowed a long time crook to teach a class in
leadership several summers ago. It is a department that is part of a college called
the College of Public Affairs and Communty Service, created by a black man back
in the early 1970s, that has such departments as Urban Studies, Social Work,
Gerontology and Criminal Justice. In the latter area they allow cops in to obtain
Master's degrees so that they (cops) can advance on their jobs.

This is the department, along with the Center for Applied Urban Research,
that leeches for federal grants and issues slanted and biased reports. They are the
ones that destroyed "The State of Black Omaha" reports that at one time were
issues by the Urban League. Once the sellout George Dillard, as director of the
League, decided to join UNO in writing the reports, the results became
generalized, distorted and virtually unreadable (by design).

With that having been said, it should be knotted that this buy Drozd is a part
of that system. This college is filled with these white boys who want to sound
urban and research black people, but whose racist skews their conclusions. For
instance, Drozd calls it progress when Omaha's percentage of black college
graduates rises to 33rd from 55th five years ago. Progress? The question is why was
it ranked thirty-third in the first place? What variables were in place that were
stifling black student progress, and what changed during that five year period? The
same people that did the stifling remained, did they not? So that means that the end
results, the outcomes were intentional!

These kinds of results are akin to the question, "do you still beat your wife"?
No matter how you answer it, you're guilty. When black people talk of "the first
black" to do that or "the first black to be appointed to that," these are insults! The
question is who was keeping track and who determined when 'the first" was going
to become a reality? They talk about who "the first" was, but they skip or gloss
over the individuals and the institutional arrangements that kept black people out in
the first place!

The Cordes article continues:

The growth in black grads also has narrowed the metro area's black-white education gap. In 2000 the white percentage of Omahans with college degrees was 2.1 times the black rate. It's 1.8 times higher now.

What was written above is not necessarily true. Just because the numbers of black graduates grew doesn't mean that the gap closes because the white group didn't just stand still – it was growing as well. But the conclusion that is drawn is that whites had no gains and blacks did all the growing. This is the kind of warped thinking and writing that World Herald reporters attempt to pawn off as "negro progress" when, in reality, nothing could be further from the truth. Their thinking is skewed and as a result, so are their numbers and the conclusions drawn from those numbers.

Moving on:

In sheer numbers, black college graduates living in Omaha have grown since 2000 from 4,300 to 7,700. There also has been marked growth in the number of Hispanic college grads in Omaha in that time. Four-year grads are up from 2,200 to 4,800, though such grads still represent only about 12 percent of the Hispanic population 25 and above, a figure that hasn't changed much.

And what are all these graduates of color doing in and around Omaha? Are they employed? Wouldn't that be a logical explanation to be included in an article of this kind? Instead, interview a bootlicker who works for Susie Buffett and the group of people who are slowly taking over the black community's land base. In this case, the person, who hails from Iowa by the way, is none other than Willie Barney:

Willie Barney of the Empowerment Network, a north Omaha community development organization, had recently noted the spike in black education levels. He said it goes hand in hand with other positive trends, including falling unemployment and poverty rates, fewer high school dropouts and an increase in black-owned businesses.

The Empowerment Network is not about developing North Omaha – it is about taking it over. And any "development" that takes place is going to financially benefit the people who are doing the developing and the planning. Those people are under the control of Susie Buffett, the Empowerment Network (which she finances) and other long-time water carriers for the system like the Omaha Economic Development Corporation (OEDC), and others who are slowly turning North Omaha's one time black Mecca into some kind of "urban village."

The black graduates are no indicator of falling unemployment because unemployment is not decreasing. Perhaps part-time and seasonal jobs might be on the rise, but full-time jobs do not exist for black people other than those service-sector jobs and the "negro" type jobs occupied by Willie Barney. The poverty rate is not decreasing because that would go against the "booty snatcher" grain and disqualify them for the social service grants and other free money that they so sorely crave. Barney knows nothing about urban planning or community development, which makes him perfect for the job he does and the position he occupies: a willing thrall for those who are working to"re-take" the northside.

Barney continues:

> "Education is critical," he said. "We still have issues to address with a sense of urgency. (But) there is a lot more focus on getting African-American kids to college and more programs and support available to assist students getting through college."

I could find nothing that shows that Barney even has a college degree. But that is not surprising. A man who was the director of the Omaha Public Schools so-called "African-American Achievement Team" was a college dropout. Several of the black men who are decision makers for nonprofit groups in the inner city lack college credentials of any kind. In other words, they have positions that they are not qualified for. This, in itself, makes them vulnerable should they ever get "uppity" and the white man seeks a reason for terminating their positions. These so-called "black leaders" do what white people tell them to do and say what white people tell them to say. Their lack of intellect is their own undoing.

Cordes, who is obviously lacking in research skills, proves just how much in the following paragraph:

> Research has long documented the barriers to college success faced by economically disadvantaged students. They often arrive as freshmen less academically prepared. They can struggle financially, many working their way through school or being forced to drop to part time or drop out due to family financial crises. Often they represent the first generation in their family to attend college, leaving them few role models and little guidance on what's required to succeed.

It didn't take "research" to learn that the previous obstacles to black graduation existed: all you had to do was know the nature of the people who were in charge of the educational system. These "revelations" were made clear by scholars who linked the nature of the white man with the issue of blacks in the American educational imagery. As Dr. Carter G. Woodson (1933) explained it,

> In history, of course, the Negro had no place in this curriculum. He was pictured as a human being of the lower order, unable to subject passion to reason, and therefore useful only when made the hewer of wood and the drawer of water for others. No thought was given to the history of Africa except so far as it had

been a field of exploitation for the Caucasian. You might study
the history as it was offered in our system from the elementary
school throughout the university, and you would never hear
Africa mentioned except in the negative (p. 21).

With such a foundation, how could the outcomes for blacks in American education be anything else but negative? But instead of placing the onus squarely on the shoulders of a white supremacist system, people like the novice John Williams are queried about it and as expected, a simplistic answer is supplied:

"When you're the first in your family to navigate the financial aid process
and to sit in a college classroom, it's a foreign land," said Joshua Williams,
a 2011 UNO graduate who now serves as coordinator for inclusion and
equity on campus.

These are the kinds of answers you get from people who carry titles like "Coordinator for Inclusion and Equity." Titles like that carry a stigma, and that stigma is like a neon sign that says, "I'm a token and you need not fear me because when all is said and done, I'm just here for window dressing." And that is exactly how they are treated. They know what to say and when to say it. And that is why people like Cordes and other "reporters" go directly to these tokens for answers to critical questions on race: the answers are going to place the blame on black people, the black family and so on – never on the white supremacist system that created both the gun and the murderer.

The best that UNO and its water carriers can come up with are generic answers that sound like they came out of a box of Cracker Jacks. For instance, note the following gutbuster:

UNO has long recognized the barriers faced by disadvantaged
students, more than four decades ago launching the Goodrich
scholarship program. Besides providing state-funded tuition
assistance,   Goodrich provides low-income students close
interaction with faculty and fellow Goodrich students, instruction
in study skills, tutoring and other support services designed to
reduce isolation and boost chances of success.

How would Cordes know whether or not "UNO has long recognized the barriers" that are faced by disadvantaged students? If this was the case, the question is what did UNO do about it? What has been learned over those "long" periods of time? Why does UNO continue to re-define minority affairs and morph it into multicultural affairs and now move it into the student center and align it with the needs of gay and transgender students, as if students of color have something in common with people with a different sexual orientation? Is it their goal to merge the two? These are questions that Cordes should have been using as follow-ups to prove his claim that barriers were "recognized" – and not institutionally constructed and then placed – by the university.

Then as examples, he shows the kind of thinking that has racism written all over it. As examples he cites the Goodrich Program and state-funded tuition. Both of these offer free tuition but what is tuition? It is an arbitrary number set to pay the bills of the university. The students see no checks, cash or stipends. In other words, it is self-serving financial arrangement. Tutoring and support services? These areas create jobs for the university and help students that probably should not have been accepted in the first place because of OPS' on-going mis-education. In other words, the examples provided are not signs of progress any more than someone who is unjustly arrested and then placed in solitary confinement can consider it "progress" once taken out of solitary and ushered into the "big yard" with the rest of the inmates.

Just as black families tend to get the blame for shortages in black graduation rates, the white man and woman get the credit when they offer up various forms of what I view as "pacification programs." In addition to the ones I've already cited and critiqued, enter none other than Susie Buffett, who continues to stick her nose and money into black folks' business and controls most of the leadership in the African-American community:

> Such efforts were significantly ramped up in 2008 when the Susan Thompson Buffett Foundation launched the Thompson Scholars Learning Community on the NU campuses in Omaha, Lincoln and Kearney. While offering scholarships for needy students and support services similar to the Goodrich program, the Thompson community is much larger. At UNO, Goodrich currently enrolls 277 students overall, 36 of them black; Thompson includes 84 black students and 923 in all.

Taking control of black lives through monetary inducements. This is an age old trick of white people historically and all across the nation. But it should be most noticeable when the daughter of one of the richest men in the world is a Johnny-come-lately to "helping" when black people have been in Omaha for about a century and a half. Warren Buffett was around and living less than five miles from the ghetto. Where was he? These white people, Bill and Melinda Gates among them, want to get involved as an "investment" because everything Susie does has a return either through the state of Nebraska Department of Health and Human Services or some kind of tax write-off.

Again, Cordes manages to find these students who are on the dole and therefore are not about to bite the hand that feeds. Take note of the following example:

> "It's a very conducive environment to be successful," said Chris
> Knight, a 2012 grad who was among the first black students in
> UNO's Thompson community. It's likely no coincidence that
> UNO black graduates have particularly spiked in the years since
> Thompson came on line.

A very conducive environment? What's wrong with this negro? You get free tuition, you see no money for your own pocket and yet the curriculum remains the same. In other words, no real change other than the fact that you get mis-educated for free. Don't these black students realize that they have an obligation to take that education and use it for community service and getting involved on campus so that the white paternalistic control of black life can be neutralized? The free tuition is great, but there are no free lunches: these people use you, like they did in order to get you to speak in this article, and will exploit you. Henry Cordes didn't pick this negro out of a random selection; they know who to talk to because they know what the person they choose is going to say. It's always the same stuff: "The white man is right as usual."

But they can't talk about UNO without also talking about the UNL campus because the "con" is to make it appear as if any black person who attends any of the University of Nebraska campuses is going to be a successful and happy camper:

> UNL has similarly seen black grads hit all-time highs. And in
> December, the school was cited in a study by Education Trust for
> narrowing the graduation rate gap for black, Hispanic and Native
> American students more than any school in the country.

But again, the equation is skewed. Narrowing a gap that only measures one side of the gap, one aspect of the variables when there are more than one variable, is a deformed equation! You can increase the graduation rates of people of color and then claim that the gap has closed – that is assuming that the white graduation rates have stood still! And since that ain't happening, and since more whites attend school and graduate in sheer numbers more than students of color, what you have is a fabrication of reality when you assume there to be a closure of any "gap." But Nebraska readers of the World-Herald are idiots for the most part, and they believe everything they read as if it was a prayer book. And that is how the "booty snatchers" continue to get away with their lies, their distortions of reality and their outright criminal and unethical behaviors time and time again.

The proof of my allegation can be found in their own words:

> Amy Goodburn, UNL's interim dean of enrollment, attributed the
> school's gains to a number of factors, including the school's
> general efforts to boost retention of all students, programs
> specifically supporting disadvantaged students and the Thompson
> community.

The school's "general efforts" to "boost retention of all students." If you throw a bunch of steaks in a yard full of wolves and there are other animals present, those other animals may inadvertently get a taste of the steak as well. The "general efforts" are aimed at the largest population of students, which is white kids. That so-called "Thompson community" is but a small smattering of kids, most of them students of color. But the larger community remains the priority and the kids of color are getting what amounts to remedial help. The end result may be graduations of non-white students, but at what level of life? Comparatively speaking, whose transcripts are the most impressive? Whose grade point averages are the highest? These are points that Cordes can't deal with because he's not an educator and judging from his writing, he's also not very *educated*.

The lie continues: "It's a game-changer for those students," Goodburn said of the Thompson program. "It's a community that creates a sense of belonging." Bullshit. How can it be a game-changer when the game is being run by the same race of people that rigged the table in the first place? How can there be a game-changing outcome when the people who planned the game know beforehand what the outcome will be, what percentage and number of "minorities" they are going to "allow" to walk across the stage, and as importantly, which students are going to get into graduate school and get jobs and which ones will NOT?

With all the grandiose quasi-truths out of the way, the article finally gets to the point that I've been making:

> However, while UNO has seen big gains in its black enrollment —
> up 30 percent over the last decade — and in its number of black
> graduates, its black graduation rates are only marginally higher
> than they were in the early 2000s. That's even as white completion
> rates at the school have climbed markedly.

White rates "climb markedly" meaning they don't remain static: black rates increase. That doesn't mean that any "gap" is closing! So how could they draw such a specious conclusion? UNO's mediocrity is well known, beginning back in the days when students said that the acronym UNO stood for "university of no opportunity." At any rate, that point is confirmed in the following passage:

> To be sure, metropolitan universities like UNO tend to have lower
> graduation rates than other types of schools. Such urban
> institutions have more open enrollment policies, higher numbers of
> students who work or go part time, and more transfers both in and
> out.

Not quite true. By "other types of schools" they must mean schools with higher rankings. Because the tier that UNO is in, comprised of schools of similar size like Portland State, STILL out-rate it! It has nothing to do with open campuses because UNO still has an entry exam geared toward weeding out the socially promoted minorities who skip through high school in the Omaha Public School system. The fact is, UNO is keeping its head above water and even Metropolitan Community College bypassed it as the second most populous college in the state of Nebraska, coming in only behind the University of Nebraska-Lincoln. UNO has dropped to third.

Now come some unproven "facts:"

> But while UNO's overall and white graduation rates exceed those
> of its peer metropolitan institutions, that's not true for black
> students. Just 22 percent of black full-time, first-time freshmen at
> UNO graduate within six years, compared with 30 percent for its
> peers.

What peer institutions are being bypassed by UNO in terms of white graduation rates? Prove it. Where are the charts and statistics? That is a lie as far as I'm concerned because if it was true, the World Herald would have been plastering it all over its front pages! The fact is, when these white UNO graduates have a cold, black UNO graduates have pneumonia.

Token efforts is all that are being offered – money spent on showcasing poorly spent activity. For instance, take note of the following claims:

> UNO officials have taken note. Two years ago they decided they
> needed to better support the school's nearly 800 black
> undergraduates, the vast majority of whom are not part of the
> Goodrich or Thompson programs. Shipp traveled with black
> students and administrators to UCLA to look at a potential model
> program there.

Why go to a mega-school like UCLA, one that had to learn on its own back in the day, the error of its ways? Judge Joe Brown, prior to becoming a TV celebrity, was an outreach worker at UCLA and testified to the low numbers of blacks that the institution had. After he got there and they began seriously recruiting, those numbers went up in a major way. But UCLA could draw from nearby Los Angeles and other major cities that dot the California coast, it can recruit nationally because of its reputation, and it can offer progressive programs and student activities that black people can get involved in. UNO cannot, so the trip that Shipp went on was just another junket since he hails from California. How can you compare UCLA with UNO? The only thing they have in common are the letter "U" in their acronyms!

When in doubt, dump the issues into the multicultural affairs junk heap the way UNO has always done. What started out as minority affairs dealing with issues germane to Black and Latino students now includes gays, lesbians, veterans and left-handed quarterbacks. Check it out:

> In the end, UNO created a new position in its multicultural affairs office whose duties include looking for early warning signs that students are struggling. The school has also created the Brotherhood and Sisterhood, gender-specific organizations that seek to provide some of the same academic services and peer connections that students in those scholarship programs receive.

I've been to a meeting of the "Brotherhood." The white man created both the Brotherhood and the Sisterhood. Now why would they do that? Their entire culture and tradition has been about denying and defiling any semblance of real brother and sisterhood among black people. Their entire modus operandi is committed to the institutional denial of black unity. So when they create groups like that, they are made of up "coon" type students who are students first and black second.

The Brotherhood is a perfect example. Their leader is a polite, well spoken young black man who – works for UNO! Naturally he's going to be passive and of the "go along to get along" variety. And the rest of the group, from what I could see, are borderline gay types who essentially don't know their asses from a hole in the ground. One of them even had the gall to have on some pink cut off jeans! And at the meeting I spoke at, one of the people in attendance was a UNO "operative" who also works for Susie Buffett and the Sherman Foundation. So in other words both groups are bullshit. The white man taking credit for "creating" such groups is an insult in and of itself.

Continuing:

> "If I haven't seen them in two or three weeks, I will go find them," said Taricka Fairgood, who facilitates the Sisterhood. "They will not fall through the cracks on my watch."

Why didn't Cordes mention the fact that Ms. Fairgood is an employee of the university and works in multicultural affairs? She's not going to make any waves. So again, UNO is so bereft of cultural competency that even when they think they are doing something "progressive" it turns out to be just another racist "scam" to control black students.

The Cordes piece then adds that, "Not all of the metro area's recent four-year black grads have been traditional students coming right out of high school. Many appear to be adult learners, including significant numbers earning degrees at Bellevue University." Of course they don't come right out of high school in many cases l- they can't! The Omaha Public Schools has been socially promoting their graduates for decades. I went to school with some of those negroes and, in fact, wrote term papers for scores of them. Many of them couldn't even put together a coherent sentence, knew nothing about a thesis statement, and sat in stone silence in the classroom during discussion times.

Continuing:

> State figures show Bellevue actually awards more bachelor's
> degrees to black students than any college in Nebraska — more
> than 200 a year — though it appears almost two-thirds of those
> degrees are going to students living in other states, taking courses
> online. Still, it appears Bellevue ranks second only to UNO in
> producing local four-year grads.

Bellevue is a quality school and is far smaller than UNO. So this school awards more bachelor's degrees per capital than UNO does. What does that say about UNO? Bellevue is not crazy about black students coming on campus and in fact, very few do. Taking courses on line is easier because some of them have people like me doing their work for them. And the reason why Bellevue ranks second "only to UNO" in producing local four year grads" (does he mean total or just black grads?), is because Creighton is an elite school and is essentially lily-white. But they teach that white nationalism with an intensity that dwarfs even the racist curriculum of UNO! I've seen it first-hand.

What Cordes and UNO deem as "black progress" is really just an assimilationist orientation of that institution and others in the area. Want proof? Take note of the following:

> Terrence Mackey, who returned to school at Bellevue two decades
> after dropping out at UNO, said he appreciated the credit Bellevue
> gave him for his real-life work at Boys Town and its accelerated
> degree program. He feels his degree is now helping him give back
> to his community in his work as an Omaha police gang specialist
> in north Omaha.

Again, Cordes finds a water-carrier who is obligated to provide the kinds of responses and answers that curry favor with the subject matter, in this case that being the University of Nebraska at Omaha. What else can this brutha say other than what he said? He works at Boys Town for one thing, and not only is it racist but it has a reputation for being a pedophile factory. Secondly, he works for the Omaha Police Division, which has a long tradition of having very few black men in their ranks, so he's concerned about keeping his job. And third, he's a "gang specialist" which means he's programmed to *fear, despise and arrest young black males*. The perfect willing thrall for the white Omaha employer.

Now comes the token negro "pledge" that these kinds of people make in order to curry more favor with white folks (like Cordes traditionally does). Read it for yourself:

> Recent UNO grads Collins and Knight say they also hope to serve as beacons for their community. Knight says he stresses education to kids while volunteering as a youth mentor for 100 Black Men of Omaha. "I tell them a lot of the things you may think are cool to do right now aren't going to be that way,'' Knight said. "The only thing that will last is your education."

Omaha is so backwards that these black men think they are making a contribution as they hand out bootlicking tips to younger black people. And they do it and call it "mentoring." Why can't there be any black nationalist mentors the way there are white nationalist mentors (who you know as school teachers, professors and scholars)? They teach white kids how to hate and how to accept segregation but black kids have to learn how to kiss ass from black people who are experts at doing it! How can you have a group that has a pre-set number in its name? One hundred black men is an insult because a percentage of those men are gay and most of them are corporate types.

So the "booty snatchers" win in terms of the curriculum, the teacher that imparts the bullshit, the programs that perpetuate the ignorance of the students and the socially promotes him, and the college that uses the student to generate more "booty" for the university's coffers.

But there are those who sicken of seeing what happened to their parents and grandparents at the hands of the public school system and even at UNO for that matter. Many of them have decided to leave, and the numbers are on the rise, despite the easily assembled lies of the Omaha World Herald and the rest of the Omaha media.

The American Student Exodus

There was a time when the Omaha slogan was, "America's Best Kept Secret." That secrecy continued on when it came to covering up the plethora of mistakes and acts of malfeasance that permeate not only the state, but also the city itself. The personnel boards who do the hiring bring people on board and evidently "forget" to tell them the whole story about what Omaha is really all about. Once on board, even when huge salaries, no one seems to want to stick around.

Following the "retirement announcements" of UNO chancellor John Christensen at the end of September 2016 (who claimed it was for family reasons), another educational executive used the same "excuse" before announcing that he would be stepping down. On October 4, 2016, Omaha Public Schools superintendent Mark Evans announced that he would be resigning. He was basically making a decision to do what increasing numbers of Omaha Public School students had already been doing, and what growing numbers of Nebraskans have now placed on the table as an option: "get going while the going is good."

According to a newscast on WOWT-Channel 6 (NBC) in Omaha,

> **OMAHA, Neb. (WOWT)** -- Superintendent Mark Evans announced Monday that he'll be retiring as Omaha Public Schools' superintendent at the end of the school year. Evens announced his decision to school board members Monday saying he plans to spend more time with his elderly parents and in-laws. Evans said some of his family members are facing health issues. He said his mother-in-law, who lives out of state, was recently diagnosed with Alzheimer's. Evans told board members that the decision has been a difficult one. (WOWT, 2016).

As I've written elsewhere, his parents were elderly when he applied for the position. They were elderly when he accepted the position. They were elderly as he performed his job as the superintendent of schools, and at no time did these elderly parents air a single complaint. This coward uses the old age of his parents as an excuse to back out of a situation that he did not have control of. The chancellor of the University of Nebraska had done the same thing and used a similar "family-based" excuse a few weeks before Evans did.

In an essay I penned for my newsletter, I looked at the real and potential impact that these twin resignations could have on black students at the college and throughout the Omaha Public Schools. What do they see taking place? Grown-ass men choosing to "cut bait" and get the hell out of Dodge. Grown men figuring that they can walk off a job that is not even close to being complete. These actions then, are a part of the reason for the student exodus upon graduating. They sicken of Omaha and its fly-by-night commitments; that is, when there is a commitment at all. They believe they can do better and that is why they leave. What is so difficult to understand about that?

Why shouldn't black students want to leave Omaha behind? They have more than enough reasons.

Even before Evans sheepishly decided to "resign," the school district hired a woman, Nancy Sebrng, who was forced to resign from her new post as the leader of the Omaha Public Schools after sending sexually explicit emails to her lover using a school account when she was at the Des Moines school district – behind her husband's back! She would have been paid $275,000 had she stayed. Here's what played out and here is what students were seeing materialize before their very eyes. So they leave the state.

> Racy: Des Moines Superintendent Nancy Sebring resigned after sending sexually explicit emails from her work account to a lover, who has now been revealed as Army Captain John Hintz … The married superintendent of a school district has left her job after dozens of racy emails to her lover were discovered in her work email account. (Daily Mail, 2012).

So the Omaha Public Schools sent money interviewing people and then decided on Sebring. And were it not for the "discovery" of the emails, she would now be in charge of the fate and future of black children. It gets worse:

> Nancy Sebring, 57, sent the emails to the unidentified man between March 26 and May 8. More than a quarter of the exchanges were sexually explicit. The school official, from Des Moines, Iowa made reference to sex acts and nude photos in the messages. (Daily Mail, 2012).

I'm going to share some of those with you in a minute because this is a white woman who was probably picked over a great number of people. Omaha Public Schools' black school board member Freddie Gray led the charge to get this woman on board. But before Gray made her attempt at a public stand (backed by her husband Ben Gray, a city council member who has seen his share of issue-flipping and questionable "deals"), another "sistah" in Des Moines (assuming she was black because of her name) also showed a great deal of naivete:

> District officials had read the emails which were sent between the couple using a school laptop and iPad. President of the school board Teree Caldwell-Johnson told the Des Moines Register she was 'sorely disappointed'. (Daily Mail, 2012).

With a name like Teree Caldwell-Jones, she's got to be Black. I checked her out on the internet: yep, she's a sistah, alright. Only a system-oriented "negro" would talk about being "disappointed" when she finds out the same thing you are about to find out about Sebring.

Now, the subject is why there is an exodus of families and students from Omaha in general and the Omaha Public Schools in particular and why that creates a need for OPS to constantly leech for free money from the government. Here is some of what that woman was saying using a public school laptop and iPad. Now remember: this is a woman who is just about to pack up and head to Omaha for her new $275,000 job. And she obviously can't control herself:

> In the correspondence, Sebring and her lover, who is also married, wrote about nipples and oral skills; how Sebring had "fallen in love with your d…"; missing each other; kissing; ass licking; horniness; sexy thoughts; gushing; 69; anal sex; late-night texts; orgasms; dick pics; suction cup dildos; and hands slipped under Sebring's dress. In an April 2 e-mail, the veteran educator wrote to the man that, "I have fallen hopelessly in love with your dick. There. I said it." Two weeks later, in an e-mail sent at 3:30 PM, Sebring wrote about a sexual encounter that morning. Referring to her use of a sex toy at home, Sebring noted, "There is a point, on my way to an orgasm, that I absolutely crave a long, hard cock being thrust into me…and I have to do without it." (The Smoking Gun, 2015).

White folks getting away with this kind of activity. Merely interject the variable of race and imagine what would have happened, what stereotypes would have been expanded on and/or referred to, if a BLACK woman had engaged in such lewd and lascivious behavior! But this is not even the issue: the issue is that the Omaha Public School board hired this woman after claiming that they conducted background checks. They were on the verge of paying this woman almost three hundred thousand dollars to lead and serve as a role model for young girls!

The saga continues:

> On May 2, Sebring recalled "how exciting it was when you slipped your hands under my dress and slid your fingers into me….OMG, just thinking about it gets my heart racing!!! I will be wearing skirts every time you see me from now on!!!" After noting that she was meeting that morning with the CEO of the Omaha World-Herald newspaper, Sebring concluded her e-mail by saying, "I have been thinking about your comments about church and God…I want to talk about that later." (The Smoking Gun, 2015).

There you have it. And she got caught. So they hired Mark Evans who took the job, lasted three years and then he "resigned." This is what the students of OPS see taking place around them. So many of them leave and the exodus is taking place although OPS tries to hide the fact because they don't want to impact Federal funding.

Remember: two school boards, one in Des Moines and one in Omaha, brought this woman on board. And look at what she was being paid at a time when both of these school systems continue to whine about "the lack of education funding."

Now let's move from public schooling to higher education.

<u>Nebraska Higher Education: In Financial Trouble Yet Again</u>

There are two major problems with the educational future in Nebraska as it relates to higher education.

First of all, community colleges are being over-run. According to PBS News Hour (April 12, 2016), only 20% of community college students graduate in three years. Modifications are going to cost money that Nebraska simply doesn't have. And the four-year institutions are faring no better

On Monday, November 7, 2016, University of Nebraska President Hank Bounds sent out a memo with the subject, "An Update on the Budget from President Bounds." The sub-heading was, "Great fiscal restraint, including a university-wide hiring freeze, is in place."

After I tried to warn him with a 50 page document the day of his swearing in, it is clear he dismissed the contents. Following is his letter with my commentary filtering in and out:

> Dear Colleagues,
>
> Recently I wrote to you about our budget planning and the fiscal challenges facing the state of Nebraska. Legislators will begin developing a state budget package for 2017-18 and 2018-19, including funding for the University of Nebraska, when they convene in January.

While hitting the ground with a plan, he now probably sees what I was attempting to warn him about. If he didn't see it then, he will see it when he gets a copy of this document, you can believe that. Dr. Bounds continues:

> You may have seen recent news reports about the state's decreased revenue projections and the likelihood that state agencies will have

> their appropriations reduced in the current fiscal year and in the next biennium. I want to be very candid with you. While we are continuing to analyze the numbers as they evolve, there is no question that we have difficult decisions ahead. Cuts to our state funding would almost certainly impact people, programs and affordability across our campuses. When you factor in unavoidable cost increases that we will have to manage in the next biennium, like health insurance and utilities, it is clear that we cannot wait to begin exercising great fiscal restraint.

The key words in the previous paragraph are "difficult decisions ahead." That is the thesis of this book: the booty snatchers have had difficult decisions to make in the past and have either avoided making them or have made the wrong ones. Nebraska leadership decisions take the easiest way out and kick the can down the road if they can but get things partially stabilized in the present. As the saying teaches, "All rivers and most men are crooked because they choose the path of least resistance." Nebraska is in a precarious position because its leadership is cowardly, ill-equipped to handle modern challenges, culturally incompetent and in many cases, downright buffoonish.

Bounds further elucidates:

> I have told the Governor and members of the Legislature that while we expect to be treated fairly and equitably, we will be a partner in navigating this downturn — as we have been historically. Following discussions with your chancellors, I have taken the following steps:
> A university-wide hiring freeze for all positions that are funded in any part by state-aided dollars is in effect immediately. This includes positions for which searches are currently being conducted. Exemptions will be granted for positions that the respective chancellor and I agree are absolutely critical to our mission.

A university-wide hiring freeze? I have always postulated that the University of Nebraska system was top heavy in administrators and manager-types all along! What they lacked were a new crop of teachers, not the fuddy-duddies who have been tenured and are now burned out and using the same out-moded classroom tactics that were used in the 1970s.

But new blood is not about to be ushered in. A tactic used at the Omaha campus is to bring n adjunct professors (part-time teachers) which represents a savings in terms of salary. But it is also a downgrade in terms of classroom quality in my view. Bounds was bought in to be a hatchet man and give the bad news as an outsider. He had toured the state for a full year before he was hired and supposedly "knew" about Nebraska. And even as he attempts to make cuts, the perks and other bullshit will remain:

> Chancellors, vice presidents and the executive directors of our university-wide institutes have been directed to move forward only on travel and purchasing that they deem absolutely necessary.

They needed to shut those "institutes" down for the most part. One of those institutes, named after Susie Buffett, could be of help: hit her up for the money. She's throwing money around as if she doesn't have a care in the world and her father is doing the same thing. Her aunt Doris, in Boston, is doling out crumbs but has access to hundreds of millions. There's the solution right there. But not in Nebraska. These hillbillies will figure out a way to find a Federal grant here or a handout there and will whittle away at the problem while never solving it. That is what their tradition clearly shows.

Travel? For what? Back in the day administrators went to conferences to discuss new and novel student personnel strategies, grant writing issues and the future of higher education. With Nebraska having been mediocre for so long, it is apparent that very little has been gleaned from these junkets. And who are they to deem what is "absolutely necessary"? These people are spendthrifts at almost every level of government, with higher education being no exception. Bounds just arrived in Nebraska from Mississippi, the one state which may be more countrified and hick-oriented than Nebraska. He is giving the University of Nebraska decision makers far too much credit.

Continuing:

> Chancellors are responsible for engaging their leadership teams to make sure they have a process in place for implementing budget cuts. Reduction processes, of course, must take into account our commitment to shared governance, in which we would seek faculty, staff and student input before making cuts. (Bounds, 2016)

"Leadership teams"? There are four chancellors in the NU system: UNOs, UN-Ls, UN-Kearney's and the Med Centers. These campuses are not known as being progressive or innovative (with the possible exception of the med center). What are these "leadership teams" producing? How can you expect progress when out of touch chancellors appoint their pals and buddies to man these teams, people who don't have a clue about having a vision. Not only that, but if they did stumble upon a progressive idea, it would be shot down by the old fuddy duddies – the chancellors. So it's a vicious cycle of Neanderthal notions and fruitless plans and that's why the system is in the position that Bounds has identified.

In order to have progressive input from faculty you need a progressive and visionary faculty. The University of Nebraska system, like the Nebraska government in general, wants to repeat the hiring patterns of the past, the same nepotism and racial preferences, the same approval of out-moded concepts so it's a clear-cut case of the blind leading the blind. Any proposals for cuts that are therefore submitted will be submitted in fear, doubt and based on what has already been proven to be played out.

Bounds adds:

> I do not expect that reducing hiring and travel alone will solve the budget challenges ahead. Two facts are clear as we consider our options. One, state appropriations and tuition are the primary sources of revenue that fund our day-to-day operations. Historically, when one goes down, the other goes up. We have been fortunate that the state has invested in its university at a level that has allowed us to keep costs within reach for students and families, and we hope that will continue.(Bounds, 2016)

They are not "keeping costs within reach for students." They jack up that tuition every other year it seems and nothing changes as a result. They rely far more on tuition than they do appropriations because the only thing that they are appropriating are contracts to construct more buildings and expand the sizes of campuses. Then they have to fill those buildings up. Those costs don't generate any revenue, which goes back again to the overwhelming need for tuition. The more students they enroll, the more money they can make. It's about making money for white folks and Bounds admits it in the following passage:

> And two, like any university, we are a people-driven enterprise. More than 80 percent of our spending goes toward salaries and benefits. Any major change in our budget, therefore, necessarily impacts people and the programs in which they serve.(Bounds, 2016)

Bounds says that they are a "people-driven university," but where do 890 percent of the spending go? To the people who work for the university! So the primary group of people that they are financially committed to are the ones who they have already hired, retained, and granted tenure! How self-centered, but now we have it in writing and these kinds of facts can be used in later lawsuits once students begin protesting the lack of commitment they receive from counselors, advisors, instructors, and administrators. After all, why be committed when you realize that the people who work at the university – not the students – are the real priority?

Bounds' memo continues:

> As we navigate this challenge, our first priority will be protecting the academic enterprise of the University of Nebraska. We will not let a temporary economic downturn damage our long-term quality, momentum and competitiveness. Rather, my goal is to use this period as an opportunity to be even more strategic and more efficient in the ways we serve students, the workforce and our state. Together with our partners at the Capitol, stakeholders across the state, and all of you, I am confident that we can identify responsible solutions that preserve the accessibility, quality and impact that Nebraskans have expected from their university for nearly 150 years.(Bounds, 2016).

No, the first priority is not to "protect the academic enterprise of the University of Nebraska." That is an enterprise that, when compared with similar universities, is mediocre at best. And Bounds knows this. *His first priority is to protect the state's investment.*

Secondly, how does he know that the economic downturn is "temporary"? There is no way he could know. (Read my section on "The Farmland Crisis"). Dr. Bounds is making this statement in order to assuage the fear of residents and stakeholders. And how can you have long-term quality when your short-term situation is so negative? And the people that he is relying on provides evidence that the economic problems are, indeed long-term. He writes that, "Together with our partners at the Capitol, stakeholders across the state, and all of you, I am confident that we can identify responsible solutions that preserve the accessibility, quality and impact that Nebraskans have expected from their university for nearly 150 years."

Why would Bounds make such a specific temporal projection? Why a hundred and fifty years? He doesn't even know how he's going to get out of debt in the next ten years – and if he's relying on the groups that he mentioned earlier, then his chances are slim and none.

The memo mercifully concludes:

> I will continue to communicate with you regarding the budget and our plans going forward. Thank you, as always, for all that you do for the University of Nebraska.(Bounds, 2016)

This memo constitutes a drastic departure from the syrup-dripping words that Dr. Bounds uttered when he was being sworn in. In my in-depth analysis of that ceremony (which I sent him and members of the administration copies of), I tried to warn him that he was from Mississippi and therefore he had grown accustomed to racism being more up-front and visible. I told him that Nebraskans are cowardly and as a result, they exhibit their racism behind closed doors and as a group (read: mobs). Evidently, he didn't listen and now he's facing a major financial crisis that was foreseeable.

"The Cultural Proficiency Journal: Response to a News Report

On July 10, 2011, the Omaha World Herald – hardly as bastion of liberal thought – ran an article by Joe Dejka titled, "OPS Buys 8,000 Diversity Manuals." This brief essay is a response to that article and an attempt to provide a deeper and more profound understanding of such a purchase, which according to my numbers means that OPS paid about $1,000 per page for a book called, *The Cultural Proficiency Journey.*

The fact is, a district that has a history as racist and discrimination-laden as the Omaha Public Schools is in no position to pretend as if it cares about "racial diversity." And it certainly has no right to spend $130,000 in federal stimulus money to order these books and then hand one out to every single member of the system, including custodians. Now, for the critique and commentary.

The article begins:

> The Omaha Public Schools used more than $130,000 in federal
> stimulus dollars to buy each teacher, administrator and staff
> member a manual on how to become more culturally sensitive.
> The book by Virginia education consultants could raise some
> eyebrows with its viewpoints.

How do you teach someone to become "more culturally sensitive" in a racially and residentially segregated context? What they really mean is how to "tolerate" people who are different while they are at work in the school system so that the system can avoid discrimination suits! Other than general truisms and glaringly obvious conclusions, the book offers little because it is apparent that the authors know little. Want proof?

> The authors assert that American government and institutions
> create advantages that "channel wealth and power to white
> people," that color-blindness will not end racism and that educators
> should "take action for social justice."

Color blindness? Do these people even have any idea what this "strategy" or "goal" really means? When white people say they are "color-blind," that is an insult. What it means is, "I don't really see your skin color" or any cultural differences, so I 'm just going to treat you like I would treat another white person." It is an admission that they can't accept someone of a different hue as a human being. And even in that, the authors turn right around and expect some kind of "acknowledgement" from these segregationist white Omahans and their fear-filled negro colleagues:

> The book says that teachers should acknowledge historical systemic oppression in schools, including racism, sexism, homophobia and "ableism," defined by the authors as discrimination or prejudice against people with disabilities.

Disabilities? Ableism? Black people kick in the door and here comes every other group - gays, the veterans, white women, the handicapped, immigrants -- claiming to be a minority. If you are white and disabled, your whiteness is rooted in privilege and you STILL have more rights than a person of color! Ableism is based on ability, not on race. It is the RACIAL dimensions of oppression that has skewed this society, and it is the variable – along with gender – that I am most concerned about.

According to the Dejka piece, "The authors argue that public school teachers must raise their cultural awareness to better serve minority students and improve academic achievement." Or else what? They've been singing that tune for decades and these white folks haven't changed yet! And what good would any change on campus be when after school ends, the blacks return to the ghetto, the Latinos to el barrio and the white folks to the suburbs? As the Yoruba saying teaches us, "You cannot shave a man's head in his absence."

The gist of my concerns, as the director of the largest African-American neighborhood group in the state, can be seen in the following excerpt:

> The Omaha school board approved buying 8,000 copies of the book — one for every employee, including members of the custodial staff — in April. The decision to buy the book was made 11-0, with board member Mary Ellen Drickey passing on the vote.

The Omaha Board of Education – the school board – was the racist vehicle that maintained segregation back in the day. After State Senator Ernie Chambers got "election by district," there were three seats that black people could occupy. And at the outset there was a modicum of progress. But that mostly consisted of quotes, quips, phrases and formulas that the newspaper could grab hold of to make it appear as if true "integration" was occurring. Today's cast of characters, which consists of three "negroes" is as non-productive as the other black political leaders who are elected by district (with the exception of Senator Chambers).

The sophistic nature of the move to buy the book can begin to be understood as we peruse the following passage:

> Janice Garnett, OPS assistant superintendent of human resources, said she could not recall another time that the district had bought copies of the same book to give to every staff member. Employees will be asked to read a couple of chapters each quarter and then meet in study groups to discuss the book using a study guide produced by the district, she said. For teachers, the study sessions will be a part of their professional development.

If what Garnett said was true, then the immediate question would have been "why now"? "Why this book?" The answer is clear once we understand that Omaha is always at least five years behind the rest of the country. So it took until 2011 for this city to come into contact with what I refer to as "the racial buzzwords of the year." White folks are good at pretending to give a damn about race relations, especially since they see "their" country increasingly getting browner and blacker. So the new buzzwords, aimed at pacification, are "multiculturalism," "inclusion," "equity," "diversity" and in this case "cultural competency" or "cultural proficiency." Hence, the purchase.

Then comes an explanation that is a total waste of time. In October of 2012, Eastfield College in Mesquite, Texas had a similar "idea" which they called, "The Common Book Project." They had staff members read a book that would be assigned and then meet on it. That idea is now dead. In like manner, four years later and in a school district far away in Omaha, there is another book that is being jammed down the throats of employees. And of what use it is?

> School board President Sandra Jensen said the district doesn't endorse everything in the book, nor does she expect employees to adopt the authors' positions. The book is intended to open a dialogue, she said.

If the district doesn't endorse everything in the book, and the points being made in the book are geared toward suggesting that the district become more "culturally proficient," then what does this say about Jensen and the rest of the decision makers? She adds that, she didn't expect the employees to adopt the authors' positions. Well in my view as a scholar, what is suggested in that book is about as milquetoast as it gets: there isn't a militant word in the whole 127 pages. So in other words what I charge is correct: white people are not going to change what makes them feel comfortable, and in Omaha, Nebraska, racial and residential segregation are the order of the day.

> "The purpose of providing this resource is to help staff see that
> people come from a multitude of different backgrounds which
> cause them to respond differently to the same set of facts,
> depending on their personal perspectives," she said in a statement.
> "Recognition that one might have a certain perspective is critical to
> treating all people equally."

This is a crock of shit and this woman, Sandra Jensen, knew it was when she was saying it. What she just described is known as "cultural relativity," and this is the antithesis of the "Omaha way." These white people treat anyone with a different view (read: progressive) with disdain-and-how-dare-you. They then banish them beyond the pale of empathy or understanding. Those with different views would be able to see this city and the school district for what it is: the people who are hired to work in Omaha are people who are more than willing to tow the company line. And that includes keeping your mouth shut, never voicing a point of view that runs counter to the racist majority, and do what you're told.

Continuing:

> Representatives of other large Nebraska school districts —
> Lincoln, Millard, Papillion-La Vista and Bellevue — said they
> have not used the book for training teachers, nor have the Council
> Bluffs Community Schools and Des Moines Public Schools.
> Lincoln officials bought copies of a different cultural proficiency
> book to train administrators later this summer, according to
> spokeswoman Mary Kay Roth.

Nebraska is a hick state and they know it. The largest city in Nebraska is about half as large as at least five cities in Texas. Omaha has barely 400,000 but lie and claim they have half a million. The second largest city, the state capitol in Lincoln, has only 172,000. These two cities also have the most blacks. So it stands to reason that they would order books and go through the motions of caring about "cultural proficiency." I believe there must be some kind of "pacification checklist" that they have, which includes ordering manuals and exposing your staff to them. But as was stated earlier, just because the books are ordered doesn't mean that they will be read – or even understood.

In what I view as a total violation of the First Amendment rights of the staff of the Omaha Public Schools, the books were not only distributed, but take note of the following:

The book that OPS bought, "The Cultural Proficiency Journey:
Moving Beyond Ethical Barriers Toward Profound School
Change," includes a worksheet for teachers to score themselves on
a continuum of cultural sensitivity. The continuum ranges from
"cultural destructiveness," as evidenced by genocide and
ethnocide, to "cultural proficiency," depicted as the highest level
of awareness.

Score themselves? This is part and parcel of the perpetuation of racism in Omaha. They continue to give themselves passing grades. The leadership should probably have carpel tunnel syndrome from patting itself on the back. When there is blame, they find a convenient scapegoat and then move on about their business. When cops shoot a civilian, right or wrong: suspension with pay. When a superintendent is hired and uses her work email to talk about sucking her boyfriend's dick, she is let go with a huge severance check, but only after a black president of the school board tried to defend her.

When a white woman steals millions from the account of the State of Nebraska Tourism Department and then put her daughter's picture on the cover of the Tourism manual. They finally terminated her, but only after suspending her for a few weeks – with pay.

And the list goes on. Back to the World-Herald piece: "Only those educators who acknowledge the existence of white privilege in America, that "white" is a culture in America and that race "is a definer for social and economic status" can reach proficiency, the authors contend." So, that's all it takes: to recognize the obvious? To acknowledge what every single oppressed person knows either directly or indirectly? I subscribe to the denotative definition of the word "proficiency," which means, "a high degree of competence or skill; expertise." How can you have a "high degree" of competence or skill in *anything* if the only criteria for it is the acknowledgement or recognition of the obvious?

And there are even more "bailouts" for these myopic-minded employees:

Those who score poorly on the worksheet are asked in the book
what they will do "to align yourself with the values
expressed."Jensen said the district will not use the book to evaluate
or judge employees.

There are no evaluations and no judging of employee reactions. Therefore, of what use is this entire exercise? What is the intended result? Where are the measurable outcomes? Take away the 39 pages of "paperwork" or drills and what you have is an 88 page book on "cultural proficiency." Therefore, now you have a book that has cost the district over $1,200 per page! A book with, as I charged earlier *no measurable outcomes!*

The issue is one of race, but these "cultural competency" people continue to link sexual preference with race. The society is already blurring the lines between male and female and the homosexuals are a powerful lobby. Not only that, but for white folks, dealing with sexual issues is preferably to dealing with issues of race, the former an integral part of their history and the latter and area they know nothing about. As the authors put it,

> The book says teachers must overcome irrational fear of homosexuality and reject the "color-blind" approach to teaching in which teachers treat all children the same. Instead, the group identity of students of color should be recognized and esteemed, the authors say.

Or else what? What are these out of town, out of touch "consultants" going to offer as a penalty if these rules or suggestions are not adhered to? I'll tell you what they're going to do: nothing. And the school district knows it, just like they know they don't have the resources, time or talent to reinforce or support any of the suggestions that were made. The so called Office of Equity and Diversity is a joke and its physical appearance is but one example of the low regard that the OPS administration has of it: small office with one staff person to assist the "director." He can no more usher in diversity and/or equity than a menu has of being the actual meal. As the African-American proverb asks, "Whoever heard of a mouse making a nest in a cat's ear?"

The power is in the hands of the traditions, history and values of white segregationists who run Omaha. The school district administration is no different. As was the case when the former President of the school board backed some malfeasant actions by a superintendent they had just hired – knowing full well that the woman was exchanging sexually-based messages with a boyfriend in another city – the board curries favor and does little else. They get elected and then sit in fear, rarely responding to letters from constituents and have worked together to whittle down community meetings from what used to be twice a month to once a month. In other words, they are not accountable.

The book further continues its high expectations:

> The authors ask readers to reflect on several hypothetical cases, including that of a gay "teacher of the year" afraid to post family photos of his male partner for his school's Family Day, an African-American parent upset by a sixth-grade Early-American Day because African-Americans were enslaved in those days, and a principal whose attempt to reach out to Muslim students backfires when he announces over the intercom that students should welcome Muslims though they "might believe in violence."

Hypothetical cases. Case studies. Comparisons of situations that gays find themselves in with those of perennial pariah groups like Blacks and Latinos. This cultural proficiency book is a crock of shit. It is filled with mundane general truisms, wording that can be re-hashed from one district to another. All they have to do is change the names of the districts and a few other tweaks within the text and voila: Mo' money, mo' money, mo' money!

You take a book and put it in the hands of the uninformed, the result is going to be increased anarchy. Now the people who are a part of the problem can accept the book, put it away, claim to have read it, and use the fact that they accepted it as example of "positive change." You've armed the people who are the problem with a tool that is going to continue to relieve them of the responsibility to ACT.

And even with what I've provided – and could have provided had I been contacted – these outsiders think that they're bullshit 127-page book is going to usher in change. Check it out:

> The authors — Franklin and Brenda CampbellJones and Randall
> B. Lindsey — all former teachers, write that their intent in the
> book is "to prepare educators to unshackle themselves from
> tradition and become facilitators for reconciliation of historical
> injustices."

Let's look at what is written above regarding the "intent" of these "educators": "To to prepare educators to unshackle themselves from tradition and become facilitators for reconciliation of historical injustices." How are you going to 'reconcile' that which has been deemed "an historical injustice"? Reconciliation is defined as, "the restoration of friendly relations" or "harmonization." How can you restore that which has never existed? How can you reconcile race relations in a city that is perfectly comfortable with the segregation and discrimination that permeate the entire city at present? Do these "educators" think that they can re-write history? And how can those who have benefited from being a part of the problem – just as their parents and grandparents were – be expected to "facilitate" anything other than mechanisms that are going to perpetuate the status quo?

The World Herald reporter then interviewed one of the authors, and I want you to pay careful attention to what was expressed in response to the reporters queries:

> Franklin CampbellJones said in an interview that although some
> issues in the book are considered "challenging" and "taboo,"
> discussing them is important to break down barriers to educating
> every child. He said the book has been well-received by other

school districts using it, including San Diego and Atlanta, and districts in Maryland and Canada.

If the author agrees that some of the issues in the book are considered "challenging" and "taboo," then what he has to ask himself is why this is the case. What is the basis for these considerations? What do the people who think this way have to hide or what are they afraid of? Instead of handing out books knowing full well that the contents are going to be challenging and taboo, why not do the right thing and work to rectify the conditions that lead to such thinking?

He then claims that he can break down barriers to educating every child. That is a lie because as an educator, I know that every child cannot be educated in the same way, by the same people, in the same situation. And if there are barriers, those barriers cannot be "partially" broken down; they have to be totally eliminated so that the student can feel safe enough to trust the teacher. Only under such conditions can true education take place.

You can't create hi-tech schools located in glamorous neighborhoods and then bus the low-income kids back to deteriorated areas of town! You have to do something about eliminating those low incomes! But again, we have to understand Omaha's tendency toward what I call "the Toys for Tots Syndrome", which I discuss later in this paper. It is better to make kids dependent on and thankful to the system than to empower the families of those kids so that all the thanks can go to the parents. Omaha intentionally devalues and divides minority families and opts instead for poverty pimp hand-out programs based on clothes, food and toys that are DONATED to them. They spend very little of their own money on relevant programs – the $130,000 on this book just one example. Those were taxpayers' dollars.

Finally, look at the other cities and areas where these consultants claim to have been: San Diego and Atlanta, and districts in Maryland and Canada. These are areas where there are sizable black and minority populations! Omaha doesn't fit anywhere in this mold – it is a town attempting to masquerade as a city! And the thinking of its population is also "town-sized." These are not urbanites: these are farmers and hillbillies in suits!

Back to the article:

> The push for cultural proficiency, sometimes referred to as cultural competence, is a trend across the country, though what's meant by these terms varies. Definitions range from encouraging teachers to understand the cultural backgrounds of students to more aggressive efforts to rewrite curricula and adapt school systems to immigrant cultures.

See? It's a "trend across the country" and that's where the non-creative leadership of Omaha gets its ideas. There is nothing original being done by the County, the City or the school system. To expect to fit the square peg into a round hole is therefore naïve and nonproductive. The schools have long been approached by Black and Latino groups for a more inclusive curriculum and programming, but it was to no avail. But this same system, one that looks with disdain upon black leadership (except for those who they have appointed or anointed) has the unmitigated gall to take it upon itself to have an out of touch school board rubber stamp the purchase of a book that has about as much cultural and racial relevance as an Archie comic book.

Moving on:

> A primary concern of critics is that schools and universities could use cultural proficiency as an ideological litmus test and that the money put toward such programs could be better spent directly on academics.

Why waste time with these institutions of higher education? They do what they do. I have taught at them and I've witnessed the laziness of the teachers once they get tenure. I've seen the athletic department work with some of them to cheat and allow athletes to skip class. I know some of the people who write papers for athletes so that the athlete can remain eligible. Institutions of higher education are in it for the money, and they use a "formula" to determine how many people of color they are going to allow on campus. They spend money on new buildings that are "handicap accessible" but most of them fall short when it comes to an atmosphere that is "minority accessible."

Then comes an example – of *incompetency*, that is:

> In 2009 the University of Minnesota-Twin Cities drew criticism when a task force proposed introducing cultural competency requirements for its teacher candidates. The task force proposed that future teachers, in order to be recommended for licensure, should "recognize and demonstrate understanding of white privilege," fight for social justice and take tests to measure their "intercultural sensitivity" and "cultural intelligence."

White people are not going to be forced to promote or believe in "inclusion" on any level. That is a key to the white supremacist machine: to exclude those you don't like and to only include your fellow race members. How can you ask these people to fight for social justice, give them tests to measure something they are totally lacking in (intercultural sensitivity) and put them in a position to flunk a test on "cultural intelligence"? It's alright to mis-educate and use tests to sabotage the lives of low-income and minority kids, but not white teachers. How dare they!

The response was predictable – and in my view, correct:

> Among the critics were the Foundation for Individual Rights in Education, a nonprofit watchdog group advocating individual rights at America's colleges and universities, which argued that the proposals intruded on matters of individual freedom and conscience.

I agree. You can't force white people to practice a "tolerance" that they simply do not have. It's bad enough they say the "Pledge of Allegiance" and sing the national anthem – both of these replete with lies – but an actual proposal where their racism would be laid bare? The Ethiopian proverb teaches us that, "The fool looks for dung where the cows never browsed."

Let's get back to the Cornhusker state:

> The Nebraska Board of Education is considering drafting teacher standards that call for teachers to be "culturally competent," a move spokeswoman Betty VanDeventer said is intended to make teachers more aware and respectful of children of all cultures. Last winter, board members authorized a 41-member committee of teachers, principals, parents and others to draft the standards.

Bullshit from top to bottom. Even if the Nebraska Board of Education DID draft teacher standards that include rules for cultural competency, what would they look like? Why would they do it? Are THEY (the Board members) culturally competent themselves? Of course not. In Nebraska being knowledgeable about farm issues and cowboy-related topics are the priorities. Most of the black people are relegated to an eight square mile area on the southeastern sector of the state (Omaha) and the Latinos are to be found out in the panhandle. Both groups are so poor they don't have time to study history or culture. And white folks sho' ain't gonna do it!

But there's more:

> The proposed standards call upon teachers to, among other things, connect with a student's traditions to move him toward academic success, use "culturally appropriate instructional strategies" and make sure tests are valid and address the diversity of students. The draft standards do not include any of the social justice goals contained in the book acquired by OPS.

To talk of "culturally appropriate" instruction strategies is nothing more than a mimicking of what black people had been telling white instructors and administrators since the 1960s. It was a reflection of the findings of Kenneth Clark during the Brown v. Board hearings, when black children were so fucked up in the head that when asked which doll they believed they wanted to be most like, most of them chose the white doll. Culturally appropriate education was what the African-American Immersion movement was about, it was what black colleges were initially aimed at (though they failed miserably) and a host of paradigms through alternative and Africentric education. White people knocked all of it as "racism in reverse."

Now that the demographics have changed and the white race is becoming a shriveling minority in the United States (and the world) they want to act as if they came up with a novel idea and start siding with the obvious paradigm.

And don't be fooled by the reference to "the social justice goals contained in a book acquired by OPS." What was produced was just more bullshit.

Under the topic "School Choice Thematic Programs," note how the concept of "social justice" has been incorporated by the Omaha Public Schools white folks. According to their website:

> **Leadership, Social Justice, Law, Government, and International Diplomacy (7-12)**
> The Leadership, Social Justice, Law, Government, and International Diplomacy programs advocate that citizens have certain roles and responsibilities to society and the environment. These programs rely on resources such as Steven Covey's "7 Habits" to develop leadership abilities in all students. These programs are found at Nathan Hale Middle School at grades 7 and 8 and at Northwest High School at grades 9-12. At the middle school level, students experience an extended school day.

All of these are areas where the white instructor at the high school level has long mis-educated and cognitively intimidated non-white students. Talks of leadership direct them to groups that are passive and system-oriented, law is a discussion of blacks as criminals, government is about the perfect approaches of the two party system, and international diplomacy favors those groups that America controls: European nations, the Japanese, India and in some cases, China. As the saying teaches, "You can't teach what you don't know, and you can't lead where you won't go. OPS instructors are home grown and in most cases, totally committed to the Omaha way of life. That is why their students graduate lagging in cultural competency: they do so because their teachers did.

The World-Herald article further informs us that,

> The state plans to hold forums this summer and fall on the draft
> standards. The Nebraska standards would be voluntary. Local
> districts could decide whether to adopt them. Paul Peterson,
> director of the Program on Education Policy and Governance at
> Harvard University, and a senior fellow at the conservative Hoover
> Institution at Stanford University, said cultural proficiency is part
> of a broader agenda advocated by people "who think that we
> should have a teaching force that has a certain political
> perspective."

That "certain political perspective" would remain a racist one, although it would be more easy to conceal with talk of "cultural proficiency." The people making the decisions would still be white, so what was going to change? They, in turn, would only hire those black people who they could control and direct so in reality, nothing institutional was going to change: an addition of a "program" over here or a "project" over there was not going to alter the system of white supremacy and discrimination in any major way. And white folks knew it.

The Harvard man that was interviewed saw and heard the same thing I saw and heard. Both of us are scholars. So then, can we both be wrong? Check it out:

> About OPS spending stimulus money on the book, he said: "That
> must be a wealthy school district." Stimulus rules allowed districts
> to spend money on teacher training, but Peterson suggested the
> money would be better spent on academic training. "I would like to
> know whether the teachers are proficient in the subject they're
> going to be teaching," he said. "It would be nice, if they're going to
> be teaching science, to be proficient in science; or math, to be
> proficient in math."

And this is a point I've addressed in other black papers. OPS is filled with long-timers who prefer the "old school" ways. These white people don't want to make ways because the new technology means that they would have to be re-trained. And that is how they view cultural proficiency as well: something new being brought in that is going to make them have to actually care, think and apply something in the classroom. These "educators" who put together that bullshit book should have understand the context, the consciousness and the conduct of the people they were dealing with in country-ass, rural Omaha, Nebraska.

What this Harvard guys says has been provided to OPS administrators since the late 1970s on a number of levels and from a number of sources:

> Peterson said it's important that teachers be aware of the traditions
> a child brings to the school, and to take those into account when

working with the pupil and deciding how to engage and motivate him or her.

White people in Omaha have been programmed to treat Black students a different way. It is a part of Omaha culture, and I have filed and won grievances pointing out some of the racist actions of the OPS administration and its teachers. In 1996 I created the Triple One Parents' Union, a subsidiary of the Triple One Neighborhood Association (and later merged them), named after the "68111" zip code in the heart of the black community of Omaha, the largest black community in the state. I have been monitoring OPS and its habits for over three decades, and what they've done is nothing short of the "mis-education" that Dr. Carter G. Woodson talked about in his book, *Mis-Education of the Negro*.

Peterson wasn't finished because he had to try to "understand" the position of his fellow whites. According to the article, "He is concerned, however, about the book's general statements about the white population. That kind of generalization can be "extremely misleading" and "it would seem it would not be the kind of book you would distribute," he said." Generalizations? Look at the relationship between the schools and black students no matter where you go in the country. The sum total of those relationships are a reflection of the way these white people act and think. Therefore, these are "populations" that are generalizable because when it comes to race, white people seem to all think alike! They just don't want to admit it.

OPS knew what it was doing when it distributed that book. They knew it was too much for their simple-minded and sophistic teaching corps to handle. They knew that their weak-minded counselors would not be able to cope. But they did it because it was a smokescreen; when confronted with yet another racist act, they could point at the purchase of this book and say, "See, we tried!"

Moving on with the *World-Herald* article:

> Jensen said there's no hidden agenda with the book study. She said she had started reading the book before the board voted to approve the purchase, and she intends to finish it and participate in the sessions.

Jensen is most likely lying. And what did the reporter expect her to say? That she hadn't read the book or had read it and hated it? Wouldn't that run totally counter to the fact that the book was being considered for purchase? Remember: these white people and their negro lackeys, once in office, forget all about the people who voted them in and put them there. This has been a long time tradition in Omaha, ranging from the County Board and the City Council to the Board of Education and other local boards as well.

Now check out the stupid answer she gives when asked an important question:

> Asked last week if she believes white privilege exists in Omaha, Jensen said: "That depends on the cultural lens that one looks through."

It was a "yes or no" question. This woman had the chance to show the reporter the depth of her understanding and commitment (or lack thereof) to the concept and conviction of "cultural proficiency." But her answer is indicative of the same type of attitude that most of Omaha's white people have when it comes to any issue that has to do with race. They feel as if a question of that type is some type of "trap." They don't mind being segregationists and discriminators, they just don't want to be discovered doing it directly. And this is a point that these "educators" seem to continually miss. Their "one size fits all" approach to cultural proficiency is as full of shit as they appear to be.

Continuing:

> The Omaha school district has a racially diverse enrollment. Last year the enrollment was 35.7 percent Caucasian, 29.9 percent Hispanic, 29.7 percent African-American, 3.1 percent Asian-American and 1.6 percent American-Indian. Students speak 93 different languages, Omaha Public Schools officials say.

The enrollment is not the issue, although the rise in students of color is a cause of concern for a lily-white administration. Not only that but the teaching corps is also overwhelmingly white. So the problem is at the top, not with the students. We can therefore conclude that the district is not prepared and that as a result, there is going to be more controversy from parents and others who understand the need for cultural proficiency. Those won't be white parents either (we've seen from Jensen what they will attempt to do); it will be the rapidly growing numbers of parents of color. And though ignorant in many cases, they will not be happy having to field complaints from their kids regarding the "racism" in their respective schools.

The lies and intentional cover-ups just keep on coming. For instance, the article says that, "The district, like most across the country, has struggled to close stubborn achievement gaps between whites and minorities." "Stubborn achievement gaps"? As if the gaps have a mind of their own and despite the efforts of "the good ol' white folks," the evil gap monsters just keep reappearing time and time again? The achievement gaps, like the various racial gaps in housing value, employment, median income, health care, and other areas, are by design. And each of those gaps generates grant funding from the federal and state government. And Omaha, being as broke and unskilled as it is, goes after that grant money like a dog after a plate of filet mignon.

Logic should reign. As an educator if I see that there is an "achievement gap," then I know that the problem is not with the students, but with the people who are supposed to be in charge of making achievement a reality! Just like the OPS "African American Achievement Team" whose leader was an idiot who was a college dropout. With this guy overlooking the hard work of the black women who were actually trying to make a difference, is there any wonder that the Team floundered and has since dismantled?

According to the article, "Garnett, with OPS, said the district will use the book as a conversation starter on topics such as social equity, cultural understanding and racial justice." That was in 2011; with the benefit of retrospect we can now see that everybody that was interviewed was telling a damnable lie. And we can also see that the OPS has not progressed one inch in the area of "cultural proficiency." So once again it was more lies to stall time until the gullible and weak-minded Omahans lose interest, much like the children that they claim to be concerned about. They know that if they can stall for a month or so, the population will be on to another "fad" or "trend" and in doing so, the city's news starved media will have something to write and report about in their quest to make Omaha look like a real metropolitan entity instead of the hick town that it really is.

Continuing:

> "We're not saying that every idea in that book you have to
> accept," Garnett said. "Not at all. What we're saying is let's explore
> this whole concept and see where we want to be as a school district
> when it relates to the diverse student population we now serve."

I can answer that for you: dump that book. That will be the conclusion of these white people who are going to feel that they are being told what to think and what to do. They do not like the same impositions on their lives that they place on the lives of minority kids. They don't like being reminded that their racism is so obvious that they have to work on studying it. They want to go back to what they are comfortable with: *pretending* that they know what they doing and *feigning* a concern "for all students" when their tradition and history clearly shows that it is one of the most racist school districts per capita, in the nation.

Garnett further explains that,

> Teachers will be asked to reflect on the book this year, and then
> next year the district will look for ways to apply some of the
> concepts in the classroom and workplace, she said. That will

include looking at "culturally responsive teaching" as a way to
improve achievement for kids, Garnett said.

More bullshit. The schools remain segregated and the same teachers that were there during 2011 are still there. They have a closed system when it comes to hiring and as was the case with the superintendent they hired and had to immediately terminate, the human resource decisions are ass backwards. And as history shows, "Ass backwards planning yields ass-backwards results."

Garnett claims that one of the ways that they would address some of what was in the book would be to include "looking at culturally responsive teaching as a way to improve achievement for kids." The question that one has to ask is what has negatively impacted on the city of Omaha and its district so much to the point where the gap existed in the first place? What was impeding achievement for kids of color? How can white kids achieve and black kids, in the same schools, cannot? The answer is clear, and yet these white people expect us to believe that the same people who created the problem and who have maintained it are somehow going to "overturn themselves" and make everything good for the poor negroes?

Next comes Luanne Nelson, the long-time apologist for the district who I had to make look like an ass a decade or so ago. But that's history. In the case of this purchase here is what she had to say:

> In defense of the district's purchase, OPS spokeswoman Luanne
> Nelson pointed to a study released by two Latino advocacy groups
> in Massachusetts calling for cultural proficiency in that state's
> schools.

Yeah, so what? Is she living in those areas? Does the OPS listen to Latino or Black groups? No. So what good is any reference by this white woman who lives in suburbia and who has been on the OPS dole for over three decades drinking the warm spit of her supervisors and the superintendent? She has no credibility and she surely is not an educator. Citing what is taking place elsewhere only makes Omaha look all the more jejune and sophistic: you would think that Nelson would know this by now.

What those studies pointed out was no different than what I pointed out in my numerous documents, memos and letters to the OPS administration and various members of the school board. In fact it was my 1980 graduate paper that served as the basis for the first official grievance against OPS, using data provided by the Urban League of Nebraska. Check out what is referred to by the news article:

> When there are gaps in achievement between whites and
> minorities, schools need to identify obstacles to learning embedded
> in school culture, policies and practices, according to the study

released by the Sociedad Latina and the University of
Massachusetts' Mauricio Gaston Institute for Latino Community
Development and Public Policy.

That is why I proposed the formation of a Cultural Consultants Commission back in 1980 and then once again in 1995. That is why my Triple One Parents' Union was formed – to empower black parents and to highlight disciplinary abuses taking place within the system. Did OPS pay any attention? Of course not. And LuAnn Nelson was there watching me kicking them in the ass. And now she has the gall to make a reference to groups that are putting in work on the other side of the country. This is what these "educators" are up against.

The news article continues with a quote from a woman who is charged with teacher education from the University of Nebraska-Omaha:

Nancy Edick, dean of the College of Education at the University of
Nebraska at Omaha, said it is "imperative" that teachers are
prepared for increasingly diverse schools. Edick has trained
Millard Public Schools teachers in culturally responsive teaching.

Talking about an "imperative" is easy to do, especially for an administrator. The question is, what has she done since she's been the dean (which she no longer is) that showed that she truly believed in what she just said? This is the benefit of retrospect once again: you can see the lies that these people used as delay tactics to offset or neutralize the overwhelmingly obvious fact that their collective ignorance and neglect have long been a part of the problem. The people who graduate from that College of Education have been taught and mentored by people who sat back and endorsed segregation. They did not fight against it. Now, when there is grant money available and buzz words like "equity," "diversity" and "cultural proficiency" flying around, here they come, hat in hand.

She continues

The hope is that teachers develop an understanding and
appreciation for diversity in the classroom, school and community,
and that they see "the increasing diversity we're all experiencing is
not a threat, it's an opportunity," she said.

And here is the key word: "hope." When it comes to any issue that has to do with race, these white people offer up the same air sandwiches and hope pudding that black ministers do. Hope? How about exchanging some of that "hope" for your next paycheck or, as Richard Pryor once said, "Shit in one hand and pray in the other and let's see which one fills up first."

When white people say "increasing diversity" what they are referring to is the "browning of America," a fact that came to the fore when Time magazine did a 1978 article directed and warning white folks about the growth of the Latino population titled, "It's Your Turn in the Sun." And ever since that time the gradual "browning" and "blackening" of America has caused white people to slightly flip the script and go into "pretense mode" and act as if they have the cultural capacity or wherewithal to treat the same people that they have run from with some semblance of respect and dignity.

The article in the World-Herald (mercifully) concludes:

> "The rich life experiences of a diverse classroom contribute to an excellent education. It's an education that helps prepare our kids for a world they're going to live in, an increasingly diverse world," Edick said.

Now all of a sudden a "diverse" classroom leads to "rich experiences." When did these white educators decide or determine that? If diversity was such a valuable asset, then why is their city residentially and racially segregated? Why is the racial gap in education, health and the legal system actually growing larger? Why is North Omaha continuing to be the target of negative media coverage and a basis for negative demographics which they (educators, legislators, politicians) then turn into appendices in the grant applications to beg for more money to "help the negroes"?

The news article was informative, although nothing new or nerve-shattering. It was an extension of what community people have been fighting against for decades. But as is the case in all spheres of life, white people listen only when they feel threatened or feel that there might be a grant involved. Let me reiterate the wise words of Malcolm X which I used earlier in this brief paper: "Of all our studies, history is best qualified to reward our research."

The Cultural Proficiency Journal: Ecological Fallacies

Jammed with personal anecdotes pawned off as "educational advice" and combined with general truisms, this "book" sounds to me like three essays combined by the authors, spread out into book form, and then given the grandiose title, "The Cultural Proficiency Journey." They made major money off of this little "exchange" from a school district that was so steeped in discrimination and racism that it may have felt it had no other choice. The purchase of the book was, in my view, an act of desperation.

But trust me: there are many more.

The primary problem with the book is that it is far too personalized. The authors claim to be consultants on some level, one of them is the former superintendent of a school district, and they all go around the country talking about cultural proficiency. But the question is: how many of them have seen positive outcomes as a result of all that talking and writing? They get paid to go into districts and tell them what they need to do. But there is no mention of any research that they did before their visits, research that would give them community demographics, poverty rate, history of race relations, the role of the banks in promoting or addressing any "redlining" or segregation patterns that might impact on mill levy and school quality. Things like that.

Without these investigatory moves, what they write is nothing more than conjecture and scholarly advice based on limited knowledge only. It's like a person with a communications background thinking that they can teach black history without first studying it. It's like someone with a PhD in mathematics thinking they can be an architect. In simpler terms, the book is the product of a group of "pals," academically qualified though they may be, who don't give the importance of "cultural education" the attention it deserves. The mistakes they make constitute the "ecological fallacy" that I mentioned earlier.

But now let me share some specific examples.

We already pointed to the poor choice of covers for the book. But if we glean the titles of the chapters, they simply do not jibe with the content of that particular chapter. For instance there are two parts to the book. Part I is titled "Cultural Proficiency and Morality." It contains four sections whose titles are: (1) Oakland Hills; (2) The Tools of Cultural Proficiency; (3) Values, Assumptions, and Beliefs Guide Our Actions; and (4) Morality, Motivation, Purpose and Intent. These chapters read like sections out of any Introduction to Sociology text or any book on Group Theory. The content is simply lacking in substance and application.

For instance, in the "Foreword," the following statements are made that are in need of critique and commentary:

> Educators are called upon to teach every child, regardless of race,
> class, gender, disability, o other markers of difference. This
> imperative has become more important in the rapidly changing
> contexts of U..S. society and education. No longer a monolithic
> society dominated by a single race, the United States is now
> populated with individuals from numerous races and ethnicities (p.
> vii).

This statement is nothing short of historical revisionism. This country was never a "monolithic society dominated by a single race." It was a country that was destroyed by a single race and then, in the wake of that genocidal campaign against the Natives, they set up a country based on race and class. The other "races" that came in were kidnapped Africans and exploited Asians. The Mexicans had already been chased out and the Native Americans had been placed on reservations. When these types of statements are made by people who know better, you know that they suffer from "the avoidance syndrome." They don't want to insult the people who are going to sign their checks to they spend more time trying not to hurt their feelings than they do dealing with the world of reality. But as the old saying teaches, "It is always better to deal with hard, cold facts than to play with pleasant, but unproductive dreams."

The book, in its quest to "sweeten" America's racist history, adds, "Thus, race and culture have increasingly become a central focus in the education of children in U.S. public schools." (p. vii). Sure, after we (black people) embarrassed the nation on international television during the civil rights movement and when we burned the country down during the black power movement. It was only then that these white people knew that "the jig was up" (no pun intended) and decided to fine tune or tweak their racist system. Not change it morally, but simply tweak it with a series of "social disguises" that would make the population think that this nation had learned its lesson.

Nothing could have been further from the truth.

Moving on:

> CampbellJones and colleagues clearly articulate the bottom line for meeting the social, emotional, and educational needs of all children: Schools as organizational structures and the educators in them must confront and change negative beliefs, attitudes, and behaviors toward students who have long been considered "other people's children." (p. vii).

"Must confront"? Or else what? These educators talk all that shit about what people "must" do or "better do" and don't have a damn thing to back it up with. This is not a moral issue or Sunday school where you point to a problematic issue and then "guilt" people into changing or addressing it. This is a system that these people are talking about, one that has made scores of quintillions of dollars being as racist as they are to this day. *Do you think they are going to change simply because you say so?*

Furthermore, they are not articulating any "bottom line." The bottom line for white administrators is revenue generation, profit and financial stability. Anything that comes after that, or that would serve to jeopardize it, is not going to be accepted on any level. The money expended on that book is just part of a smoke screen where the pretense of being concerned is far less costly than change itself.

Omaha as a city and OPS as a district has been successfully using this tactic for centuries.

The "foreword" also claims that, "These issues point to the need for cultural proficiency at all levels of education, but especially in the classroom." (p. viii). These issues may "point to a need for cultural proficiency," but that need is in the eye of the beholder! If Omaha saw a need, they would have addressed it. So evidently the "need" is not shared by the people who make decisions for OPS: not the superintendent, not any of his "Assistant Superintendents" and not the Board of Education. If things remained the way they were none of these entities would give a shit. What is written in that book may be plausible in progressive cities with sizable minority populations, but not in Omaha, nothing more than a glossier version of Hooterville.

Next comes the "Introduction," written by Dr. Linda C. Tillman out of UNC-Chapel Hill, who shares the following:

> The essence of the book can be summed up in the authors' five essential elements of cultural competency – namely, that teachers and leaders are competent when they believe in and have a commitment to social justice, advocacy, the mentoring of underserved students for access to educational opportunity, the mentoring of more privileged students for historical awareness of inequity, and a commitment to leveling the educational and societal playing field for all students regardless of race, class, gender, disability, or other markers of difference. Armed with these commitments, teachers and leaders can fulfill their responsibility to educate every child (p. viii).

These are not "commitments;" these are suggestions or recommendations that have to be decided on. Only after the decision is made can we determine how deep any "commitment" is. So once again, in vintage "horse before the cart" fashion, outside consultants come in (as they do at the city planning level), fast-talk these hicks in suits, pick up a check and take off laughing all the way back to the city they hailed from. And then the local media does a "report" to make it look like OPS is doing its job and is on the "cutting edge" of something. What that could be, I have no idea.

At any rate, let's take a look at was shared in the previous excerpt from the book's "Introduction."

Throughout the book there are references to leveling the playing field. Later in my analysis I expose this cliché for its lack of substance and value, but as a metaphor for social action, it means nothing. First of all, this is no "game" so anyone who is "playing" with the futures of minority kids is an asshole in my book. Secondly, as I point out later, if the game is rigged, it won't matter how "level" the playing field becomes. The same decision makers function as the commissioners, the referees and the coaches. Low income people and minorities are simply "players" whose very presence shows those in power that they still have total control.

Another point from the "Introduction" is the claim that these teachers have to give a shit about social justice or have some semblance of an "historical awareness of inequity." Who do these out of town educators think they are dealing with? The key to Omaha's on-going mastery of racial discrimination is its ability to dupe outsiders into thinking that they (Omaha leadership) actually gives a shit! They have the money and are therefore rife for the plucking as outside consultants know, but other than that, both sides are disingenuous and that is why nothing gets resolved that will improve the life chances of the low-income and/or minority.

As a result, you cannot expect people of this ilk to give a shit about morals or social justice, two terms that continue to appear throughout the book on cultural proficiency. They even go so far as to quote Bible scripture. Why? If the shit in the Bible worked, there would be no need for cultural proficiency consultants! Let me tell you something: Omaha has 458 churches and of that number 116 of them can be found in North Omaha. And yet North Omaha, and eight-square mile area, has more poverty, unemployment, drug abuse, gang abuse and health-related problems than any other area of the city?

The book's "Preface" also includes some issues that are somewhat nebulous. For instance, at the very outset of the preface is a statement that I refer to as "color-coded." It states that, "Our deepest fear is not that we are inadequate. Our deepest fear is that we are powerful beyond measure. It is our light, not our DARKNESS that most frightens us." (p. iv – emphasis added).

Say what? How are you going to address the gradual decline of pink skin (white folks) and still use terms that stigmatize darkness. In my 25 year longitudinal study of the words "dark," "black," "checkered" and others, I've proven beyond the shadow of a doubt that these are terms and images that are here to stay. That is why I have labeled them as being "color-coded." You are what you think; and if you think black is negative and white is good, then that is going to be reflected in everything ranging from your movies and headlines to your everyday conversations and the way you teach your children.

The preface continues by claiming, "In this book, we approach cultural proficiency as a moral framework that helps educators respond in ways that educate each child to achieve high academic standards …" (p. ix). And that is precisely why these educators are going to fail when it comes to traditionally conservative and racist cities like Omaha. Their school district is aimed at producing students who think a certain way: and no 127-page book is going to alter that. This is a point I prove quite cogently in the pages ahead.

The "preface" further opines that,

> The path of cultural proficiency is an *inside-out* approach that professes a transformation of values and beliefs that affect the actions of all members of the school community – administrators, counselors, teachers, students, parents, psychologists, custodians, technicians, secretaries, office managers, and so son (p. ix) (emphasis original)

And this concept of *inside-out* is again mentioned on page 11 where it is written that, "Cultural proficiency is an *inside-out* approach to change, where the individual and the organization intentionally engage in transformational processes to effect change. Moreover, applying this approach requires school system members to critically reflect on the moral underpinnings of school and address, the structures and tactics for which these moral foundations support." (emphasis original). On page 113 we again see the concept of *inside-out*: "A fundamental premise of this book is that we, as educators, must change in order to provide high academic education for each child. Through Cultural Proficiency, we seek an inside-out transformational approach to change for educators.

Let's deal with this inside-out approach, which is almost as ridiculous as the "level playing field" analogy that is also over-used in the book.

A transformation of values? Is there a magic wand hidden somewhere in that book that I might have overlooked? Why would white people change their values when values are a product of their culture? And as we know, "Culture is the basis of all ideas, images and actions. To move is to move culturally, i.e., by a set of values given to you by your culture" (Karenga, 1967). Of course when they say "transformation" they don't mean from negative to positive or from wrong to right: what they really mean is "modify" – change them so that those who are watching them won't be able to see what is taking place *underneath the façade.*

White people don't change unless it is to a better situation that will bring them more money, status or success. In light of this, poor and minority people don't fit into this equation. These 'educators' and their "inside-out strategy is too reliant on introspection, soul-searching and self-scrutiny that white people are not going to engage in when all that will result is treating a few low-income kids or minority students in a different way. In their view, it's simply not worth the effort. Again, OPS's own history and traditions bear this out.

The preface also contains a sub-section where they quote from an article called "Proud Flesh." This quote is ridiculously jejune and far too generic and philosophical to have any real relevance in a book that is about the human condition. As a writer, it appears to me to be nothing short of "padding" or "fluff" and perhaps to give a shout out to the authors (cited as Noli & Jones) who may well be pals or acquaintances of the authors. Who knows? And at this point, who gives a shit?

The preface is followed up with acknowledgements and in my view, it is an indicator of what is taking place throughout higher education in general and secondary level education in particular: white folks with power and black folks with what Dr. Harry Edwards once referred to as "niggerologist" positions.

For instance, three people are acknowledged, one of them is an associate professor and the second is an assistant professor. The third, the only brutha, has the title of, get this: "Coordinator of Cultural Diversity and Extended Learning Opportunities." Ain't that a bitch? I don't know if the two women named are black or not, but that's not my point. My point is that the very existence of titles such as the one for the "coordinator " (not "director") is for a particular reason: and that reason is to show the public that these school systems have "special token positions" and that the person in that position need not be viewed as a threat to those who make the real decisions. In fact, the position may not even be linked to the organization chart!

Following the Acknowledgements is a section labeled, "About the Authors." I don't really care if they're black or not; they are good people with good intentions and they are making a living talking about cultural proficiency to institutions and entities that they full well know don't give a shit about it. They know that despite their claims, the fundamental fact is white people are going through the motions when it comes to educating youth of color. It's going on all over the nation so all the "consulting" in the world is nothing but a smokescreen that the schools are located in use to make it appear as if "we care about the Blacks and the Latinos." *But the practices of elementary, intermediate, secondary and even post-secondary decision makers and teachers, clearly show just the opposite.*

I have sued and filed grievances against school districts – and won. I brought this very school system to its knees twice for civil rights violations: placing black kids in EMH programs and not enough in Gifted and Talented Programs. That was in 1980. *Then I had to do it again in 1981.* I had to file a grievance to get "Black Pete" taken out of the Christmas handout kits that were distributed first of all, throughout the Milwaukee Public Schools and then, a year later, in the Omaha Public Schools. In both cases I was thanked and promised that the sidekick of Sinter Claus, as is the myth in Holland, would no longer include "Black Pete," a black dwarf with horns who beat kids that misbehaved with a birch rod!

And there's more. But the point is that I know what I'm talking about. These people in educational administration think in long-range terms with their white supremacy programs and teaching approaches. At the same time people like these authors – as well-meaning as they may be – are just coming to town to jack these racists off, make them feel good, pick up a check and then get out of town by sundown. If what I write is not true, then let them come here and publicly debate me – an award winning educator – on the subject.

I say this to inform you, the reader, that I can see through the bullshit. I was in Milwaukee when the African-American Immersion School movement was underway. I opposed it because it was too gender biased – they wanted the bruthas but not the sistahs. I was editor of the black newspaper in that city and I wrote about it. Do some research. I led community movements to get principals fired and got rid of one Assistant Superintendent in Milwaukee. I spearheaded bringing an end to forced busing in Omaha, and I closed town a proprietary school in Milwaukee – Technology Institute of Milwaukee – back in 1990.

So when these "scholars" make certain statements, I can immediately spot the ecological fallacies inherent in them. For instance Brenda CampellJones, one of the authors being introduced is described thusly: "Through the lens of cultural proficiency, she coaches and facilitates the change process in school districts that are making systemic changes for academic achievement" (p. xi).

She can do all the "coaching" and "facilitating" she wants to, but it is only going to last until she leaves town. Then it's going to be back to business as usual. Another author, Randall Lindsey "has a practice that is centered on educational consulting and issues related to diversity. And here is how he is described:

> All of Randy's experiences have been in working with diverse populations and his area of study is the behavior of white people in multicultural settings. It is his belief and experience that too often white people only observe multicultural issues instead of being personally involved with them. To that end, he designs and implements interventions that address the roles of all sections of the society (p. xvi).

Do these people really believe that they are ushering in change or do they just write this shit as a reference to give to future contractors?

By the time we mercifully get to Part I, the first area are the Oakland Hills which is totally irrelevant and despite author claims, is no indicator of what is taking place in education anywhere else. I lived in Oakland back in the late 1970s, right behind Castlemont High School, and all we heard about the Oakland Hills was that they hated any niggas coming up there. If there's been a change, then that is good for those who can afford it. The fact that Oakland is majority black and yet only 15% of the Oakland Hills-area is black speaks volumes about race relations in a city that at one time truly "had it going on" (headquarters for the Black Panther Party over on Grover, for instance).

When scholars use the word "dilemma," I have to believe they chose that word intentionally. A dilemma is more than a problem: it is the choice between two or more equally undesirable alternatives. Therefore when these writers talk about the "Oakland Hills Dilemma as Emblematic" (p. 10), this bothers me. The word again appears on pages 70-71. In the former case is another sub-heading, "Mastering the Dilemma" (an oxymoron if I ever heard one) and in the latter case in the following statement: "Educators are plagued with dilemmas on a daily basis where they face conflicting "right" choices resulting in competing "right" actions …"

These are supposed to be "educators" meaning that they are supposed to know the meanings of certain words that they use. When you put those words in a book, it implies that you are so confident in that selection of the words that you don't mind widely circulating it. If these buttheads are dealing with "dilemmas," then they are beaten before they start. This word implies that the situation is intractable, and if that is the case, then why are they selling these white people a bill of goods knowing beforehand that nothing is going to change for the better?

The sophistic chapter concludes with some workbook "assignments" if that's what you want to call them.

The second session of Part I claims to be about "Tools of Cultural Proficiency" – as if the authors have a monopoly on knowing what all the tools are, regardless of context or situation. For instance, the following statement is pontificated on page 16:

> Profound school change is an organic, nonlinear process comprised
> of two overlapping and interactive phases: The recognition of
> development of a moral consciousness for doing what is right …
> An ethical framework of moral principles to guide one's behavior.

Reading more like a textbook on Moral Philosophy and Reasoning, the chapter appears to be plagiarized from books that address these philosophical topics. But the real error comes in terms of applicability of these concepts. Who do these authors think they are? Where is their magic wand? These are white supremacy systems we are talking about, not some schoolyard bullies who need a time out! Page 28 makes my point rather cogently where they stated that, "Competency is when an educator or school has incorporated the essential elements into their practice to the extent that they develop at least these five commitments." And then they list the following on page 28:

- A commitment to social justice that addresses the educational needs of every current and emerging cultural group in the school and community.
- A commitment to advocacy that is natural, normal, and effective.

- A commitment to mentoring the historically underserved and to give them educational opportunities that allow them to thrive academically and socially.
- A commitment to mentoring those historically well served by current practice to become aware of and responsive to those historically underserved individuals and cultural groups.
- A commitment to leveling the playing field so every cultural group can participate as colleagues, students, and/or members of the community.

As one educator to a trio of others (the ones who claim to have written the book on cultural proficiency), let me offer some responses to the previous five commitments that are a chapter that they titled, "Cultural Proficiency and Morality."

Who developed these "essential elements" and where have they been? Were they in existence in the 1950s? The 1960s? Do they exist in black colleges or high schools that are predominantly black? Do the teachers know about these and are teacher colleges informing students that these are "essential"? I think the only thing about these five points being "essential" is that the authors SAY that they are. So let's take a look and then compare them with the world of reality.

First off, this "commitment to social justice." Why is that essential to the teacher in the classroom when that same teacher and his neighbors lack this commitment in the greater community? A segregationist is going to believe in segregation no matter what their occupation is. Therefore, what makes these white teachers any different? And isn't it a fact that any black teacher ("Negro," as they called us then) that got involved in any activity would be dubbed a "communist" or a "rabble rouser" and would therefore be fired for such actions? Where do these "educators" get this bullshit from? Certainly not from the world we are living in!

Secondly, an essential element has to be "advocacy that is natural, normal and effective." What kind of advocacy? Back in the day the common theme was, "The key to the classroom is the key to the bedroom." How about "segregation now and forever," as espoused by George Wallace? What about former OPS administrator and teacher Harry S. Burke (who has a high school named after him) saying that "No negro will ever be a principal as long as I'm in this system"? Aren't these forms of advocacy? Without saying what TYPE of advocacy, these educators are making a grave omission. What is most frequently and most vehemently advocated by white people is exactly what we are seeing now: pervasive whiteness.

Third, this "mentoring" thing that seems to be the craze. These white people in Omaha are capitalizing on it – and they are also getting paid to do it. I don't think that white people can mentor black kids. Even these educators have put together a book promoting "cultural proficiency" and that is because of the lack of it on the part of white folks! Black people don't culturally mistreat white kids! So then, calling for mentoring is moot unless that mentoring has a culturally relevant message and magnitude – two points again overlooked by these "educators."

Furthermore, who are the "historically underserved"? Is it Black and Latino kids? Or wouldn't white kids also be considered "underserved" since what they are learning is not going to endear them to any person of color and may well lead to them getting their asses kicked? An entire section on the "underserved" should have been included because many of these white teachers are experts at "playing dumb" and pretending that they don't know who the "underserved" are. After all, since they don't see lynchings, night riders and "no negroes allowed" signs, many of them think racial progress has actually been made!

Fourth, more mentoring in terms of the well served becoming aware of the underserved, which touches upon my previous point. My question is: why? This is a nation that is rooted in capitalism and in that kind of system there are "the haves and the have nots". Why should white teachers and students give a shit about those who are lacking or who are underserved? This book needs to give some reasons why such concern and why such mentoring is somehow an "essential element."

Fifth and finally, is the element that contains that phrase that I detest so much: "Level playing field." White people and their negro lackeys continue to use this phrase (it is also used in the book) and it is actually a phrase that shows how foolish the people using it are. To talk about a level playing field implies that there is only one: the one owned and controlled by the white man. If we are playing cards and you pull out six aces, and I continue to want to play that game with you, I am no longer being "fair" I'm being "foolish." If the field is not level then we have to realize that it is for a reason: and that is reason enough to get the hell out of their game and establish a "playing field" of our own choosing!

Furthermore, as I've written elsewhere, a "level playing field" means nothing when the white man controls the bats, the rules, the balls, the goals and the referees calling the game! And "participation" is not evidence of fairness: Black people participated in slavery *but at what level of life?*

The next section of this chapter on "Cultural Proficiency and Morality" is section 3 and it is titled, "Values, Assumptions, and Beliefs Guide Our Actions." Again, sociological concepts transferred to the realm of education.

This section begins with a 1995 quote from Lis Delpit: "We do not really see through our eyes or hear through our ears, but through our beliefs." That is bullshit! Our eyes show us what is around us and our ears give us the skill to listen to how what we see is interpreted. Only THEN can we determine what we choose to believe or disbelieve. And the Omaha Public Schools shelled out more than $130,000 for this kind of sophistic drivel?

This chapter begins by revolving around a "Ladder of Inference" which is a hierarchical step by step "guide" that sounds sociological in its foundation. There are supposedly seven (7) rungs on this ladder and every step is nothing short of a general truism. So jejune is this mish-mash that as examples I will show what these educators have to say about two components: (1) values and (2) beliefs.

In regard to values under the subheading "What I Value Most," it is written on page 43:

> When you consider an action by another and something inside
> says, "That's really not me," most likely you have felt a twinge
> from a deeply held personal value. *Values* are deeply held view of
> what we appreciate, respect, or cherish. They come from many
> courses as a part of the socialization process – parents, caregivers,
> religious teachings, schools, peers, people we admire, and culture.
> Many are grounded in our childhood experiences while we take on
> other views as adults. (emphasis original)

Playing with sociology is like playing with matches; if you don't know what you're doing you'll get burned. The previous definition is sugar-coated bullshit. Values are not only rooted in "appreciation, respect" or things we cherish. They can also be negative. For instance, in his listing of American values, sociologist Robin Williams added "racism" to the list. This is definitely an American value, but Americans often deny it exists.

When white people describe all that is bad or negative, they use terms like "dark," "black," "shadow," "tainted," "checkered" and so on. This is based on their value system. When they want to talk about something being good or positive, it is reflected in their color-coded values: a "white lie" is a little one; "angel food cake" is white, "fair-skinned" means light and so on. What the educators wrote about is misleading and piecemeal. People reading this book deserve, "the truth, the whole truth, and nothing but the truth." Not someone's manipulated manifestations of reality.

Next are "beliefs." The educators write that, "Beliefs are principles by which we live. They give us confidence that the actions we take are correct and true." But that doesn't mean that they ARE true. At one time white people thought that black people had tails. This was a belief. Was it true? Of course not. I do not accept this definition of the word "beliefs." They need not be correct or true even though it is a given that they "give confidence" and they constitute "principles by which we live."

As was the case with the definition of "values," these educators are catering to white educators and administrators. So careful are they not to offend, they tiptoe around the very issues and variables that they themselves introduce! I've just given you two examples.

The fourth section is titled "Morality" and again it begins with a quote, this one dated from 1981, and it is as ambiguous as the others they selected. Check it out:

> Although the role of government is important, the enforcement of civil rights transcends federal actions. Enforcement is rather a larger responsibility of American society; its failure lies within the confines of the nation's morals and mores (p. 59).

Say what??! How does enforcement of something as vague as "civil rights" become the role of the society to enforce? Those were the people who, by and large, negated civil liberties, created and affirmed segregation, and then had to have civil rights laws imposed on them BY the government! The previous paragraph sounds to me like a call for "state's rights," and that term is always a red light for people of color because the states are going to do what the white majority calls for.

A second point that needs to be corrected is the claim by the educators that the failure of American society lies in the confines of the nation's morals and mores. What? American society has not "failed" as far as they are concerned. Those in power and those who control education have a plethora of lies at the ready to counter any call for "civil rights" that might be made. From "we're a work in progress" and "we didn't know" to "we can't find any qualified minorities" and "we need more inclusion, equity and diversity," this nation has always been able to sidetrack its racist ways. And I believe that these educators are aware of that. So what they opt for is a chance to promise to help maintain the ersatz goal of "equity" by appearing before groups, giving away books and then blaming it on the masses of parents who are too busy to give a shit about either.

The concept of "moral purpose" as continually reiterated in this chapter, is also questionable. Quoting from others (namely Fullan) who wrote a book called *The New Meaning of Educational Change*, the educators, like Fullan, fall far short. Take note:

> Fullan (2003) argues rather convincingly that moral purpose should be front and center of all professional actions in the educational setting … "let me be explicit … The only goal worth talking about is transforming the current school system so that large-scale, sustainable, continuous reform becomes built in" … Moral purpose of the highest order is having a system where all students learn, the gap between high and low performance becomes greatly reduced, and what people learn enables them to be

successful citizens and workers in a morally based knowledge society" (p. 62).

What society is he talking about? These utopian ideals have nothing to do with the "new meaning of educational change" that is the title of his book unless that change is going to take place on some faraway planet in some galaxy that exists only in his mind! Fullan talks about "the only goal worth talking" about and then outlines what HE thinks that goal should be. Those in power know what they want the goals to be, and that is creating more obedient workers that will submit to authority, report to work on time, and never complain. So this is in direct contradiction to his search for "a morally based knowledge society." That kind of society never existed in the United States!

All students learn and the gap is "greatly reduced"? These "dreams" run counter to the money that is generated by poverty grants and bullshit remedial programs! These schools pimp the handicapped and the allocation of money provides them with more money if the student has a disability. Don't these educators know that? Moral purpose? In America, politics aren't becoming more moral; morality is becoming more political" (Karenga, 1967).

Now we come to Part II of the book, and the title is "Case Studies: From Reflection to Action." To tell you the truth, I don't give a shit about a case study unless first and last names are shared, and some type of demographic data is given. What is the person's race and ethnicity? When was the information gathered? In far too many instances as I analyze these white reports and review books written by so-called scholars, they come up with these people with first names and then they make up a "life" for them.

There are three sections in this part of the book. The titles are named after what the authors view as "barriers." So to begin with, they are admitting that barriers do exist, but they don't point the finger at any specific group. They don't even have the term "racism" or "white supremacy" in the index. In the entire book they don't even refer to Brown v. Board of Education, which essentially paved the way for the race-based educational considerations that this country has yet to live up to. So that's another barrier: cultural ignorance by people who should know better.

At any rate, the three chapters are: (Chapter 5) Barrier 1: Systems of Oppression; (Chapter 6) Barrier 2: Resistance to Change; and (Chapter 7) Barrier 3: A Sense of Privilege and Entitlement. The first part, "Systems of Oppression" really contains nothing of criticism, although there are a plethora of debatable points surrounding the title. And why? Because if they admit there are "systems" then these educators should know that they can only be effectively countered with an equally powerful "systemic" approach. That was what "black power" was all about in the 1960s – the aim was to counteract "white power." So these little programs, workbooks and skits don't mean shit when you're going up against a system that has hundreds of years of racist success controlling and dominating the very people that this book purports to want to defend and develop.

The second section, "Barrier 2: Resistance to Change" is, like the first section, graph and chart-heavy and filled with workbook type pages that the reader is supposed to respond to. Yeah – fat chance of that happening. One somewhat relevant point lies in the definition of "change" that is offered. The authors write, "Resistance to change is another of the three barriers to cultural proficiency. This barrier emanates from the perspective that change needs to happen as the result of others' actions, not by the actions of one's self." (p. 87). This is a moral philosophy issue, but let me drive home a point about Omaha, specifically.

In Omaha there is racial segregation. With or without busing the utopian concepts espoused in the book The Cultural Proficiency Journey are going to waste. The context promotes segregation, the media endorses it, and the politicians build around it. Race in Omaha comes in handy only when they beg for more poverty and social service or community development grants. Having a sizable Black and Latino population qualifies an otherwise lily-white city for free money from the government. Once that money arrives, the white decision makers hire their own race members (and family) for jobs and dole out token dollars to a few "negro" groups who claim to be about "community development."

The largest school system in the state, also located in Omaha, uses a similar formula. As the black student population grew, so did the intensification of their segregation. So they build schools in within the boundaries of the black community to pacify the ignorant negroes. Even when there was busing, those kids still returned to the black community. Omaha remains segregated by design, and the public schools are part and parcel of that method of operation.

Therefore, when it comes to the collective consciousness of whites in Omaha, the concept of "we" IS "me," and vice-versa. If there is one thing that almost all of them agree on it is the fact that North Omaha (where the blacks reside) is a dangerous place to avoid. By extension, you can't hate the root of a tree and not hate the tree itself. If North Omaha is to be avoided, then so too are the people who live there.

The concept of "resistance to change" therefore becomes synonymous with "maintaining tradition" and "keeping the white way of life." The "hiring" of these consultants and the purchasing of this book are small prices to pay in order to pacify OPS workers who are gullible enough to believe that "OPS truly cares." Nothing could be further from the truth, and in my book, these "educators" need their asses kicked for profiting on racist scams like the one that OPS ran on them.

The third part of this section of the book deals with "Barrier 3: A Sense of Privilege and Entitlement." The educators, so afraid to make racial references, refer to the issue as just being one of "privilege" when, in reality, the proper name is "white privilege" and neither Christine Sleeter or Peggy MacKintosh – the two leading advocates who are most widely published in the area of "white privilege" – are not even mentioned in the book and therefore not cited in the index. Again, selective research limits holistic results. Backwards ass OPS administrators, teachers and counselors would not know this: a true scholar, such as myself, *would.*

The section of the book begins on page 101 and it is this page that contains all of the points (three major ones to be exact) that I find most worthy of addressing.

To begin with,

> A sense of privilege and entitlement arises from indifference to
> benefits that accrue solely by one's membership in a gender, race,
> or other cultural group. This barrier encapsulates the practice of
> denying one group's societal benefits while awarding those same
> benefits to others. It recognizes that benefits gained by the
> dominant group accrue over time and passed from one generation
> to the next. (p. 101).

What other group has a sense of privilege on the level of these white people in America (and the ones in Europe)? It might be argued that women as a group feel a sense of privilege, but linked to that sense are a slew of institutional arrangements that defile and degrade them at the same time. The issue is white supremacy, and these "educators" are lumping in a bunch of other members of "protected classes" whose members may themselves be racist! The white handicapped, the white veteran, the white lesbian, the white gay, the white Slav, Jew or Italian: they all had a hand in black oppression on some level, from back in the day up to the present. This seems to be a point that the educators don't want to address: the *historio-genetic* basis for the oppression that they purport to be combating! (See Michael Bradley's *The Iceman Inheritance* for a more detailed analysis)

Secondly is where the following insipid tidbit is shared by the educators under the section on "Privilege and Entitlement":

> It is common to see historically oppressed populations of children
> – African American, Latino and native American – clustered in
> low-level academic courses while upper-level courses are filled
> with historically advantaged groups, primarily Euro-American.
> The clear distribution of academic benefits for Whites and lack

> thereof for people of color is evident in the achievement data
> reported over the past two decades … (p. 101).

The disparities in academic benefits may be "evident in the achievement data," but that is after the fact. Such realities are also evident in the histories of these school system. Their recent Britney Spears-like claims of "oops I did it again," continue even after it has been established by the courts that discrimination was the name of the game. And as has been proven elsewhere, OPS hated the idea of allowing black people some semblance of fair play that even after the 1954 decision was rendered, it wasn't until 1976 that OPS complied with the desegregation order and only did so then after spending in excess of $300,000 fighting the order! Why? Because of the very feelings of "privilege and entitlement" that these educators want to attribute to everyone who is a victim without lying responsibility for a system full of beneficiaries of both at the door of the people at the top – the people who purchased those books!

My third and final concern with this section of the book lies in what the authors refer to as "key questions":

> Key questions associated with this barrier include:
> - Are there practices or policies in place that serve one group better than another? Are certain families served better than others? Are schools in one zip code served better than schools in another?
> - Do some groups purposefully have unfair advantages over others? What beliefs support this practice?
> - Do new teachers get the last support? Are they forced to move from room to room, due to space issues, while certain teachers stay in a single room? Do veteran teachers get their choice of students? What are the underlying values that support these practices?

Let's deal with these questions as they specifically relate to Omaha and its chances for some form of "cultural re-conversion (which is what I believe it needed).

In regard to the first set of questions, of course there are policies in place that serve one group better than another. In fact, there are informal policies, *defacto* policies that served to exclude entire groups so that the white students could have advantage in a segregated setting. The next query asks if certain families are served better than others? Evidently so: Omaha ranks number one in the nation in black child poverty and also ranks number on black youth homicide. Then comes the question, "are schools in one zip code served better than schools in another." The answer is again yes. In a segregated context, zip codes are the most efficient way to determine the life-chances of residents. In Omaha that would be 68104, 68110, 68111 and 68107, the latter representing *el barrio.*

The second set of questions is even more ridiculous with the first one asking if some groups "purposefully have unfair advantages over others"? They need not have used the word "unfair;" just the fact that one group has any kind of advantage over others, when added to unbridled white discretion that permeates decision making all over the school system, means that the end result will be a racially skewed set of rules, policies and resources! The second inquiry is, "What beliefs support this practice"? It is a quid pro quo, a mutually supportive system: white supremacy is the umbrella with discriminatory practices maintaining it – as is the case all over America. Why do these educators ask such insipid questions to these ignorant blue collar racists?

The third set of questions is more teacher oriented and directed. The first one asks if new teachers get the least support. Of course they do, but that is based on race. So a new blonde in a short skirt and a tight blouse is going to be catered to while a black woman, new to Omaha, is going to receive short shrift in the same way that she would when she shops at a store or encounters any act that has to do with human decency. There are businesses in Omaha where white people behind the counter still refuse to put your change directly in your hand, but would rather place it on the counter.

Are new teachers forced to move from room to room due to space issues while "certain teachers" stay in a single room? This could be a logistical issue, not one based on race. But in a racist environment anything is possible. And if you have segregated schools, then that school is isolated beyond the pale of being concerned about the rights of the teachers in that school (unless they are white). So this question, like the book for the most part, is a waste of time. And again, a dumb general question that asks, "What are the underlying values that support these practices?"

Can there be any doubt that we know what those values are? Have I noted schooled you on the relationship between values and culture? Have I not provided you with supportive snippets of the history of this racist town masquerading as a metro area? If you understand these things, then there is really no need to understand or ask what these racist relationships tend to produce. It doesn't matter if you're talking about Omaha or Orlando, Oakland or Oak Cliff (TX), it's the same when the white man is calling the shots. The purchase of these 8,000 books was nothing more than a smokescreen, plain and simple.

With the questions having ended the gist of the book, the final section of the rather insipid cultural proficiency book is titled, "Heuristic Reflection" and again, it starts off with a quote that is moot unless directed at a group that is a part of the oppressor class. The quote, from Kempis (1980) reads as follows: "Who hath a greater combat than he that laboreth to overcome himself? This ought to be our endeavor, to conquer ourselves, and daily to wax stronger." (p. 113).

What? If it sounds Biblical it is because it is. The quote comes from a book by Thomas Kempis titled, *The Imitation of Christ*. Now here are educators who are talking about equity and cultural respect and here they are quoting from the very instrument that has assisted in the oppression of people of color all over the United States. Finally the use of the word "wax" has a Greek and a Jewish history and once again, a book that is supposed to be about cultural proficiency quotes from a book that has been used to oppress and from two groups – Jews and Greeks – who were intimately involved in the exploitation and co-opting of African culture and history.

Or didn't the "educators" know that?

The book (mercifully) winds down and on page 115 is a quote that places blame but an invisible oppressor (no as not to jeopardize book sales and piss off their white oppressors). Here is what these "educators" wrote:

> The culturally proficient journey requires that educators question tradition, or , more forcefully stated, question the truth about how we educate children. We face a reality that many of us are educated by schools that created, maintained, and propagated
> - racial segregation,
> - gender inequality,
> - academic tracking systems,
> - religious disparities,
> - homophobia, and/or
> - ableism

If these writers and the systems they claim to seek to change are willing to admit to the previously stated conscious, on-going and traditional actions that the schools were responsible for, and they are willing to admit that during the sponsorship of all of the previously cited "isms" that the schools nevertheless continued to receive mega-funding and generate grant money in other ways, then what is the purpose of "the cultural proficiency journey"? No system can condemn itself. The only thing that has gotten these white people to change in the small ways that they have were the threats of violence, threats of cutting their funding or actual violence. Read the history, "educators."

Then, as if to add insult to injury, they attempt to offset the facts that they previously listed with a quote from the so-called "Prince of Peace":

> Dr. Martin Luther King, Jr. (1963) reminds us, "Never forget that everything Hitler did in Germany was legal." King's observation urges us to give attention to our moral obligation to humanity more

> so than legal mandates for forced responsibility … During his
> campaign for President of the United States of America, Senator
> Barack Obama's speech in Philadelphia echoes King's sentiment
> … However, without our willingess to act from these principles,
> they are simply seeds without soil (p. 115).

These Omaha white people in the schools – the ones that the educators don't want to mention by race -- have a lot of gall making any reference at all to a quote from a pacifist about the race-hating Hitler. For one reason, this country had laws that made segregation by race legal. This country was lynching and castrating black men and raping white women for centuries. This country had a system of legalized enslavement which was replete with on-going campaigns of dehumanization and cultural brainwashing.

Secondly, quoting Martin King Jr., and his campaign of what I call "one-way integration" only shows the mealy-mouthed, passive, milquetoast "we don't want to offend the decision makers" approach employed by the educators and hence, their book. If this book is a reflection of a "cultural proficiency journey," then that journey is headed for failure because the "captains" of the ship – in this case these well-meaning "educators" are steering these white people toward a course that is only going to further perpetuate mis-education of children of color. The book, *The Cultural Proficiency Journey*, only serves to pacifies them and mis-diagnose the racial situation. *And either the people who ordered the book and commissioned these "educators" were idiots, or all of this is by design.*

You choose.

PROPERTY TAXES AND LAND MANIPULATION

As stated elsewhere, without property tax relief, the state's population has no real reason (other than "tradition") to remain in Nebraska. It appears that the majority of Nebraska's state departments and the institutions that depend on funding and resources from these entities is deteriorating at an unabated rate. By offering tax reductions and various tax-related incentives for people to come to Nebraska and construct building, this state is going to wither away like the last leaves of a painfully prolonged autumn.

A story in the April 2, 2015 issue of the Omaha World Herald titled, "Nebraska's Property Tax Credit Fund May Grow to $200M Per Year" provides some information that will show the true state of Nebraska and its population. According to that article,

> LINCOLN — Nebraska property owners would share $200 million
> a year in tax reduction under a tentative budget decision reached
> Wednesday. Members of the Appropriations Committee voted to
> increase the state Property Tax Credit Fund by $60 million
> annually. That's up from the $45 million increase the committee
> had included in its preliminary budget and matches the amount that
> Gov. Pete Ricketts has been pushing lawmakers to approve.
> Ricketts applauded the committee's action while saying more
> could be done to ease the tax burden on Nebraskans. (Stoddard,
> 2015)

Ease the tax burden on Nebraskans as the state is bleeding money? Ease the tax burden when revenue streams are drying up? Ease the tax burden on citizens when the people who were chosen to run various agencies are begging, busted and forced to resign because of theft, mismanagement and malfeasance? What kind of fantasy world is governor Ricketts living in?

He adds,

> "I will continue to work with the Legislature to prioritize tax relief
> and stop tax increases this session," he said, in a nod to the full
> Legislature's vote to advance a gas tax increase earlier Wednesday.
> State Sen. Heath Mello of Omaha, the committee chairman, said
> the Appropriations Committee has made property tax relief a
> priority. (Stoddard, 2015)

Ricketts and Heath Mello readily admit that they are going to work with the lawmakers to "prioritize tax relief and stop tax increases." In other words, he is going to deny the reality of Nebraska's financial problems and continue to work to pacify the voters so that he can stay in office. The old maxim teaches us that, "You cannot alter until you first admit." Nebraska's leadership, from back in the day of Charles Thone to the present, have been able to successfully pacify Nebraskans with their lies, which is why you see political flip flops in terms of political party; one era it's a Democratic governor, another one is a Republican. It comes down to who can tell the biggest lie, and one of the most successful fabrications has been to promise to provide tax relief.

Continuing, Senator Heath Mello offers the following:

> He said the committee opted for the $45 million annual increase in
> the tax credit fund in its preliminary budget, issued in late
> February, while waiting to see what property tax proposals might
> be put forth by the Revenue and Education Committees. Now, with
> agency budget hearings completed and the picture on other
> legislation clearing, committee members wanted to opt for the
> larger amount, he said. (Stoddard, 2015).

That was then and this is now, a year later. Now they're whining about a potential $900 million budget shortfall. (Remember earlier where Dr. Hank Bounds of the University of Nebraska system claimed that he had things under control and the budget problems faced by the NU system and the state would be eradicated in 150 years?). So in this case it was Sen. Health Mello who lied and used stall tactics and political rhetoric to pacify the weak-minded Nebraska citizenry and it worked. Here's what Senator Mello claimed:

> Mello said he was working on a plan to offset the increase in the
> property tax credits within the larger state budget proposal. He said
> he was committed to leaving $42 million for other legislative
> actions. That's the amount that the state revenue forecast exceeded
> estimated spending in the preliminary budget. (Stoddard, 2015).

Wishful thinking, because what he is proposing can't possibly consider "unforeseen circumstances." And because of the graft and grifting that takes place all over the Nebraska administration, there's a lawsuit being filed or a scandal being exposed on a monthly basis. The residents leave it to the people they elect or who are appointed and those people take advantage of their respective posts and use those positions to "run with the money." If Sen. Mello doesn't understand this basic tradition of Nebraska politics, then it only stands to reason that he would continue to see the "sunny side of the street," as attested to in the above paragraph.

And yet the Senator continues with his utopian "There's-no-place-like-home" believe in the Nebraska economy:

> Mello said he was looking at reducing other areas of the budget, as
> well as at tapping cash funds and unspent appropriations from the
> current year. "I think our final product is shaping up to be a
> responsible budget that prioritizes property tax relief, investments
> in economic development and investments in education" while
> addressing problems such as the corrections system, he said.
> (Stoddard, 2015).

If you reduce one area of the budget, you impact on the jobs related with that area. When you impact those jobs, you impact on the people who have those jobs. Once you do that, you begin to retard and distort the political landscape. Once that is done you have more upheaval because you flood the system with applications from various exploiters who capitalize on economic weakness and seek to get their foot in the door. One of my Master's degrees is in Political Science, with an emphasis in Nebraska politics: I've studied how these "men" flip flop, change parties and will do almost anything to stay on the government dole. Considering this, Sen. Mello's optimistic view should be tempered with a deeper understanding of the history of his state.

Giving these hicks "property relief" is a pacification measure that sounds good but merely splices into the long-term economic development potential of a given area – the way Omaha is doing with its on-going abuse of Tax Increment Financing (TIF). In the eye of the Nebraska politician and the Omaha exploiter of those politics, "short term pleasure yields long term pain." But do they care? No. They're tradition is one of kicking the can down the road. That is why the problems are recurring, perpetual and will eventually be the undoing of the Cornhusker State.

Instead more ideas that lead to programs and plans that don't work seem to be the tendency and tradition. For instance:

> The Property Tax Credit Fund was created under former Gov.
> Dave Heineman in 2007. It provides credits directly to property
> owners, which show up as a line on their annual tax statements.
> The $60 million increase would provide about $45 more in credits
> for the owner of a $150,000 home if the total valuation of property
> in the state was unchanged. (Stoddard, 2015).

Of what good are Property Tax credits in a state where the property is being under-valued? Of what good are these credits to homeowners whose homes are hocked to the hilt? All of this sounds good (not really), but you have to remember that implementation and application are paramount to a plan's effectiveness. And so despite approaches that might work in other parts of the country, the decision makers have to keep in mind that Nebraska's residents don't think clearly in most cases. Nebraska's financial planning is now, as it has been for a century, an on-going "work in progress."

Continuing:

> Mello noted that the Appropriations Committee has work yet to do
> on its budget package and that decisions made so far could be
> revisited. The committee's budget package is due to the full
> Legislature by April 28, the 70th day of the session. By then, the
> state's official revenue forecasting board will have met again and
> other legislative committees may have taken additional action.
> (Stoddard, 2015).

"Has work yet to do." "Decisions made could be revisited." These nebulous references stall time and show that once again there is nothing definitive in the planning process. There are no concrete, time-lined oriented, outcomes. Nebraskans don't know much about the type of planning that will lead to concrete solutions, which is why they encounter the same problems time-and-time again. That which cannot be co-opted, confiscated or plagiarized from neighboring states simply is not on the planning table. They spend millions bringing in fellow white "experts" who come in, take the money and offer up piecemeal programs which don't work because the experts didn't stick around long enough to oversee the implementation of those ideas. Why? Because they (the experts) knew that after meeting the Nebraska "braintrust," there was no way that the programs would work.

In 2015 the following claim was made:

> So far, the Revenue Committee has advanced a bill that would provide exemptions for people paying personal property taxes. But a measure to reduce the assessed value of farm and ranch land is stuck in committee. The Education Committee, meanwhile, is looking to next year to make changes in the state aid formula that could offset property taxes. School districts receive the bulk of local property tax revenue. (Stoddard, 2015).

And just look at the quality and caliber of its largest school district: begging for federal money and using remedial approaches to stabilize and otherwise moribund system. And yet there is where "the bulk of local property tax revenue" goes? Since Tax Incremental Financing rapes areas of their tax base, as does the construction of all of these nonprofit buildings that find themselves hunkering down in the poverty zip codes of North Omaha, where is the tax revenue going to come from for the long term?

An old cultural nationalist once wrote, "To go back to tradition is the first step forward." In the case of Nebraska and its tax problems, history is best qualified to reward our research, as Malcolm X taught. If these two points can be taken seriously and followed, then the gravity of the situation can be better understood. And from there, more sane and serious planning, policies and procedures can be developed.

The Farmland Crisis

According to an episode of "Elementary," diabetes kills four million people every year. When I heard that number I researched it – and guess what? A 2012 article from United Nations radio said that in 2012, the United Nations health agency estimated that 3.4 million people died every year from diabetes, and that almost 80 percent of the deaths occur in developing countries (United Nations radio, 2012). And according to the American Diabetes Association, 1.4 million Americans are diagnosed with diabetes every year.

You may ask, what does diabetes have to do with the farmland crisis. I blame farmers DIRECTLY for the rise and proliferation of diabetes because of what they have been placing in their crops and their livestock, that's what it has to do with it! In order to make more profit, these hicks are injecting their animals and their crops with all kinds of steroid-type ingredients and are genetically engineering bigger and larger crops and animals. What goes in is what comes out. And once we digest it, the human body cannot adjust – the result is diabetes and related diseases.

Nebraska is a rural state, which means that the concept of "agribusiness" and the commitment to farming are vital to the state's survival. In February of 2016 it was learned that the farm economy's values were plummeting. According to the article,

> FOURTH QUARTER 2015
> Farmland values in the Tenth District softened in the fourth quarter of 2015 as farm income continued to weaken. Looking ahead, bankers generally indicated they expect further moderation of both farmland values and cash rents alongside relatively low prices for agricultural commodities and low farm income. Reductions in farm income continued to affect credit conditions, and bankers expected loan repayment rates to deteriorate further in the coming months. (Kauffman & Clark, 2016).

When bankers talk about anticipating "further moderation" of anything, that's going to affect the way they loan money in the future. With no loans, the farmers are screwed. In the past they've been able to borrow money and repay it using the interest that was generated after they deposited the loan in an interest generating account. With that scam over, what are they going to do? They can't "rely on their wits" because the track record makes it clear that Nebraska farmers are also lacking in *that* area. What to do, what to do?

When credit conditions are affected, the state's overall economy is also impacted. Once again, the state is falling short, continuing to make the same kinds of projection-related, hiring and management errors, and they pay the price each and every time. I believe that Nebraska's best days are behind it. But the only way to break the news to a low-intelligence public is to piecemeal out the bad news, to break it up so that the situation won't sound as catastrophic as it really is. For instance, note the following:

> Farmland values in the Tenth District dipped again in the fourth quarter. According to respondents of the Tenth District Survey of Agricultural Credit Conditions, values of nonirrigated and irrigated cropland decreased 4 percent and 2 percent, respectively, from a

> year ago … With the fourth quarter declines, irrigated cropland
> values have fallen modestly in four consecutive quarters, and the
> value of nonirrigated cropland generally followed the same trend
> through 2015. (Kauffman & Clark, 2016).

What is being posed as an issue in the "Tenth District" or "the fourth quarter" is a piecemeal way of hiding the fact that Nebraska, as a state, is in trouble. The key word above is "trend" and you know what the old maxim teaches us: once is a fluke, twice is a coincidence and three times is a trend (or a pattern)." Nebraska's on-going woes signal a trend, and the source of that trend is easy to pinpoint once you take note of certain decision making policies, hiring policies and the on-going greed and malfeasance of political officials. The "invasion of the booty snatchers" is a survival tactic that brings in money for the state. And they will pimp whomever or whatever they have to in order to keep the farmland state solvent.

Continuing:

> Growth in the value of ranchland also stalled in the fourth quarter
> alongside sharp declines in cattle prices that persisted to the end of
> the year. From January 2015 through December, feeder cattle
> prices plunged more than 25 percent, causing profit margins in the
> cattle sector to deteriorate significantly. Alongside these price
> declines, year-over-year growth in the value of ranchland dropped
> from an average of 8 percent in the first three quarters of 2015 to
> zero in the fourth quarter. (Kauffman & Clark, 2016).

When the "growth in the value of ranchland stalls," then this only proves the point I made earlier. Texas is now the beef capital – not Nebraska. So the farmers are in trouble which leads us to the issue of genetically engineered food. The bigger the cattle and the larger the stalks of corn and the more soybeans, the more you can make up for any perceived or actual losses. But when you spray that food, feed those cattle and genetically alter those foodstuffs, you are poisoning the people who consume it. When you ask why America is getting so fat, just look at what the farmers are providing in the form of food, meat, vegetables and so on.

They are killing not only Americans because their genetically engineered food leads to diabetes, high blood pressure, cancer and other diseases, but they're shipping these foods out to the rest of the world – just like they did with cigarettes. Once banned in America, these white men immediately found markets in the Philippines, China and other Asian nations. The international version of "the invasion of the booty snatchers."

Look at how other states are doing:

In contrast to most other District states, farmland values in
Oklahoma continued to rise modestly. Oklahoma was also the only
state where bankers reported increases in average cropland values
when compared with the previous year. Ranchland values also
continued to rise modestly in Oklahoma, in addition to the
Mountain States (Table). Changes in farmland values in most other
states, however, generally were consistent with average changes
for the Tenth District as a whole. (Kauffman & Clark, 2016).

Oklahoma's farmland values continue to rise, albeit modestly. Why? Proper fiscal management at the state level. Even when it comes to "most other states," according to the article, the farmland values were consistent. But not Nebraska. So then what can you say? What can they do to get the values back on par and at the same time, bolster a dying economy? It's time for "invasion of the booty snatchers" and they have been doing it for decades but their management and leadership teams are so inept, so morally bankrupt, that they can't seem to get their acts together. So instead they cover up failure with glossy pictures of renewed tourism, the construction of new soccer and football fields, and other fluff pieces that the media just loves to air and place in print.

Is it going to get any better? You be the judge:

Survey respondents expected farmland values to fall further in the
coming months. In fact, bankers expected the value of each land
type – non-irrigated cropland, irrigated cropland and ranchland – to
decline again in the first quarter of 2016 (Chart 2). However,
between the three land types, more bankers expected further losses
in the value of non-irrigated cropland. Moreover, bankers expected
slightly larger adjustments in non-irrigated cropland values in the
coming year than what was expected at the same time a year ago
(Chart 3). (Kauffman & Clark, 2016).

When bankers start worrying that is when the farmland economy is really in trouble. Those farmers are constantly leeching for loans, using their land as collateral, and then depositing the loan in interest-generating accounts and using the interest off the borrowed money to repay the banks. It's a game that's been going on for a long, long time. Also known as "dryland farming," there are certain crops that use the winter water stored in the soil and don't depend on rainfall during the growing season. These include grapes, tomatoes, pumpkins, beans and other summer crops. Corn is not one of them.

And then there is the issue of land leasing and rents, another revenue steam for the farmers. Farm rents, quite simply, take place when a farm is rented for a fixed amount per acre for all acres in the farm (e.g. 160 acres in a quarter section) regardless of the number or acres of cropland, pasture, buildings, or waste. This is referred to as a whole-farm rental rate. Or, the farm may be rented for a fixed amount per cropland acre (i.e., 145 acres cropland in a 160-acre farm) with a different rental rate for any pasture or buildings (Edwards, 2016). Once again, the same white people that pointed fingers at black people getting welfare subsidies knew all the time that the "food stamps" were basically welfare for farmers. After all, who grew the food that was in the supermarkets that black people and others were purchasing?

But even deeper than that, look at how these farmers leech for loans and then "rent out" their farmland – land stolen by their ancestors from various Native American tribes. And it's easy money. Edwards (2016) explains,

> Cash rent lease agreements are popular because the lease is simple, the rent is fixed, and the owner is relieved of making operating and marketing decisions. Likewise, the tenant has maximum freedom to plan and develop the cropping and livestock programs. The risk and returns from changing prices, yields, and costs are all borne by the tenants.

What "risk"? They either make the money or lose it but they still retain the land. And land, no matter where it is located or how white boys manipulate the market, never loses value. The farmers who rent the land do so banking on there being a profitable crop. Just like they did the black sharecroppers just after slavery when everything rested on "trusting" and having faith in the white landowner. Now they know how it feels. Put into a more contemporary context,

> This squeeze is starting to attract more attention, even outside of agriculture. Recent reports hint at farmers "walking away" from land leases due to the inability to pay high cash rent rates with corn, and soybean profitability falling into the red. If that happens, it could dramatically change the land market in areas where highly productive land fetches up to $400 an acre cash rent. (Caldwell, 2015)

This is just what the black sharecroppers had to do back in the day – pack up with their families and "walk away." They would then head up north hoping for a better way: no land, highly visible because of their black skin, and without a clue about what to do about "finding work." The white farmer is white in a nation that is predominantly white and therefore benefits from some semblance of "white privilege." He can still "muster" up enough capital to survive, sell his land or use his "contacts" to lobby the legislature. He can continue to plant his poisonous crops, spray them with toxic insecticides and if those crops don't pass government muster or inspection, peddle the food overseas to some developing nation – even as he is now doing is tobacco crops.

Caldwell (2015 adds that, "Supply and demand will decide rental rates as they have before. It may reduce rental rates, or it may change the players. But it will be a competitive market as before," adds Farm Business Talk senior contributor ... "What made rental rates high was people willing to pay it, and that will be as always." (Caldwell, 2015).

The key words are "people willing to pay." In a capitalist system, that is the way it will always be. Greed begets more greed, which is why Ponzi schemes are so successful. These farmers get by on their image of being "people of the soil" and "down to earth folk," but they've been bilking various state governments – Nebraska being no exception – for centuries.

While consoling "Black Bart," fast draw Jim (Gene Wilder) has a line in the movie "Blazing Saddles" that not only points to the racist reaction of the farmer-type townspeople to the new black sheriff but also their overall mentality on social issues. It goes like this:

> **Jim**: [*consoling Bart*] What did you expect? "Welcome, sonny"? "Make yourself at home"? "Marry my daughter"? You've got to remember that these are just simple farmers. These are people of the land. The common clay of the new West. You know... morons.

And because the leadership of Nebraska is equally bereft of management skills, creativity and innovative leadership, they continue to capitulate to these farmers, cater to their every need and then when the economy begins to sink, they bail them out. Even with farmland going down, what reputation would a state like Nebraska have without its hayseeds? Speaking of farmland, Kauffman & Clark (2016) posit,

> The volume of farmland sales also dropped in 2015. Historically, changes in the volume of farmland sold and farmland values have moved together (Chart 4). Landowners may be less inclined to sell when prices have recently fallen, in hopes that prices might rebound in the future. A more limited supply of farmland available for purchase, then, may partly explain why farmland values have retracted only modestly, as demand has remained relatively strong in the meantime. (Kauffman & Clark, 2016).

So what can be done? The Nebraska economy's main industry, the farmer and the land, is being threatened. They know this because they have agricultural committees, agricultural leaders, they air TV shows on "agribusiness" and they have a multitude of farmer types being voted into the Nebraska Legislature every election. They have no choice but to engage in what I call "the invasion of the booty snatchers." They'll make up for any losses at the expense of the poor and ignorant. They only have one real black community, so they exploit it to the hilt (as I show in this book), the Indian reservations are paying hundreds of thousands in management fees and taxes to the system and the alcohol that these white boys keep plying the reservations with, and the various Latino enclaves around the state are rife for exploitation.

Free federal grant money and on-going poverty pimp programs help to offset some of the shortfalls, but the Cornhusker State still has a long way to go. It's tourism is failing and the only real source of statewide entertainment is its lackluster college football team, the Nebraska Cornhuskers. In my view, the future does not look good. Read it for yourself:

> Farm credit conditions in the Tenth District also deteriorated somewhat alongside lower farm income. Farm loan repayment rates slipped further in the fourth quarter while farm loan demand remained high (Chart 10). Moreover, both loan demand and repayment rates moved in similar directions in all District states … (Kauffman & Clark, 2016).

Loans slipping. Farm credit conditions deteriorating. Farm income waning. Such conditions require extreme measures, and again, it's time for the state to rely on its largest city and the mis-managers at the state level to find new ways to pimp, exploit and bleed dry the social service money and the poor people whose poverty generate that free Federal funding. Just as the Democratic party relies on" the black vote" and just like the enslavers of old relied on "negro labor," the state of Nebraska is relying on social service block grants and related monies being allocated so that they can turn around and "divert" those funds to pay bills or to help out white farmers and others.

The banks are no friends to these people because they have no honor or commitment to the community. They only care about the bottom line. For example,

> Through the fourth quarter, softening repayments rates and strong loan demand appeared to be a reflection of persistently weaker farm income and reduced cash flow. Yet, commercial banks generally continued to report low delinquency rates on agricultural loans, as shown in the Federal Reserve Bank of Kansas City's first quarter (Kauffman & Clark, 2016).

This same Federal Reserve Bank of Kansas City, which has a branch right here in Omaha, nevertheless has a "community" division where token negroes are sent out to talk these hicks and small business "negroes" into believing in what they (the Federal Reserve Bank) has dubbed, "entrepreneurial momentum." This is putting a band-aid on a cancerous sore. It is a pacification measure aimed at keeping Nebraskans constantly believing that "this is only a temporary condition." But it's not. Nebraska is on its way out because its main exports are inferior to other areas of the country (corn and beef from Kansas and Texas, respectively). Their home grown products are anxious to leave and see "the real world" and the old guard has been exposed so many times for their outright buffoonery and ineptitude that banking interests and others don't want to give them the time of day.

Skipping past a lengthy and repetitive paragraph in the Kauffman and Clark article, we (mercifully) arrive at the conclusion:

> The effects of weakening farm income continued to ripple through the farm economy in the fourth quarter. Reduced income pushed cropland values lower and developments in cattle markets halted growth in ranchland values. In addition, lower farm income trimmed cash rents somewhat and was expected to continue to pressure agricultural credit conditions in the coming months. (Kauffman & Clark, 2016).

And there you have it. The "invasion of the booty snatchers" will continue on, unabated, with the targets being low income areas, from the Native American reservations and the small Latino areas in the panhandle to the state's only real "black community" in Omaha, Nebraska. As long as poverty can generate free money from the federal and state governments, then poverty will be maintained by the powers that be. The money will be used to pay bills and to promote antiquated tourist attractions. Abuse of Tax Incremental Financing and other enticements and inducements may lure businesses to the state, but it won 't last long.

The state's leadership should come clean – or go away dirty.

HEALTH CARE INDUSTRY

Quoting from a report, Dr. Onyema Nkwocha, Program Analyst for the Office of Minority Health and Human Services for the Nebraska Department of Health and Human Services provides telling information about what the reality is and what needs to be done to correct it:

> According to the March 2002 Report, Unequal Treatment: Confronting Racial and Ethnic Disparities in Healthcare … published by the Institute of Medicine (IOM), racial and ethnic minorities across the nation are prone to recieve lower-quality health care services than whites do, even when access-related

> factors, such as patients' insurance status, income, age and
> severity of health conditions are comparable. Thus …[r]acial and
> ethnic minorities tend to receive a lower quality of healthcare
> than non-minorities, even when access-related factors such as
> patients' insurance status and income, are controlled …
> Disparities in the health care delivered to racial and ethnic
> minorities are real and are associated with worse outcomes in
> many cases, which is unacceptable … ***The real challenge lies
> not in debating whether disparities exist, because the evidence
> is overwhelming, but in developing and implementing
> strategies to reduce and eliminate them,*** " said committee
> chairperson, Alan Nelson (p. 42—emphasis added).

The fact that was written above in 2002 remains true today in 2016 – some 14 years later – should clearly show the health care is not only big business all over the nation, but its leading patients, clients (and victims) remain the poor and minority.

When it comes to serving people of color, Nebraska has probably the most biased medical system in the region, and as a result, the concept of "invasion of the booty snatchers" is hardly more evident.

Loaded down with doctors from other countries, you might get good service from one of them (before they are "briefed" about the insurance-first orientation of the white American doctors). But if you don't then you get delayed and inferior care. That is the reputation of these hospitals if you ask black people. Creighton/St. Joe's hospital is referred to as "killer joe," for instance because of the number of black people who die on their watch.

As another example of lax priorities as it relates to the public, the University of Nebraska Medical Center spent $350,000 on its new (and ugly) logo, and another $250,000 on its bullshit slogan, "Serious Medicine. Extraordinary Care." More recently they've added, "Our Identity is Priceless." That's a lie and furthermore, who gives a shit about their identity: their services sho' ain't "priceless"!

Health care is a good way to "divest" poor people from the system in a number of ways. First of all, they have to go to bullshit programs and small clinics to get health care. Secondly, their credit is sabotaged by the medical profession because of exorbitant charges for everything, even a glass of water. But even before that, every gunshot wound that a person is rushed to the hospital for is a $20,000 charge. Did you know that? So with North Omaha being number one in the nation in black youth homicide and related shootings, that means every single one of those kids is going to have that shit on his credit report. What does that mean? Credit and insurance are the first things that the medical profession looks at when you enter the hospital.

The health care industry is a literal proponent of the concept of "invasion of the body snatchers." They pay for themselves with all those fees. And, once the under the table payments from the pharmaceutical industry kick in, these hospitals, medical centers and major clinics make a killing. Add to that their on-going exploitation and abuse of the Medicaid system, and there are more than enough unhealthy people to continue to pay. These rich white farmers can afford it, and Nebraska is one of the oldest states in the union: some 13.6% of Nebraska's residents are 65 years of age or older according to the Population Reference Bureau.

The "bill you later" expense associated with the ambulance ride to the hospital also damages credit of those who already are lacking in insurance. The health care industry has long discriminated against the poor and minority of Omaha. That is why their health care and health access is so bad and it's been that way for a long, long time.

Blacks in Douglas County continue to fare worse in almost every single major health indicator than did their white counterparts, usually anywhere from 30% to 50% worse. As Nkwocha (2003) noted just over a decade ago, "It is therefore no wonder that one-fifth (20%) of Black adults statewide (with the overwhelming majority living in Omaha) rated their health status as either "fair" or "poor," compared to 12.3% of white Nebraskans" (p. 7).

The "booty snatchers" have been "invading" the lives and life chances of black Omahans for a century. Recent history is but one indicator. After all, it should be remembered that in 1978 it was reported in the State of Black Omaha that health care was an indicator of the quality of life of a community. Thirty-eight years later, in 2016, life remains the same for the most part. What was said in 2003 about black women continues to ring true when Douglas County made a similar comment as it addressed an ultra-high infant mortality rate among black women:

> Infant mortality is a critical indicator of the health of a population. It reflects the overall state of maternal health, as well as the quality and accessibility of primary health care available to pregnant women and infants. Despite declines in the 1980s and 1990s in the United States, the infant mortality rate in Douglas County has been steady, averaging approximately eight deaths per 1,000 live births over the last ten years. In most years, the infant mortality rate in Douglas County has exceeded the United States rate. The disparity between races is prominent in infant mortality where the rate for the black race is almost three times the rate for the white race (Douglas County Health Department, 2003: 3).

When we fast forward to the present day we find little change. Based on results of a 1993 Nebraska survey, African Americans report higher prevalence of cigarette smoking (32%) and physical inactivity during leisure time (34%) than Nebraskans in general. They are also more likely to report having no health insurance (21%).

Health care provides an indicator of the quality of life, not only of those who are contemporaries, but also serves as a potential projection of future health. After gleaning the data provided by the Douglas County Health Department, an argument can be made that the future health care of the Black family, and that of the black female in particular, is gloomy indeed. And as gloom hangs over the heads of black people all over North Omaha and beyond, the coffers of the booty snatchers continue to get filled, buildings continue to go up, new programs that employ white Omahans continue to get created and in sum, the poor remain poor while the wealthy seem to get wealthier.

As was the case with the lead paint "discovery" and the ailments that afflicted black and poor children who lived in older housing in North Omaha, money was made to remove it, money made by white agencies. When it comes to black women, their lives are controlled and manipulated from "the womb to the tomb." Black babies do not fare well in Omaha; in fact in 2015, Omaha ranked number one in the nation in black child poverty. The facts clearly show why this is the case.

For example, not only does Douglas County rank high in black infant mortality rate, but also when it comes to black babies dying of Sudden Infant Death syndrome. According to its own data, once again, we find the rate for blacks in 2003 was three times the rate that it is for blacks (Douglas County Health Department, 2003: 4). And it remains close to this number today in 2016.

As for Low birth weight (LBW), which is the risk factor most closely associated with neonatal death, in Douglas County, the rate for Blacks is 50% higher than that seen in both whites and Hispanics (Douglas County Health Department, 2015). In regard to pre-natal care during the first trimester of pregnancy, Black women fared worse once again; Black women are 28% less likely to receive early prenatal care than white women (Douglas County Health Department, 2015).

When it comes to pre-term births (the leading cause of neonatal deaths not associated with birth defects), the percentage of preterm deaths among Blacks is 38% higher than that seen among whites and Hispanics (Douglas County Health Department). On a more generic level, "complications" during labor and delivery impacts on black women much worse than it does white women in Douglas County; black women are 13% more likely to have complications than are white women (Douglas County Health Department). And what do those complications mean? More money for the health care providers, who jack up prices on the poor, pimp their Medicaid insurance and mis-diagnose large numbers of them. This latter allegation is a national phenomenon.

Future generations appear bleak as well, since being a teenaged mother is, in itself, a risk factor. The proportion of adolescent births among the black race is five times higher than that for the white race (for Hispanics, it is three times that seen for the white race). In one study from 2003, "a … study reported by the *New England Journal of Medicine (NEJM)*, found that being a young mother may by itself be a risk factor favor premature delivery. In previous studies, experts speculated that because teen mothers are often poor, not well educated or are from racial minorities, their living conditions – not their age – accounted for their poor pregnancy outcomes (Nkwocha, 2003: 89).

Notice, when "risk" is discussed, there is no mention of the risk of having a group of people from a segregated area of the city, a group of people with a long history of disdain for low income people of color, and the impact and stress that this fact in and of itself places on black people in need of medical care. The shortage of minority doctors (from this country) makes matters all the worse.

When it comes to health and the negative impact on black women, the past is prologue. As if black women don't have it hard enough, Nkwocha (2003) reports that statewide, "African American females are 2.9 times as likely as whites to die from diabetes-related causes" (sic), and 1.8 times as likely as whites to die from breast cancer during 1998-2002 (p. 8). Speaking of diabetes, based on responses to the Nebraska Behavioral Risk Factor Surveillance Survey, African Americans (11.4 percent) were far more likely than white Nebraskans (5.7 percent) to indicate they had been told by a doctor that they had diabetes (Nkochwa, 2003: 111). And when it came to deaths due to diabetes-related causes, between the years 1998-2002, Blacks experienced an increase of 13.7% in diabetes-related mortality rates compared to the previous five-year period a—2.4 times higher than that of whites (Nkochwa, 2003: 113).

In terms of heart disease, Blacks in Douglas County is 40% higher than the rate seen for whites. Blacks in Douglas County have a cancer death rate that is 32% higher than the white population. Other health factors include:

◆ Blacks in Douglas County are twice as likely (50%) than whites to die from stroke;
◆ The lung cancer death rate for blacks is 29% higher than that of whites

Health care is so poor for African-Americans in Douglas County even when it comes to preventable diseases, blacks appear to fare worse. Take the case of high blood pressure and obesity.

As far back as 2003, Nkwocha (2003) found that, "Among those who ever had their blood pressure checked, 22.3 percent of Nebraskans indicated that they had been told it was high. African Americans continued to have the greatest prevalence of high blood pressure, placing this segment of the population "at higher risk" (p. 60). And, 33.4% of African-Americans in Nebraska (the overwhelming majority living in Omaha) were obese, with much of this having to do with physical inactivity, and the prevalence of it was higher among African Americans 31.6 percent than among whites (27 percent).

Why would it be any different now when groups like North Omaha Area Health have data and even power point presentations that clearly show that when it comes to access to medical care, even clinics, the black community is in the middle of what is called a "medical desert." There are clinics all around the fringe areas, but in North Omaha, a scant few. How can this be an accident when the money made by the "booty snatchers" and their on-going exploitation and invasion of the black community has persisted over time. It is no accident; *it is by design.*

An article that appeared in the June 2004 issue of the *Omaha World Herald*, based on a report issued by the State of Nebraska, shows that racial factors do play a role in obesity. According to the article,

> Nurses collected height and weight data from more than 40,000 children in grades kindergarten through grade 12 during the 2002-2003 school year. The report found that: American Indian and Hispanic students are far more likely than their black, white and Asian peers to be overweight … While black and white boys are equally likely to be overweight, black females are 47 percent more likely than white females to carry extra weight … Poverty may be one reason why American Indian, Hispanic and black students have higher rates of obesity (Hopkins, 2004: 1).

Notice how the racist perpetrators protect themselves by stating that poverty MAY be a reason for the higher obesity rates. Not only poverty, but the "corner-cutting" farmer who is shooting his crops up with every kind of genetic altering herbicide in the world, not to mention the hormones and steroids that he feeds to his cows, pigs, chicken and goats. Then they turn around and eat his genetically altered feeds. A combination of all of this is what we, as humans consume. Hence, just as the farm animals get larger and the crops are bigger, the human body grows in the same way. These white people know this; but since Nebraska is an agricultural state that is farm-dependent, no one is saying anything about it.

The article on youth obesity adds that,

> Differences in culture, such as how one group socializes or what is considered an acceptable appearance, can also play a role …

> Another puzzler is why blacks were the only population to have
> a higher rate of females overweight than males. [Corri] Hanson
> [a Visiting Nurse Association dietician] … said she faces
> resistance from any of her black female clients when it comes to
> dieting because the cultural preference is a curvy body (Hopkins,
> 2004: 1).

The fact is, America is getting fat and much of the blame goes to farmers who are genetically engineering the food and crops to get more profit. What goes into those farm animals and those plants, which we ingest and digest, is what goes into us. As Stengle (2005) explained,

> The prevalence of obesity among adults is well known, with an
> increase of 75 percent since 1991. So is the problem with school-
> age children, reaffirmed by new statistics showing that nearly
> four million children ages six to 11 and 5.3 million young people
> ages 12 to 19 were overweight or obese in 2002. But the findings
> among preschoolers are a strong indication that kids' weight
> problems are beginning even earlier (p. 5).

Elsewhere in this book I charge the farmers with this obesity problem. I charge them with genetically engineering their food and livestock and not caring about the fact that the same drugs and toxins that make foodstuffs larger and cattle fatter is going to do the same thing to human beings. Premature growth among young people, 12 year old girls with 36 inch breasts, 12 year old boys tall enough to post up Kareem Abdul Jabbar – all because of what they consumed in my view. Obesity, high blood pressure – the farmers know what they did. And by exporting their food around the world, *they are infecting every nation that they claim to be committed to "saving."*

Then there are respiratory problems. According to a 2003 National Urban League "special report," "across the United States, 71 percent of African Americans live in polluted counties, compared to 58 percent of the white population. In another report issued by the Uhuru Sasa Research Institute located in Omaha, Nebraska, a number of reasons were cited as to why the North Freeway should not be built. The report stated, in part,

> In addition, the politics of freeways clearly shows that such roads
> can dilute or fracture the potential of the black vote because of
> the relocation of residents. In urban planning this is known as
> "population transfer." Residual affects from these roads and the
> relocation that takes place includes the harm to black businesses,
> who lose long-time customers, ***increased air and noise pollution
> in an area already rife with asthma and other respiratory***

> *problems, and the confusion that years of bulldozing and*
> *construction often demand* (Stelly, 1980: 48—emphasis added).

That was thirty-six (36) years ago. The national picture shows that asthma impacts on black people disproportionately more than it does whites. According to the National Urban League,

> Asthma is 26% more prevalent in African American children than white children … African Americans are three times more likely to die from asthma … African Americans aged 15 to 24 are 6 times more likely to die from asthma than white Americans (2003, p. 3).

Today, in Nebraska, the asthma rate among blacks is double that of whites. Some 13 years ago, Nkochwa (2003) wrote,

> In Nebraska, an estimated 112,100 persons have asthma. The Nebraska 2000 BRFSS estimated a statewide self-reported prevalence rate of approximately a6.6 percent of adults aged 18 years and older. In 2000, there were asthma self-reported prevalence rates of 8.4 percent of females ages 18 years and older and 4.2 percent of men I this age category. During 1999-2001, the age-adjusted asthma prevalence rate among African Americans (13.8 per 100,000 population) was more than double when compared to whites (6.1) (Nkwocha, 2003: 145).

Not only that, but the same report concluded that, "African American children had 1.8 times the risk of having asthma as children of other races" and "27 percent of African American children … had an asthma action plan on file with school." Furthermore, in Nebraska during 1998-2002, 218 people died from asthma … Of the total, 195 asthma deaths occurred among whites at the rate of 2.0 (per 100,000 people), while 20 of the deaths were among African Americans at a high rate of 7.7 deaths per 100,000 population (Nkwocha, 2003: 146 & 148).

While the same report boasts of decreases in the number of asthma deaths among African Americans statewide, in Douglas County – where the overwhelming majority of Blacks in Nebraska reside -- between 1987 through 1999, 238 residents died of asthma and, of those, 52 were Black (Nkwocha, 2003: 149). And the figures appear to again be growing all over North Omaha as developers dig ditches, mix cement and continue to pollute the environment. Adults and children alike inhale these pollutants and the vicious cycle of respiratory ailments persists. Pneumonia and various other forms of lung ailments appear to also be on the rise.

Remember what I wrote earlier about the "medical desert" that existed in the Omaha black community? The same was the case nearly forty years ago. At that time *The State of Black Omaha Report 1978* concluded that, "no major health care facilities exist in the black ghetto, while hospitals of the city lie at distances not readily accessible to an area in which fully 45% of residents lack automobiles (Urban League of Nebraska, 1978: 20). And in 2003 it was noted then – just as it is now in 2016 – that on a statewide level, African Americans were more likely to have had a routine check-up in the past year (76 percent) than white Nebraskans (67.8 percent) (Nkwocha, 2003: 5).

But accessibility is more than just a matter of proximity or access to transportation. There is also the issue of insurance, and when it comes to health insurance, 16.3 percent of Blacks, 18 years and older, have no health insurance, and 16.4% of Blacks could not afford to see a doctor due to cost (Nkwocha, 2003: 1). Those figures have hardly changed over the past 13 years because of the regular draining of insurance by the booty snatchers: area hospitals and the like. One health clinic (Charles Drew Health Center) demands payment before they render any services.

Out of a total of 3,088 primary care physicians in Nebraska, only 36 are black, compared to 165 that are classified as "Asian-Indian," 76 Chinese, and 33 listed as "other Asian." When it comes to Registered Nurses, out of a total of 11,937 statewide, 97% are white and only 110 (0.9%) are African-American (Nkwocha, 2003: 38 & 41). It's just as bad today in 2016.

Is there any doubt as to why blacks believe that the health care industry is not sensitive to their needs? In one survey by the Chamber of Commerce, the Minority Division found that, "a substantial proportion of racial/ethnic minority Nebraskans (ranging from 30% to 48%) stated that race or ethnic origin is a barrier to receiving health care in their area."

Finally, just as the farm industry exports its genetically engineered food and livestock, and just as the pharmaceutical industry continues to dupe doctors into prescribing drugs (over-medicating) to low-income and minority residents, we cannot forget the tobacco industry and the millions of deaths that it is responsible for. Nebraska hasn't avoided that particular "cash crop," either.

Tobacco use is the leading cause of preventable death in the United States. In 2004 it was reported that, "In Nebraska alone, nearly seven people die every day as a result of smoking (Omaha Star, 2004: 12). According to 2001 data, 23% of whites nationally smoked; in Nebraska that figure was 19.9%. When it comes down to blacks, 22.6% smoke nationally and the figure is 22.8% for the state of Nebraska (Kaiser Family Foundation, 2004). Nationally, among white smokers, Marlboro was the brand used most often … followed by Camel. Marlboro was also the brand used most by Hispanics, followed by Newport. Among blacks, Newport was the brand used most often, followed by Kool (Office of Applied Studies, 2004).

In any given store in North Omaha, cigarettes are readily available. Specialty stores, such as the Tobacco Hut and Four Aces, offer cartons of cigarettes at reduced rates. Stores in big cities sell individual cigarettes for a quarter, in direct violation of consumer laws. The "invasion of the booty snatchers" is national, pervasive, and targeted at using the low income and minority to make up the slack left by declining state, county and city budgets.

The Triple One Neighborhood Association and Parents' Union think tank, the Uhuru Sasa Research Institute, concludes that the data provided paints a picture that health care for African-Americans is not going to see measurable improvements until Blacks themselves become a more active part of the service-providing process.

When the variables mentioned above are accounted for, and when they are comparable, and when Blacks STILL receive lower quality health care, what is the constant? Racism, pure and simple. Racism in lack of access, racism in application and racism even in the billing process. In Omaha, Nebraska there should be a Grand Jury hearing conducted on the horror studies that come from the mouths of relatives of those receiving treatment from the likes of St. Joseph's Hospital and the University of Nebraska Medical Center, to name but two. These two institutions, more than the others, have been mentioned time and time again as being involved in the "accidental deaths" of black men and women, many of whom only visit these institutions for routine checkups.

A SKEWED DEPARTMENT OF CORRECTIONS

Whether young and in prison or young and being held in juvenile detention facilities, Nebraska's maltreatment of young males – especially black ones – proves that racism is alive and well and the grant-motivated booty snatchers are working feverishly to create a group of mentally damaged people to be let loose on the community to become fodder for missionary-minded social workers and racist cops.

First, the prison system.

On January 9, 2015 there were clearly problems at the managerial level as it relates to the Nebraska Department of Corrections. In an article from the Nebraska Legislature website titled, "State Senator Heath Mello Introduces Budget Reform & Planning Legislation," it was clear that something had to be done:

> LINCOLN, NE – Yesterday, Nebraska State Senator Heath Mello
> (District 5, South Omaha) introduced LB 32 and LB 33, key
> legislation that will enhance the Legislature's efforts towards
> performance-based budgeting and sound planning for fiscal
> uncertainty. LB 32 would require the Nebraska Department of
> Corrections to develop programmatic strategic plans and
> performance benchmarks as part of the biennial budget process.
> (Nebraska Legislature website, 2015).

The invasion of the booty snatches depends a great deal on the revenue generated by the prison system. Not only is labor pimped out to corporations who bid for whatever can be manufactured from behind bars, but the on-going leeching for more money, more funding, more grants is one way to pay without actually having to insult lazy Nebraska taxpayers. Again, if the funding that deals with human issues cannot be gotten for free from the Feds, then lily-white Nebraska doesn't want to commit.

Though mistake-prone, the decision makers continue to look the other way while the Department of Corrections commits one glaring miscue after another. As it was reported in January of 2015:

> "The recent investigations into the various scandals surrounding
> the Department of Corrections has convinced me that the
> Department should continue to face a greater level of scrutiny
> during the biennial budget process," said Senator Mello, who
> serves as Chairman of the Legislature's Appropriations
> Committee. "After passing LB 974 last year to create these
> strategic plans and benchmarks for a troubled Department of
> Health & Human Services, LB 32 is a natural step to help the
> Legislature in evaluating the agency's ongoing performance." LB
> 33, a bill also introduced by Senator Mello, would require the
> Legislative Fiscal Analyst to produce a state revenue volatility
> report. (Nebraska Legislature website, 2015)

What good does any of this do without proper oversight? What good can any improvements represent if the new plans are being handed to idiots for implementation? Time after time recommendations have been made by State Senator Ernie Chambers calling for immediate investigations into the protocols, procedures and practices of the Department of Corrections. Then when a riot breaks out because of some administrative impropriety, these white people want to cry "foul" and start blaming the lack of money for causing the problem.

Then they want to run to out-of-state "consultants," "advisors" and others to tell them what to do, which is a perfect example of the blind leading the blind. You can't get people to help you "craft" a state budget when the problem, as I have pointed out, is that the "booty snatchers" are too stupid to implement a budget without co-mingling funds, directly stealing revenue or otherwise engaging in nepotism to hire unqualified relatives and buddies for various positions. Be that as it may, the website made the following claim (promise?):

> "Creating the new planning instrument will assist the Legislature in both preparing for the next economic downturn and for strengthening the state's fiscal policy," Mello said. "This best practice fiscal policy, promoted by The Pew Charitable Trust, will serve future Legislatures in both crafting state budgets and understanding the volatility of our tax system." (Nebraska Legislature website, 2015)

Now, fast forward. Even as I polish off this book, and despite Sen. Mello's valiant attempts to improve the situation, Nebraska's on-going mis-management and lack of intelligent application of rules of the penal system remained rampant. And here is one more thing I'll share before moving on. It has to do with the concept of "solitary confinement" and what I view as its on-going abuse within the correctional system

White people, in general, use terminology to dupe the public. In this analysis of the solitary confinement situation you will see it referred to as "restrictive housing." What??? These guys are in prison which is the ultimate form of restrictive housing. But not referring to it as "solitary confinement," the oppressors want to avoid public criticism and scrutiny because of the brutality inherent in the terms "solitary" and "confinement." This is indicative of the kinds of tricks that the "booty snatchers" exercise in their on-going quest to leech for free money, pacify the public and work to keep their state, county and city budgets afloat.

Now for the article regarding solitary confinement.

A November 3, 2016 article in the Omaha World Herald once again showed that the state of Nebraska and its treatment of inmates was a day late and a dollar short. What studies had found three and four years ago, and what other legislatures had been acting on was just now coming to the fore in the Cornhusker State. Can there be any doubt as to why the state finds it hard to find qualified corrections workers?

The name of the article in question, which appeared more than a year and a half after Sen. Mello offered up "improvements" in the Corrections system, was, "Nebraska Prisons House 'Alarming Number' of Inmates in Solitary Confinement, but Reforms Are Promising, National Think Tank Says." Again, outside sources offering information that should be tailored to meet the hillbilly-like approaches and procedures being conducted by the Nebraska Department of Corrections.

The article, by World-Herald reporter Martha Stoddard was partially informational (as it relates to Nebraska's Neanderthal application of solitary confinement as a punishment), and part bullshit in regard to those studies and how "promising" any reforms are. Furthermore, it was clear that the racism that permeates the state was being reflected in the people who made up the inmate population, a point made for more than three and a half decades by State Senator Ernie Chambers.

According to the article:

> LINCOLN — Nebraska's prison system houses an "alarming number" of inmates in solitary confinement, according to a national think tank. The Vera Institute of Justice, based in New York City, said the state uses solitary confinement at more than twice the national rate and nearly half of all inmates spend at least one day in "the hole." (Stoddard, 2016)

There's a reason for that "alarming rate": racism and the lack of cultural competence. The same thing is done on a different level at the elementary, middle school and high school levels: when you can't control black people, lock them away from one another lest they may organize against you. Do you think this is a quirk? And furthermore, these white people know that while in solitary they are actually making matters worse for the inmate because no human being was ever created to live in isolation for a long period of time.

Moving on:

> But, in a report released Thursday, the institute praised recently launched reforms and offered several recommendations for doing more to reduce the use of solitary. "It is Vera's hope that these recommendations will provide helpful guidance for (the Department of Correctional Services) to successfully build upon the promising steps it has already taken," the report said. (Stoddard, 2016).

This is nothing but a bullshit smokescreen. As long as the people at the top remain of the same background, and as long as those being locked up represent what scholar Michelle Alexander called "mass incarceration" (The New Jim Crow: Mass Incarceration in the Age of Colorblindness, The New Press, 2012) all these "recommendations" do is stall time and serve as a façade. After a few months, the same situation persists. And it is a situation – abuse of the use of solitary confinement – that has existed in the prison system for centuries.

All these white "booty snatchers" do is get paid. They get paid for the studies they conduct, for the time they spend analyzing the data, for the publishing of their material, on the lecture circuit claiming to be "consultants" and "experts" and so on. The goal is not substantive change, and never has been. As long as there is solitary confinement money can be made inside of the prison and outside of it. The prison benefits from recidivism: when these people return after being released, the prison financially benefits. As do the people who make the shoe strings for the guard's shoes, the uniforms, the batons, the food that is sold in bulk, and so on:

> The report follows a yearlong study of how and when Nebraska prisons use what is called "restrictive housing." Department Director Scott Frakes sought the institute's help after working with them in his previous position in the state of Washington. He said that work led to significant changes in Washington and he expects it will help Nebraska develop alternatives to restrictive housing. (Stoddard, 2016)

"Restrictive housing." Was it "restrictive housing" when they jammed those Jews into concentration camps back in Nazi Germany? Was it "restrictive housing" when the former Soviet Union put together labor camps from 1930 to 1955, where thousands died? Regardless of solitary confinement or not, are not the oppressive and hellish conditions in prisons like Marion (IL.), Angola (LA.), Rikers (NY), Leavenworth (KS.), or Folsom (CA) "restrictive housing" as far as the inmates are concerned?

To call solitary confinement "restrictive housing" within a context that is already degrading and brutal is like referring to Charles Manson as "the nice one" out of the entire Manson Gang! These white people are aware of the degradation that is heaped upon the heads of inmates which explains why more than 70% of all inmates are either Black or Latino! And they also know that this kind of confinement only makes the mind more warped. Let me give you an example.

In her book, *A Taste of Power*, Elaine Brown writes about Huey P. Newton (late founder of the Black Panther Party for Self Defense) and his experiences. While describing him she offers some insight on one of his experiences that transformed him into the man that he would become:

> Thus he agonized over and sought ultimate answers to ultimate questions. Before the *Soul Breaker [maximum security cells in Alameda County* specially designed to break the spirits of men] ... and after, before the Party and now, he pushed life to see if it would reveal a hope of eternity. He tested life's edge every day, daring, challenging, hiding, and seeking at once. It was his best and worst attribute. It was what elevated him and diminished him. (Brown, p. 299 –emphasis added).

The concept of a "soul breaker" was designed specifically for inmates who didn't tow the line. And on some level they exist in all of these prisons. Even in hick prisons like the Lincoln Penitentiary, the solitary confinement that these racist decision makers refer to as "restrictive housing" are nevertheless "soul breakers" on several levels.

First, such "confinement" isolates people from human interaction and communication which is about as barbaric a psychological punishment as one can receive. Secondly, they isolate the inmate from his family and any letters he may receive from "the outside." It's bad enough that most of these new prisons are being built in lily-white, rural hick towns where black mothers, girlfriends, wives and others have to travel hundreds of miles and risk being pulled over by redneck cops every step of the way. And third, the idea of isolation only pisses the inmate off more and makes him more of a "hero" in the eyes of his fellow inmates once he gets out.

Even the usually day-late-dollar-short warden of the Lincoln Penitentiary had to admit to the following:

> "The best reform of restrictive housing is reducing the need for restrictive housing by improving the quality of life within prisons and reducing idleness, which is a priority for this agency," Frakes said. (Stoddard, 2016).

This is basic Penology 101 – this guy cracks a book and reads a few chapters and then impresses the reporter with general truisms and she documents it as if it is tailor-made creative thought. State Senator Ernie Chambers has been telling these white people since the 1970s that they were abusing the inmates and documented it with hundreds of pages of memos, letters, and reports. They did nothing. Even as they change wardens the system remains the same when it comes to maltreatment of inmates and the on-going hiring of unqualified prison personnel. Hence, the following re-invention of the wheel:

> Doug Koebernick, Nebraska's inspector general of corrections, said the report reinforced previous recommendations for change, such as addressing staff shortages, increasing programming and improving mental health care. (Stoddard, 2016).

Take note that the human recommendations – like more classes for those seeking college credits, more culturally-based courses in Black Studies, Latino studies and the like – that is totally overlooked. These white people are in it for the booty (sometimes literally) and what they can snatch from a non-vigilant Federal government in terms of free money. And in typical acquiescent manner, what is the conclusion? Koebernick tells the reporter, "I think it gives the department a lot of ideas," he said. "Now we'll see what they do with it." (Stoddard, 2016)

> The use of solitary confinement, particularly its long-term use, has been a concern in Nebraska in the wake of the Nikko Jenkins case. Jenkins, a mentally troubled inmate, killed four people in Omaha shortly after his 2013 release from prison, where he had spent years in segregation. (Stoddard, 2016).

If Nebraska was not morally bankrupt, their concerns about solitary confinement would have come to the fore following the 1971 Attica uprisings, following the previous complaints and riots from their own Nebraska penitentiary, and other prison riots around the country which were informing the white man about the conditions of the prison system. But they turned a deaf ear, using "financial restrictions" as the reason for not taking any action. This is one reason why the "booty snatchers" are always having problems with their prison system. They hire incompetent wardens to lead, and then they turn a deaf ear to the problems of the prison culture. The problems inevitably snowball and create increasingly larger debt.

Why do you think that the prisons are overwhelmingly filled with black and brown people when the vast majority of the money being stolen in America is being ripped off by white collar whites, disproportionately Jewish, who are given time to stash money, hide it in off shore accounts, send it to Israel and then when and if caught, end up doing time in prisons that look like Club Med? Those in charge take their time with black poverty at any level whether it be the ghetto or the prison system. For instance,

> The Vera Institute report noted that his case led to public and legislative scrutiny of the prison system and to efforts at reform. Among the more recent changes was a 2015 law aimed at limiting the use of solitary confinement. (Stoddard, 2016).

One man who killed four white people got those in power to begin thinking about what was going on in the prison system. One man had them scurrying all over the state with a petition to reinstate the death penalty. The collective cowardice of these white men, combined with their hatred of black males, can be the only reasons why so little attention is paid to an institution that boasts of being about "rehabilitation."

Laws made by lawless men. They make one statement to gullible reporters and the public while continuing to "do dirt" behind the prison walls. For instance, Martha Stoddard (2016) writes, "It [reform efforts aimed at limiting solitary confinement] … was followed by new agency regulations that eliminated the use of restrictive housing as a disciplinary sanction and required that restrictive housing be used only when all other options have been exhausted. The regulations took effect in July." (Stoddard, 2016).

When prison inspects take place by the government – which is very rare – the government warns the prison that they are coming. This gives these racists more than ample time to "clean up their act" as is the case with most government inspections. The inspectors don't want to find anything wrong and the wrongdoers want to keep that federal and state funding coming so they do whatever is necessary to bamboozle the overseers. And it works, which is why the problems that generate funding for "the booty snatchers" keeps on coming year in and year out.

There's always an excuse – like the following one:

> Frakes, at a legislative hearing last month, said the number of inmates in solitary confinement has not changed since July, but only because of a string of prison assaults and disturbances that have sent more inmates to segregation. (Stoddard, 2016)

Why didn't Ms. Stoddard ask about and print what the sources of those "prison assaults and disturbances" were? Wouldn't that be germane to the topic of why solitary confinement was being used? Of course it would. But remember, this is the Omaha World Herald and their tendency is to take information straight out of the bureaucrat's mouth and off the police blotter. Investigative reporting? Only when another newspaper somewhere else in the country stumbles across something and dares to print it. Only then does the World-Herald come forth with an expose. Again, that is how the money continues to pour into the Cornhusker state and how the "booty snatchers" continue to keep their jobs, their power, and their undeserved privilege.

Continuing:

> As of Oct. 12, there were 324 inmates confined in restrictive housing, many for assaults but also many (42 percent) as a precaution because prison officials perceive they are a threat to staff or other inmates. The Vera Institute study looked at the use of various types of restrictive housing during the two-year period ending June 30, 2015, before the recent reforms. The different types of restrictive housing varied in their purpose, but all involved living in isolated cells with little out-of-cell time or access to social interaction, recreation or constructive activities. (Stoddard, 2016).

Nebraska's financial woes and its tendencies toward on-going abuse of minorities both have long traditions. And solitary confinement only makes matters worse. Even without the use of restrictive housing, the prison system is nothing more than a university where many inmates learn new tricks of the trade and where hardened criminals become harder. There is nothing about "rehabilitation" taking place because once inside, those who have been arrested can only look forward to being stigmatized once released. They can only get hired at pointless jobs, menial labor and in far too many cases the employers exploit them, having hired them only to get some kind of federal tax break.

Again, the "booty snatchers" capitalize on black pain and create jobs and use the money to bolster their sagging economy.

How can you not be "perceived as a threat" to staff when the staff is white and as a black inmate, they despise having to work in your presence? Even the black staff are usually sadistic losers who barely have high school diplomas. And what makes them so "white" in the mind is the fact that most of these prisons are located in lily white, hick areas where the residents in the nearest town despise black people across the board, inmates as well as staff.

Following are five of the report's alleged "findings", which I will quote and then analyze point by point:

> Among the report's findings:

> » The daily population in any type of restrictive housing averaged 13.9 percent of the prison population, more than twice the estimated national average of 5 percent to 6 percent.

So Nebraska guards and decision makers were not only more lax, but they were more punitive. And when these white people do this, these inmates are writing home and the word is getting out about the abuse and maltreatment. This builds up a deep resentment for a "justice system" that metes out justice based on race, a point made clear by numerous scholars over the years. The only people who can't see this fact or who choose to avoid it seem t be these Nebraska decision makers.

A second "finding" in the "report" reads as follows:

> » African-American, Latino and Native American inmates were disproportionately likely to be in restrictive housing. Men were more likely than women and younger men more likely than older ones to be in such housing.

Again, we find the variable of race. The previous facts in and of themselves constitute grounds for a major civil rights lawsuit. And when Nebraska loses, how are they going to pay it off? They have no money! They're as guilty as sin and they know it. And they wonder why they are the laughing stock of neighboring states, including such lily-white bastions as South Dakota, Kansas, Wyoming and Iowa? Young minority males are the targets and the victims, and yet Nebraska uses these facts and the relatives of these young people as fodder for submitting grant application after grant application leeching for that free Federal money. Hence, the "invasion of the booty snatchers."

Continuing with the report findings:

> » Inmates averaged 44-day stays in disciplinary segregation, but
> 311 days in protective custody, a type of restrictive housing used to
> protect inmates from the general population.

"Protective custody" must be where they keep the snitches and the white boys. Why not go into detail regarding the "characteristics" of the ones who get "protective custody"? What could they have done that was so bad that they have to be protected? Could it be gang related? Or, as I charged earlier, could it be people who worked with the cops and who dropped dimes? Again, either give full details that provide specifics about this "protective custody" (full disclosure) or why write the damn article?

Racism in the decision making is the result of the discretion given to people who have the power. Also involved are forms of bitch-like pettiness which white men exhibit (Donald Trump) when the variable of race is interjected. This helps to explain the following "finding":

> » Low-level rule violations accounted for 91 percent of all
> sanctions that led to disciplinary confinement. The most common
> sanction was for disobeying an order.

Disobeying an order? Again, the issue of discretion. These white guards, most of barely graduated from high school, get to wear uniforms and then they look down their noses at those who have it worse than they do. It is clear that most of these guards cannot handle the responsibility. How can you obey an order that is given by someone who himself is seen time and time again violating the rules, making exceptions, discriminating against certain inmates and the like? Again, without specifics, the article may sound bad but it is a whitewash compared to the picture that would be painted with focus and specifics. No one knows the gutlessness and callousness of white men better than other white men – and black men.

Finally,

> » Rates of hospital or nursing home admissions were significantly
> higher for inmates living in restrictive housing compared to other
> inmates. Studies show that solitary confinement has harmful
> effects on physical health, as well as mental health.

This last point is well known. And that's why it's also applied at the juvenile level. In January of 2016 the American Civil Liberties Union came up with some findings that prove that race, control and abuse work hand in hand when it comes to Nebraska corrections. According to one news report under the heading, "Some facilities send young people to solitary for as long as three months, despite medical evidence that extreme isolation can permanently damage adolescents' brains,"

> LINCOLN, Neb – Today the ACLU of Nebraska released Growing
> Up Locked Down: Juvenile Solitary Confinement in Nebraska.
> The report presents first of its kind comprehensive research
> regarding solitary confinement in Nebraska county and state
> facilities. *The ACLU found that a young person in some Nebraska
> youth facilities can be held in solitary confinement for as long as
> 90 days.* Mental health experts have found that the depriving
> young people of contact with others for over 4 hours can have
> devastating *long-term impacts on children's health and wellbeing.*
> Placing a juvenile in solitary confinement leads to psychological
> damage, increase suicide rates, hampered educational outcomes,
> and *overall stunted development* (ACLU, 2016 – emphasis added).

Look at what appears above and you can see both the short- and long-term impact of what these institutions are doing to black youth. They are not only impacting on these individuals but also on entire black families and the future of the black community. Bear in mind that these people knew what they were doing all along, and they did it with malice aforethought and intent.

Recall what former Black Panther Elaine Brown recalled about the Alameda County version of solitary – the *Soul Breaker, which was a maximum security cell* "specially designed to break the spirits of men." But in my view the concept of the "soul breaker" is the prison system itself and the sadistic guards who may have gotten their asses kicked in high school by some black or brown kid, or had their girlfriend taken from them by these kids of color, and can now use their jobs as prison guards to vent their frustrations on these men.

So there is a historical tendency and purpose for these prisons and detention centers once the populations become increasingly black and brown. Let's take a brief look at what is taking place before we move on with the rest of the ACLU's "findings."

First, the issue of long periods of time in solitary confinement. As I make clear, these white people knew what they were doing. They have been using black people for "experimental purposes" for over a century. These black inmates are coerced into signing away their rights and taking experimental drugs and the like. So if the system is willing to do this to them, then solitary confinement is a piece of cake by comparison. These long periods of time in isolation only serve to make these kids even more deviant than they already were; it makes them hate the system, hate all forms of authority and take that time to map out various types of "payback" on everybody involved. That's why so many of them get released and then come right back – it's called "recidivism."

Secondly, the issue of "long-term impact on children's health and well-being." Again, the ACLU is a day late and a dollar short with this information. Since the days of enslavement these white people knew about the punitive impact of isolation on the human soul. After that the "ghettoization" of black people created a collective form of isolation in the guise of residential and racial segregation. Today, the same "isolationist" mentality exists through educational segregation and employment discrimination. Long-term impact is therefore assured.

Third, the issue of "overall stunted development" as it relates to these young people. Following any war, America takes in its soldiers and "de-briefs" them in order to acclimate them to the American climate. But following 300-plus years of enslavement, black people were never "de-briefed" and believe me, it was a war, with black people being nothing short of POWs. Following so-called "emancipation," we were just tossed out into a racist society wearing skin color that the majority envied and hated and were expected to literally "pick ourselves up by our own bootstraps."

This situation has led to a form of collective "stunted development" because black people still have the "slave" mentality. The white man's position remains that of "master" and his on-going maltreatment, as documented in this report, makes it clear that the "master-slave tradition" is still alive and well and living in Nebraska and its largest city, Omaha.

The ACLU findings continue:

> "Before they are old enough to get a driver's license, enlist in the
> armed forces or vote, some children in Nebraska are held in
> solitary confinement for days, weeks, even months. As the stories
> in our report show, the youth placed in solitary confinement are
> often in need of support – not a cage. The experts agree – what
> Nebraska is doing is harmful to youth and does nothing to improve
> public safety. This research makes clear that the policies and usage
> for solitary confinement among vulnerable Nebraskans truly

shocks the conscience. We can and must do better," said Danielle
Conrad, ACLU of Nebraska Executive Director.

The ACLUs findings are nothing but a re-hash of what black scholars
around the nation have been pointing out for decades. These Nebraskans act
shocked but since it can be proven that all of this is by design, it's a conspiracy of
sorts. It's attempted genocide, plain and simple. How can such damaging realities
be anything short of race-based death warrants? According to the report, Lancaster
County (Lincoln) permits use of solitary for rule violations such as "too many
books in room" or "digging for cookies."
If these were white kids being subjected to this, Nebraska would be up in
arms about it. But they're kids of color, and nobody really cares because the long
term residual effects will guarantee future grant-based mental health, behavioral
and social service programs that, in turn, will generate more jobs for white folks.

CRIME, THE JUDICIARY & THE PENAL SYSTEM

According to a report issued by the National Urban League in 2003, the
incarceration rate for white males was 649 per 100,000 residents, but for black
males it was 4,810 per 100,000 residents. For white women, the rate was 68 per
100,000 but for black women, it was 349 per 100,000 (p. 12). According to this
same report, approximately one in three black males born in 2001 will go to prison
during his lifetime. Compare this with 13.4 black males going to prison who were
born in 1974.
In Omaha, Nebraska as in most major cities, black males are the fodder used
to justify everything from negative news stories and police overtime to the
construction of more prisons. Although blacks make up less than 6% of Nebraska's
entire population, the following chart shows you the numbers and percentages of
those incarcerated:

TABLE 8. Incarcerations by Race (2000)

	Nebraska (FY01)		National (CY00)	
African American	987	25.3%	633,777	46.7%
Asian	20	0.5%	8,205	0.7%
Hispanic	405	10.4%	170,928	12.6%
Native American	193	4.9%	16,408	1.4%

White	2,293	58.8%	517,323	38.2%
Other	2%	0.1%	9,324	0.7%

NOTE: All National figures are drawn from the 2000 Corrections Yearbook

Not only are blacks disproportionately represented in the penal institutions, those institutions are grossly overcrowded. And they will continue to be overcrowded because the "police state," particularly the ones in Omaha and Lincoln, will continue to concentrate their efforts on black communities.

These social scientists well know the link between the population density of an area and the tendency toward conflict; the more people who have to share a given area, the greater tendency there is for negative interactions. Experiments on fruit flies in jars have shown that the flies, when crowded, ignore the fruit and begin attacking one another. In the case of human beings, reliable sociological studies clearly show the link between greater density and human conflict. In light of these facts, if prisons are crowded, what will be the inevitable result?

Table 9. POPULATION vs. DESIGN CAPACITY(December 18, 2001)

	Design Capacity	Actual Population	% of Capacity
CCC-L	200	272	136.00%
DEC	160	385	240.63%
HCC	152	183	120.39%
LCC	308	519	168.51%
NCCW	139	277	199.28%
NCTC	90	90	100.00%
NSP	768	1,216	158.33%
OCC	396	707	178.54%
CCC-O	90	143	158.89%
NCYF	68	73	107.35%
TSCI	960	32	3.33%

TOTAL DCS:			
12-11-01	3,331	3,897	116.99%
12-11-00	2,371	3,776	159.26%

The 2000 Nebraska Crime Commission reports that though individuals ages 12 through 17 represent only 10 percent of the state's total population, 19.2 percent of total arrests were committed by persons under the age of 18. The Omaha Police Department indicated during 2001 there were 1,739 suspected gang members involved in 19 suspected gangs. In 2001, gang-related activity included 4 criminal homicides, 40 drug possession/traffic and 507 defacing property crimes. Furthermore, 2002 statistics indicate that the numbers of gang members and gangs in Omaha are increasing, and the amount of gang activity is on track to increase by 14 percent.

The use of drugs including tobacco, alcohol, and marijuana among students in Nebraska generate concerns. For example, the 1999 Youth Risk Behavior Survey results show that 31 percent of respondents, grades 9-12, report having used marijuana at least once, as compared to 19 percent in 1993. Additionally, 37 percent reported smoking tobacco in the past 30 days, and 65 percent of respondents reported using tobacco in their lifetime. Eighty two (82%) percent of teens reported having used alcohol at least once in their lifetime, while 58 percent and 54 percent of males and females respectively, reported having a drink during the last 30 days. Furthermore, the prevalence of methamphetamines is another concern. To illustrate, the number of methamphetamine labs discovered in Nebraska has soared from 45 in 2000 to 251 as of October 2002.

In Omaha, Douglas County Department of Health reported that 290 teen girls ages 17 years and younger gave birth during 2001, and nearly 15 percent of those births were repeat pregnancies. Moreover, the number of teenage girls giving birth in Douglas County has averaged 290 over the past five years. The state of Nebraska recently released statistics from the Nebraska Crime Commission Report that document a 21 percent increase in juvenile arrests in the state over the past two decades and an increase in juvenile crime (murder, manslaughter, rape, robbery, and aggravated assault) for every year since 1990.

In February of 1998, the Omaha Police Department released the latest Police Crime Statistics for 1997 and this report indicated that as of December 1997, there were 2,262 suspected gang members involved in 15 suspected gangs. The number of drug possession/trafficking incidents among gang members was 239 for 1997, while the number for defacing property was 653. The report also indicated an overall increase of 3 percent in violent crimes. In 1997, gang-related activity included 5 criminal homicides, 4 sexual assaults, and 19 felony assault/drive-by shootings.

The use of drugs including tobacco, alcohol, and marijuana among students in Nebraska is also increasing. The 1997 Youth Risk Behavior Survey results show that 31 percent of respondents, grades 9-12, report having used marijuana at least once, as compared to 19 percent in 1993. Similarly, 40 percent reported smoking tobacco in the past 30 days, up from 34 percent in 1993. Eighty percent of teens reported having used alcohol at least once in their lifetime, while 56 percent reported having a drink during the last 30 days, up slightly from 52 percent in 1993.

In Omaha, Douglas County Department of Health statistics for 1997 indicate that approximately 325 teen girls, ages 17 years and younger, give birth each year and about 15 percent of those births are repeat pregnancies.

While the black community of Omaha is literally a place of police occupation and mass sweeps and roundups, the rest of Omaha is experiencing declines, according to the Nebraska Crime Commission. More specifically,

> Crime in Omaha decreased 6 percent (from 29,049 offenses reported in 2002 to 27,349 offenses in 2003) … Cities under 5,000 population as a group was the only area of the state to experience an increase, from 1,820 offenses reported in 2002 to 1,910 offenses reported in 2003 … Adult arrests (involving persons age 18 and over) decreased 3 percent from 78,436 arrests in 2002 to 75,859 arrests in 2003). Adult arrests accounted for 84 percent of the total arrests made statewide … Juvenile arrests decreased 9 percent, dropping from 16,290 in 2002 to 14,805 in 2003 (Omaha Star, 2004: 8).

Of course, the preceding numbers do not address the racial issue in Nebraska or Omaha, since disproportionate numbers of people being arrested are African-American and Latinos who reside both in Omaha and out in the western panhandle.

SOCIAL SERVICES

Throughout this document a form of "social services" has been outlined. The concept of "invasion of the booty snatchers" basically translates to mean social services for the powers that be: rich farmers, corporate decision makers, politicians and others. This form of "welfare" is widely accepted as normal business practice in and around the state of Nebraska and in its largest city, Omaha.

In this brief section the issue is the Department of Health and Human Services, formerly known as "the welfare department." Black people during the days of welfare used those stipends to raise families, and although there were far more white families on welfare than black ones, it is the black community that these racist whites pointed out as welfare frauds. White female social workers inspected black houses and apartments looking for any evidence that a man was present and slowly but surely the cash stipends were pulled back and while food stamps and housing assistance remained, the white man claimed that the day of "the welfare Cadillac" was over.

He was wrong. It is the entire state of Nebraska and the city of Omaha who are the welfare recipients and the leeches of Federal grant money. One of the keys to maintaining a system that keeps a section of its population poor so that it (the system) can continue to get free government money can be found in a principle called Campbell's Law. This is a law that holds that,

> …the more a social indicator is used for social decision making, the more subject it will be to corruption pressures, thus distorting the social processes it was intended to monitor … Nonetheless, calls for greater accountability – from the federal government, from state legislatures, and in particular from philanthropic organizations putting large sums of money toward efforts that they believe will increase competition … (Brawer, 2013: p. 418).

A case of Jesse James being called into investigate the dealings of his brother, Frank James. And this is how the system perpetuates itself. Subject to corruption pressures as well as a tradition of knowing that you can get away with murder, Nebraska leadership has been bilking its rural thinking population for over a century. And once black people migrated here from the South, they were perfect targets for the "booty snatchers" to exploit in the areas of housing, mass arrests, mis-education, health care manipulation and the like; another form of "taxation without representation," one might say.

Back in the day we used to call social workers "poverty pimps," a term made popular in a 1977 movie that starred Bill Cosby and Sidney Portier, titled, "A Piece of the Action." Although said in jest by some, the term becomes a reality and is therefore meant in earnest when one looks at the actions, programs, plans and policies that impact upon the poor as social workers and others work to *maintain* poverty so that, in turn, their city and state can continue to qualify for free grant money from the Federal government.

In October of 2010, a candidate for governor stated publicly that the Department of Health and Human Services for the state of Nebraska was "horribly broken" (Ruggles, 2010). Following are excerpts from an article that appeared in the Omaha World Herald. My commentary will filter throughout to provide context and evidence that when it comes to ineptitude, poor fiscal management and outright financial buffoonery, Nebraska reigns without rival.

The October 7, 2010 article begins, thusly:

> "Health and human services in this state is horribly, horribly broken," Meister said. The Democrat, who is running against Gov. Dave Heineman, spoke in front of the Douglas County Youth Center, a juvenile detention facility. He said that's the kind of place where children end up when families don't receive adequate support. (Ruggles, 2010).

This statement was made by someone who got drubbed in the gubernatorial race and more likely than not he was saying it as an act of desperation. After all, the truth doesn't come easy for the typical Nebraska politician. But the truth is still the truth when all is said and done. But the DHHS does not function as some kind of force field of sui generis spirit; it is manned and operated by inept human beings and what the Department is viewed as is a culmination of the buffoonish acts of the people who work within and work for that department. In the words of Forrest Gump, "Stupid is as stupid does."

The issue is not that families don't receive adequate support; the issue is what are the factors that place families in a position to need this state aid in the first place. Where there are social services and welfare there are white people who have jobs all over that system. And the key is to make sure that a pool of impoverished people remains available so that those jobs can be justified and therefore maintained.

Continuing

> Meister also called Thursday for a series of debates over the next three weeks.Dean Dennhardt, financial director for the Heineman campaign, said he believed there would be debates. "We're just working through the time and timeline right now," Dennhardt said. (Ruggles, 2010).

See? All this guy wanted was some publicity by way of debate. He really didn't give a shit about the horrible condition of DHHS and had he become the governor, he would have done what the other governors before him had done – what Norbert Tiemann, Charles Thone, Kay Orr, Ben Nelson, Mike Johanns, Dave Heineman and now Pete Ricketts had all done. Nothing.

But facts – akin to the ones I had been making for a decade that exposed the DHHA – are facts no matter how well they are shrouded in impious ceremony:

> Meister said the Nebraska Department of Health and Human
> Services' child welfare reforms, which have privatized some
> services, have failed. The evidence of the failure, he said, is the
> fact that some agencies have terminated their involvement or been
> terminated by the state. (Ruggles, 2010).

Here is what you have to consider after reading the previous excerpt: Nebraska ranks number one in the nation in black child poverty. Since there are relatively few "black children" in the state, then it is clear that these kids are targeted. And they are targeted because the "booty snatchers" are grant hungry and looking for free money (read: Community Service Block Grants). So the Black and Latino kids are the ones who are focused on in order to get the money but once the money comes, these white people hire their own race members and do all that they can to make sure that the poverty and the dependence on the system continues so that they (the decision makers) can continue to have jobs.

There are internal and external problems, but it is much easier to focus on the minor ones, the problems that won't impact the free money that the state continually leeches for. Check it out:

> He also said the fact that the health and human services' head,
> Kerry Winterer, is called a "chief executive officer," reflects the
> misguided belief that the state agency should function like a
> corporation. Winterer said it wasn't the agency's decision to call
> him a CEO. That's determined by state law and is "nothing we've
> chosen," he said. (Ruggles, 2010).

It doesn't matter what the title on the door says; it's the job description and what is done to achieve measurable outcomes. And that is why the department continues to fail: the lack of leadership, not what the name plate says. But this is the kind of "critical analysis" that you can expect from even the supposedly "brightest" of Nebraskans, which is why throughout this document you see where I have documented them bringing in, retaining, hiring and using ideas of outside "consultants" and then pawning it all off as "progress" or some kind of "new direction." In reality, it's the "same ol' same ol' with a different program title and budget number.

DHHS is a loser because it is manned by people lacking in vision, creativity and commitment. It's as simple as that. As a result, take note of the following excerpt:

> Winterer said child welfare reform has been a "rocky road" in
> some cases. That doesn't mean it's a failure, he said.

"We've learned from going through the process," he said.
(Ruggles, 2010)

Nebraska has been sucking at the government teet for decades. All this going on while the white people point to minorities and low-income people and label them as "welfare cheats." Let's take a look at some of the programs that enable a hick state like Nebraska to continue receiving free money from the Feds.

And what is the result of all of this? The "booty snatchers" continue leeching, getting paid and ensuring that the poverty that is at the root of their livelihoods, continues on unabated. On March 30, 2016, State Senator Bill Krist (busted later in the year for using the state computers to surf for porn) stated, "Nebraska has experienced an Increase in child poverty … and the rate has increased 118 percent since 2000 in Nebraska."

And it's not going to get any better. The governor is going to cut social services in the next budget session. So all those social workers who claim to be overburdened in terms of their case loads now are going to have it much worse in the years ahead. Nebraska is in trouble because once the poor get neglected, the result is going to be calamity in the streets. And the state's leadership will only have itself to blame.

Goodwill Industries, Susie Buffett, and Big Bucks for White Males

What a scam that was run, and the dual "reports" that I am about to quote from don't even deal with the real thrust and pervasiveness of the problem. I'm talking about Goodwill Industries, the leeches who claim to be about helping the poor, employing the physically challenged (read: underpaying them) and helping the community. They were scamming all along, as many of us suspected, but now it comes to light and none other than Susie Buffett was providing this so-called "social service agency" with funding.

But let me not get ahead of myself.

During my application for General Assistance, I had to attend these meetings with other people. My motives and purpose were far different, as I had always intended on making white people pay my way just as black people had always paid theirs. It worked. At this meeting these people were telling us about how and where to look for jobs. But one organization was continually emphasized: *Goodwill Industries*. The speakers continually droned, "Go to Goodwill and volunteer and they'll eventually hire you," "Goodwill is a great place to start" and so on.

In other words, not only were these pimps getting major funding from the weak-minded Susie Buffett (just as she had "given" two bruthas $150,000 a few years back to "finance parties at the YMCA to give black kids something to do" – no contract, no receipts), they also had the Department of Health and Social Services promoting their stores to the poor. Big donations on the one hand, cheap exploitable labor on the other. Sounds like a new version of enslavement to me.

With that having been said, now comes two World Herald articles, the first appearing on October 28, 2016 under the headline, "Susie Buffett, Now Ex-Donor, Calls Goodwill CEO's Defense of Pay 'Outrageous.' The second article, which appeared six days later in the same paper, was titled, "Goodwill Omaha CEO Frank McGree Resigns Following World-Herald Investigation Into Executive Pay." I will dissect both articles and link them to the "Invasion of the Booty Snatchers" thematic pattern that permeates this book.

The daughter of one of the world's richest women gives away cash money ($150,000) to two black men to sponsor parties at a local high school as a crime deterrent for young black kids. Knowing this and the fact that she has a host of "negroes" on her payrolls, from Edu-Care Child Care Center, Northstar Recreation Center, the Sherwood Foundation, the Women's Fund and so on, what you are about to read about her donations to Goodwill Industries represents the height of gall and temerity. But I cite it as one example of the kind of financial chicanery that permeates Nebraska in general and the city of Omaha, in particular.

The following October 28, 2016 article by Henry Cordes provides context, although my commentary, which filters in and out, will provide context, background and relevance. The headline of the article is, "Susie Buffett, Now Ex-Donor, Calls Goodwill CEO's Defense of Pay 'Outrageous.'" The article begins:

> The CEO of Goodwill Omaha defended the charity's executive compensation Wednesday, calling his leadership team one of the best in the country, but his first statements in response to a World-Herald investigation fell short of satisfying some in the public — including one significant Goodwill donor. (Cordes, 2016).

There is nothing in Omaha or Nebraska that even comes close to becoming "the best" in anything. Even their so-called Business Ethics Alliance is comprised of people who believe in and endorse racial segregation, refuse to hire minorities, treat women like crap and use "the bottom line" as the justification for all of the above. They hide out in gated suburban communities and then have the unmitigated gall to attend church on Sunday. What Goodwill was doing was par for the course, as was Susie Buffett's complicity as a funding source.

The article continues:

> The nonprofit's board also issued its own statement, indicating that it was taking a serious look at the issues raised by the newspaper

and would respond after going through "our due diligence."But CEO Frank McGree broadly defended the charity in his statement, even as he confirmed many of the newspaper's findings. (Cordes, 2016).

That's one thing about the "booty snatchers." They always pacify the public with claims about what they're going to "look into" or "investigate." These lies buy them time to cover their tracks and, with the assistance of a mindless public, they can get away with crime after crime. These types of actions have been taking place in Omaha for over a century and apparently the public has become numb to these malfeasant activities.

Moving on:

> He called Goodwill's executive pay fair and deserved, arguing that the Omaha charity is unique and so complex that it can't be compared to any other nonprofit organization here or elsewhere. He also defended the employment of close relatives within Goodwill's upper ranks — *including his own daughter* — saying the charity is lucky that it gets referrals "from friends and family that already bleed Goodwill blue." (Cordes, 2016 – emphasis added).

Grandiosity. So convinced are these white men that they deserve what they have that they have actually begun to believe their own fabricated stories. The fact is, Omaha simply does not compare and cannot compete. There is no way that these hicks could deserve such incredible pay for doing so little to so many. They simply walk about in ice cream suits, chasing after under aged women and living the life that is impressive on the outside but rooted in filth and frolic once you take an introspective look. They know it and it is their job to work to do what they can to make sure that only fellow "insiders" find out.

Nepotism is rampant as I've established elsewhere in this report. Back in the 1980s when I was attending UNO I went through the staff and faculty handbook and found scores of husband and wife teams. Now while this is not unheard of among the ranks of faculty members, I found actual staff persons who were related who held jobs at UNO, from the janitors to the mid-line staff. Even today there are two chancellors – Christine and BJ Reed – who work side-by side (at one point she was his boss) and their son runs the public relations division.

And in the case of Goodwill, the Omaha World Herald's "day-late-and-a-dollar-short" reporting nevertheless uncovered the following:

> Asked whether the public should be concerned about family ties among top Goodwill executives, McGree said no. Not only is

> McGree's daughter, Shannon, a retail executive at Goodwill paid
> over $100,000, the charity has a vice president of retail who has a
> sister working under her as a retail director and a board member
> whose daughter-in-law is paid $130,000 as a vice president. Until
> recently, the chief operating officer had a son who ran Goodwill
> stores. (Cordes, 2016)

And,

> Carol Miklas of Omaha was particularly struck that McGree
> seemed to defend the hiring of relatives at Goodwill. "It's a joke,"
> she said. "I will no longer give to them — maybe when it's all
> settled and they get rid of them. I think the man's ready to retire
> after 30 years of being there." (Cordes, 2016)

All this while black people in and around Omaha languish in relative squalor. This is information that has to be shared with outsiders who have the power to do something about it. Where they can be found is still up in the air, but one thing is for sure: this document will be shared with people who will never see Omaha, Nebraska in the same light.

Now, enter Susie Buffett. I have written about her father under another label where I document his racist activities around the nation as well as the maternalistic racism of his sister, Doris. At any rate, such bombast apparently runs in the family, as the following excerpt bears out:

> The statements from McGree and the board were blasted by Susie
> Buffett, whose Sherwood Foundation pledged $140,000 this year
> for a Goodwill program training youth in construction skills. "I
> think his statement is outrageous," Buffett said in an interview. "I
> think the board should be embarrassed. I think (McGree) should
> have been fired Monday or earlier. I don't know why he's still
> there.."They will never get another penny from the Sherwood
> Foundation. There is my statement." (Cordes, 2016)

It's called "white privilege." When you mix it with racial paternalism you have a low regard for black kids and an undeserved and inflated ego for white people who claim to want to "save the negroes." Both Susie Buffett and McGree are guilty of both. She's just pissed because her investment – which was a tax write off since Goodwill has tax exempt status – was made public. She'll get her money back as she always does when she "donates" funds to these programs that just so happen to focus on low-income black kids.

Like her father, she wields that money like a whip, and uses it to control the people who she uses to control other people. Her negro lackeys range from political figures and religious folks to lesbians and college professors. Her ego and Type A personality can be seen in her statement, "I think (McGree) should have been fired Monday or earlier. I don't know why he's still there.."They will never get another penny from the Sherwood Foundation. There is my statement." See? She even talks as if she thinks she's the Queen of Sheba.

"There is my statement"? That's it? Your statement was the money you donated; your statement is your incursion into the black community of Omaha with your father, buying up properties and using "negroes" to serve as your prospectors. These are the statements and this is your legacy, regardless of what these submissive black people in Omaha hear or believe. What she says doesn't make it so – the proof, as the saying goes, is in the pudding.

The booty snatchers are alive and well as the following passage makes most clear:

> Capping a four-month investigation, The World-Herald reported this week on McGree's corporate-styled pay package, which in 2014 included a $519,000 retention bonus that pushed his total pay close to $1 million. Even without the bonus, his pay was more than double that of Omaha's other prominent social service nonprofits and the Goodwill affiliates in our region most comparable in size. (Cordes, 2016).

What took four months to find this out? This is akin to those cops who sit on a drug house for months, sometimes years at a time, and "wait to compile more information." In this case all they needed was McGree's tax returns. But once again, when you have Jesse James investigating Frank James, what can you expect? Just like when the FBI was about to bust former mayor Mike Boyle's brother and informed Boyle of it, he called his brother to warn him. This stuff has been going on in Omaha for untold decades and the citizenry does nothing about it.

The booty snatchers keep on getting paid:

> An analysis of the nation's largest Goodwills also found that none could match Goodwill Omaha in the percentage of budget that it put into CEO pay and the rate at which it paid six-figure salaries to its leaders. Goodwill Omaha last year had 14 executives and managers paid more than $100,000, three times more than would be expected for a Goodwill its size. (Cordes, 2016).

All those white people making all that money and living in the suburbs and expanding that tax base with their illegally gotten gains. No sense of conscience at all. They just do as they please and when they get caught they know that because of their skin color they will be able to land another job. But remember that

Goodwill is a nonprofit that is supposed to be committed to helping the poor. But as you can see, what they do is help themselves TO the poor. If you need any additional evidence, pay close attention to the following:

> The paper also found that despite Goodwill's slogan that shopping at and donating to its thrift stores help the charity assist the disabled and other needy job-seekers, just a fraction of its store profits fund such job training programs. Instead, those dollars are being largely consumed by its administrative overhead, including much of the pay for the charity's leaders. (Cordes, 2016).

So they comingled funds, engaged in various forms of malfeasance and no one went to jail. And yet they made off with millions. That is the way things are done in America. Look at those guys who ran Tyco, Enron and Worldcom into the ground: do you think they spent all that money? They went to prison but their families are taken care of for life. Bernie Madoff? He's a Jew: you know he sent some of that money to Israel and they hid it for him. And he may do time but his family is taken care of for generations to come.

And in the case of these Omaha shysters, it's the same method of operation: even when they get caught, they do so only after getting rich and greasing enough palms so that their family members can continue to live their segregated, suburban lives. All of these at the expense of the poor. The veritable "invasion of the booty snatchers" continues on, apparently unabated.

CONCLUSION

> There is so much good in the worst of us,
> And so much bad in the best of us,
> That it hardly behooves any of us
> To talk about the rest of us.
> Edward Wallis Hoch, *Marion (Kansas) Record*
> *(1849 – 1925)*

I wholeheartedly disagree.

When the variable of "race" is interjected into the equation, and when white people continue to beat down, pimp, exploit, kill off, rape and denigrate black people and black lives, then exposing them for their crimes is of paramount importance. After all, "to be forewarned is to be forearmed."

In Nebraska, the "invasion of the booty snatchers" is a mandatory requirement in order for there to be any semblance of fiscal and financial survival. One man's "disparity" is another man's "gold mine." There is a long and successful tradition of denying black people in and across the state and turning those denials, denunciations and subsequent disparities into financial growth, new revenue streams and jobs for those who would otherwise be too stupid to qualify for employment.

According to a nationwide report, despite a more than 50 percent decline in the welfare rolls overall, racial disparities in caseload decline persisted. After implementation of Temporary Assistance to Needy Families (TANF), the proportion of blacks and Latinos on the caseload increased, particularly for children (National Urban League, 2003: 23).

The State of Nebraska's Health and Human Services System perennially ranks among the worst in the nation mainly because the people who are in charge of important divisions in the area of family welfare are not adequately prepared to engage in long-range planning or cross-cultural planning. The pervasive lack of creativity in addressing the needs of the low-income in and around the State of Nebraska has actually created more problems than the division itself, has solved.

In 1970 and 1980, nearly a third of Omaha's black families were at or below the federally defined poverty level currently $10,650 for a family of four. According to David DiMartino, a UNO researcher, that many or more blacks probably were at or below poverty level in 1986 (Omaha World Herald, 1986).

Welfare has long been a source of survival for residents in the black community. While today those who have jobs look down their noses at it, many of those same people were raised on it. Figures from 1985-86 give you an idea of the welfare state in Omaha:

> Nebraska Department of Social Services figures indicate that 35 percent of Douglas County's black households received food stamps last year [1985] ... Five percent of the county's white households received the stamps. In fiscal year 1985-1986, food stamps valued at $6.8 million were distributed to black households in Douglas County. The value of all food stamps issued that year in the county to blacks and non-blacks was $17.2 million. The same year, $16 million in Aid to Dependent Children was distributed to blacks in the county. The countywide total was $27.6 million. (Omaha World Herald, 1986).

Then there is child welfare, the status of black children in Omaha. It was noted by child welfare advocates in February of 2004 that the failings in Nebraska's system contributed to the deaths of 33 children in six years and could not be addressed by adding staff alone (Stoddard, 2004: 1). The shortcomings noted in the system included a need to restructure in order to "create accountability and bring intake, investigation and prosecution together under a common organizational roof" (Stoddard, 2004: 1).

Some in the black community see all this as just another way to create more jobs for unqualified whites, jobs that put white folks in charge of the lives of black clients. While blacks are being "re-trained" for employment, even less qualified and experienced whites are provided with jobs that are created by the construction of prisons, jails, and in the case of social welfare, "investigation and prosecution centers" that would be headed by county attorneys and assistant attorneys. But it is clear that jobs as custodians, guards and food service workers, all with benefits, would be created and then handed out to non-minorities.

> Moving on:

> The survey ranks 86 cities on the basis of six factors:
> unemployment, education, income, housing, poverty and the
> proportion of the population younger than 18 and older than 64.
> While Omaha ranked well in the survey, not everyone in the city
> is enjoying prosperity. Hardships abound for many Omahans
> struggling to find housing, jobs and food. Rich Koeppen, director
> of the St. Vincent DePaul family shelter, said every day the city's
> homeless shelters are unable to meet the demand.
> "Conservatively speaking, 150 women and women with families
> a month have to be turned away," Koeppen said. In nearly all
> cases, lack of space is the cause, he said. Shelley Kiel, director of
> Together Inc., said her organization is receiving 700 to 1,000
> calls a month asking for help to pay rent. "We are seeing record
> numbers of people looking for emergency food," Kiel said.

Even when these racists address "problems" in Omaha, they attempt to divert attention away from the city's complicity in the creation and perpetuation of those problems. Omahans struggling to find "housing, jobs and food" is not the primary issue: the primary issue is the reason WHY it is taking place. And for the majority of those involved in this search, the reason is because they have skin color! And Omaha makes money even in that because those housing shelters get donations and federal help to stay open. One shelter, Siena St. Francis House, continues to use the social security numbers of the homeless even after the people have been long gone from the facility. Why? Federal dollars. This is how Omaha, a true "poverty pimp," continues to qualify for national funding.

> The study results, though, were hailed by Greater Omaha
> Chamber of Commerce President David Brown, who offered a
> caution: "We are mindful that there are areas of the city that are
> in need of specific economic and community development
> efforts. Hopefully, the results of this study reflect the progress
> being made in that regard."

Progress being made? Debt still looms like the Sword of Damocles, over the heads of Omaha's decision makers.

Omaha is in major trouble with its financing despite the easily assembled lies of the city's financial officers. The general population tends to forget what takes place which assists the financial people in their on-going perpetrations against those residents. Let me provide an example that sounds bland, but it is essential to the fate and future of the city.

An article by Erin Golden appeared in the March 14, 2013 issue of the Omaha World Herald titled, "Omaha Sewer Project Could Top $2 Billion; More Rate Hikes on the Way."

> With about one-tenth of the city's massive sewer system overhaul
> completed, Omaha officials say they're working to get a better
> handle on how big a financial burden the city can afford to take on.
> (Golden, 2013).

And even while they have all this debt and all of these infrastructure obligations, they still seek out more money to construct leisure projects. This kick-the-can-down-the-road financial management is digging an ever-deepening hole, and yet strapped for answers, they spend even more money on fly-by-night consultants who come in, give them some crazy ideas that won't work, take the money and leave town. For example:

> The city is working with a consultant from the University of
> Cincinnati Economics Center to see how higher rates related to the
> project are affecting and will continue to affect residents and
> businesses. Marty Grate, the city's environmental services
> manager, said Thursday the city still estimates that the federally
> mandated project will cost at least $2 billion. But as construction
> and financing costs rise, he said, the final price tag will be higher.
> (Golden, 2013).

Costs go up as does debt. The "booty snatchers" are strapped and they take it out on the poor in hopes of gaining free money to pay for their rising social service problems. The tax money that is supposed to be spent on projects such as this one is squandered on salaries for unqualified department heads.

The future does not bode well for the River City:

> Grate said the city is working on a rate plan for 2015 to 2018,
> which will likely go to the City Council in the next few months. He
> said rates are likely to increase by 10 percent to 12 percent each
> year because of the sewer project. That's a lower jump than

ratepayers have seen in recent years. In 2006, he said, the average
residential customer paid $10 per month. Now, that's closer to $30
and by 2017, it could be over $50. "The largest of the increases —
we're past those," he said. (Golden, 2013).

People like Grate buy time so they can continue to collect their paychecks
and get ever closer to their retirement pensions. There are no real solutions other
than to pad the coffers of as many white people as they can find. The $900
milliion dollar deficit that is predicted for the year 2019 looms ominously over the
state of Nebraska. And with the tendency to repeat past mistakes, to kick the can
down the road, and to yield to short-term pleasure (which yields long-term pain),
the times are not going to get much better, despite the easily assembled lies of the
oppressor.

Hence, *the need for the continuation of "the invasion of the booty
snatchers"* in an attempt to address the impeding $900 million deficit that the State
of Nebraska faces in the years ahead.

REFERENCES

ACLU. (2016, January 4). ACLU finds dangerous overuse of solitary confinement
for Nebraska Youth. Retrieved from https://www.aclu.org/news/aclu-finds-
dangerous-overuse-solitary-confinement-nebraska-youth

Akstarben.blogspot (2016, August 2). Dean of NE legislature slams AG, Gov. for
GOP cover-up of Kintner sex video on state laptop. Retrieved from
http://aksarbent.blogspot.com/2016/08/dean-of-ne-legislature-slams-ag-gov-
for.html

Archive.org. (2016). Full text of "The Franklin Cover-up by Former Green Beret
John DeCamp"
Retrieved from http://archive.org/stream/TheFranklinCover-
upByFormerGreenBeretJohnDecamp/the_Frankklin_cover-up_-_ebook_djvu.txt

Barton, P.E. & Coley, R.J. (December 2009-January 2010). Those persistent gaps.
Educational Leadership. 67, (4). p18-23.

Bradley, M. (1978). *The Iceman Inheritance: Prehistoric Sources of Western
Man's Racism, Sexism and Aggression.* New York, New York: Kayode
Publications.

Brawer, F.B.C.A.A.M. (2013). *The American Community College*. Wiley. Retrieved from http://www.ebrary.com.

Brown, E. *A Taste of Power*. New York: Pantheon Books. 1992

Caldwell, J. (2015, February 25). Are farmland cash rents going to fall or not? Agriculture.com. Retrieved from http://www.agriculture.com/news/business/are-farml-cash-rents-going-to-fall-not_5-ar47694

California Black Women's Health Project (2004, December). Stress of racism may lead to low birthweight babies. Retrieved from http://www.cabwhp.org/resources/newsletters/december_2004/stress_of_racism_may_lead_to_low_birthweight_babies

Charles Drew Health Center (2016). About Charles Drew Health Center. Retrieved from http://www.wicprograms.org/li/ne-charles_drew_health_center

Cole, K. (2005, February 14). Nebraska: Area ranks high in risk of STDs, youths are told. Retrieved from http://www.thebody.com/content/art25483.html

Cordes, H. (2010, February 21). Omaha data left out by mistake. Omaha World Herald.

Cordes, Henry (2016, February 22). Omaha sees spike in black college grad rate, as outreach programs aim to close education's race gap. Omaha World Herald.

Cordes, Henry J. (2016, October 28). Susie Buffett, now ex-donor, calls Goodwill CEO's defense of pay 'outrageous.' Omaha World Herald.

Cordes, Henry J. (2016, November 3). Goodwill Omaha CEO Frank McGree resigns following World-Herald investigation into executive pay. Omaha World Herald.

Daily Mail (2012). Married school superintendent, 57, resigns after sending sexually explicit emails to lover using work account. Retrieved from http://www.dailymail.co.uk/news/article-2154443/Married-school-superintendent-57-resigns-explicit-emails-sent-lover-work-discovered.html#ixzz4M715spni

Davis, B. (2016, July 23). CEO rebukes those behind flier advocating for 'white man.' Omaha World Herald.

Duffy, E. (2016, February 28). OPS has eye on Sherwood Foundation grant to boost number of district's social workers. Omaha World Herald. Retrieved from http://www.omaha.com/news/education/ops-has-eye-on-sherwood-foundation-grant-to-boost-number/article_e16a2fc4-176e-59da-8704-655ccd12cf06.html

Edwards, William. (2015, May). Computing a Cropland Cash Rental Rate. Iowa State University Extension and Outreach. Retrieved from http://www.extension.iastate.edu/agdm/wholefarm/html/c2-20.html

Ghosh, P. (2014, January 27). Omaha, Nebraska: The most dangerous place in America to be black. Retrieved from http://www.ibtimes.com/omaha-nebraska-most-dangerous-place-america-be-black-1548466

Gines, D. (2016, March 31). Improving Nebraska's entrepreneurship momentum. Retrieved from https://www.kansascityfed.org/en/publications/research/ne/articles/2016/1q2016/improving-nebraskas-entrepreneurship-momentum

Golden, E. (2013, March 14). Omaha sewer project could top $2 billion; more rate hikes on the way. Omaha World Herald. Retrieved from http://www.omaha.com/news/omaha-sewer-project-could-top-billion-more-rate-hikes-on/article_4c3fcbac-ca1c-56e6-93bc-8b4050c17c14.html

Golden, E. (2013, April 22). Feds looking into alleged bias in Omaha youth jobs program. Retrived from https://www.google.com/search?site=&tbm=isch&source=hp&biw=1258&bih=866&q=community+development+block+grant+program

Grant, S. (2016, March 27). Why more students are leaving for the U.S. for college. MSN.com. Retrieved from http://www.msn.com/en-us/news/us/why-more-students-are-leaving-the-us-for-college/ar-BBqMzxc?li=BBnb7Kz&ocid=iehp

Hammel, P. (2016, April 30). Auditor: State tourism commission 'took advantage of the Nebraska taxpayers'. Omaha World Herald.

Himes, C. L. (2003, April). Which U.S. states are the 'oldest'? Washington, D.C.: Population Reference Bureau.

Hopkins, K. (2004, June 14). Region, race factors in obesity: South-central Nebraska kids heaviest in the state. *Omaha World Herald.*

Kauffman, N. & Clark, M. (2016, February 11). Farm economy tightens further. Federal Reserve Bank. Retrieved from https://www.kansascityfed.org/research/indicatorsdata/agcreditsurvey/articles/2016/2-11-2016/farm-economy-tightens-further

Kiersz, A. (2015, March 3). Ranked: The 50 US state economies from worst to best. Retrieved from http://www.businessinsider.com/state-economy-rankings-q1-2015-2015-3.

Malcolm X (with the assistance of Alex Haley). *The Autobiography of Malcolm X.* New York: Ballantine Books. 1965.

McGraw, D. (2006, January). Tax Increment Financing: A bad bargain for taxpayers. *Reason Magazine.*

MedLibrary.org (2016). African-Americans in Omaha, Nebraska. Retrieved from http://medlibrary.org/medwiki/African_Americans_in_Omaha,_Nebraska.'

Nelson, R. (2011, July 11). OPS book has little more than noble goal. *Omaha World Herald.* p. 1-B.

Nkwocha, O.G. (2003, September). *Health status of racial and ethnic minorities in Nebraska.* Lincoln, NE.: Office of Minority Health and Human Services.

NORML.org. (2000, November 2). New study reveals blacks arrested for marijuana at more than twice the rate for whites. Retrieved from http://norml.org/news/2000/11/02/new-study-reveals-blacks-arrested-for-marijuana-at-more-than-twice-the-rate-for-whites

Omaha World Herald (1978, February 21). DeCamp Apologizes for Racial Comment.

Omaha World Herald (2016, November 23). Editorial: Work can help Tourism Commission Earn Public's Trust.

Reed, C. (2016, June 17). Christensen is namesake for Early Childhood Welfare Community Chair. UNO Public Relations Department.

Ruggles, Rick (2010, October 7). Meister: HHS 'horribly broken.' Omaha World Herald.

Saul, S. (2016, March 21). A Middle Eastern tension point: Pocatello, Idaho. New York Times. Retrieved from http://www.msn.com/en-us/news/us/a-middle-eastern-tension-point-pocatello-idaho/ar-BBqK7ct?li=BBnb7Kz&ocid=iehp

Simpson, K. (2012, June 15). Community-university partnership aims to optimize birth outcomes. University of Nebraska Medical Center public relations.

Skankman, Samantha (2013, July 17). Skift. The Haves and Have Nots of U.S. State Tourism Budgets. https://skift.com/2013/07/17/most-state-tourism-boards-get-peanut-budgets-in-comparison-to-the-top-ten/

Stelly, M.C. (1982, June 7). Minorities can help build Omaha. Omaha World Herald.

Stengle, Jamie. (2005, January 6). Obesity is rising sharply among U.S. preschoolers. ***Carolina Peacemaker.***

Stoddard, M. (2015, April 2). Nebraska's property tax credit fund may grow to $200M per year By Martha Stoddard / World-Herald Bureau . Retrieved from http://www.omaha.com/news/metro/nebraska-s-property-tax-credit-fund-may-grow-to-m/article_64c3e987-bae7-58bd-88d0-7b812590cb08.html

Stoddard, Martha (2016, July 15). Nebraska ended last fiscal year with $95M less revenue than expected; Ricketts orders agencies to tighten belts. Retrieved from http://www.omaha.com/news/nebraska/nebraska-ended-last-fiscal-year-with-m-less-revenue-than/article_6b13d730-2211-5562-af1c-82da15ca4568.html

Stoddard, Martha (2016, November 3). Nebraska prisons house 'alarming number' of inmates in solitary confinement, but reforms are promising, national think tank says . Omaha World Herald.

The Smoking Gun (2015, June 4). Schools Boss Is Sacked Over Explicit E-Mails Racy exchanges sent from woman's work account . Retrieved from http://www.thesmokinggun.com/documents/superintendent-sex-emails-769341

Tinuoye, K. ()2014, January 29). Omaha, Nebraska: Highest rate of black murders says new report. Retrieved from http://thegrio.com/2014/01/29/omaha-nebraska-highest-rate-of-black-murders-says-new-report/

Tysver, Robynn (2016, June 23). Sanders supporters and Latinos smooth rift. Omaha World Herald.

United Nations radio (2012, November 14). Diabetes kills 3.4 million people every year: WHO. Retrieved from http://www.unmultimedia.org/radio/english/2012/11/diabetes-kills-3-4-million-people-every-year-who/

Wesley and Perry, quoted in Woodson, C.G. (1933) ***Mis-Education of the Negro***. Trenton, New Jersey: Africa World Press.

Wikipedia (2106). Phillips County, Kansas. Retrieved from https://en.wikipedia.org/wiki/Phillips_County,_Kansas#Demographics